Joseph Addison

Remarks on several parts of Italy, &c. in the years 1701, 1702, 1703. By Joseph Addison, Esq

Joseph Addison

Remarks on several parts of Italy, &c. in the years 1701, 1702, 1703. By Joseph Addison, Esq

ISBN/EAN: 9783742850997

Manufactured in Europe, USA, Canada, Australia, Japa

Cover: Foto ©Andreas Hilbeck / pixelio.de

Manufactured and distributed by brebook publishing software (www.brebook.com)

Joseph Addison

Remarks on several parts of Italy, &c. in the years 1701, 1702, 1703. By Joseph Addison, Esq

REMARKS

ON SEVERAL

PARTS

OF

ITALY, &c.

In the Years 1701, 1702, 1703.

By JOSEPH ADDISON, Esq;

Verum ergo id est, si quis in cœlum ascendisset, naturamque mundi & pulchritudinem siderum perspexisset, insuavem illam admirationem ei fore, quæ jucundissima fuisset, si aliquem cui narraret habuisset.
Cicero de Amic.

DUBLIN:

Printed for T. WALKER, at CICERO's HEAD, IN DAME-STREET.

MDCCLXXIII.

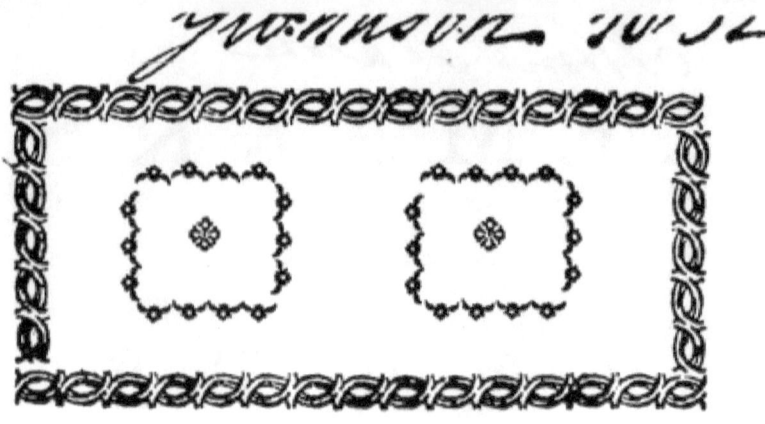

To the Right Honourable

JOHN Lord SOMMERS,

BARON of Evesham.

MY LORD

THERE is a pleasure in owning obligations which it is an honour to have received;

but

DEDICATION.

but should I publish any favours done me by your Lordship, I am afraid it would look more like vanity, than gratitude.

I had a very early ambition to recommend myself to your Lordship's patronage, which yet encreased in me as I travelled thro' the countries, of which I here give your Lordship some account: For whatever great impressions an Englishman must have

DEDICATION.

have of your Lordship, they who have been conversant abroad will find them still improved. It cannot but be obvious to them, that, tho' they see your Lordship's admirers every where, they meet with very few of your well-wishers at Paris or at Rome. And I could not but observe, when I passed through most of the

DEDICATION.

the protestant governments in Europe, that their hopes or fears for the common cause rose or fell with your Lordship's interest and authority in England.

I here present your Lordship with the remarks that I made in a part of these my travels; wherein, notwithstanding the variety of the subject, I am very sensible that I offer nothing new to your Lordship, and can have

DEDICATION.

have no other design in this address, than to declare that I am,

My LORD

Your Lordship's most obliged and

most obedient humble Servant,

J. ADDISON.

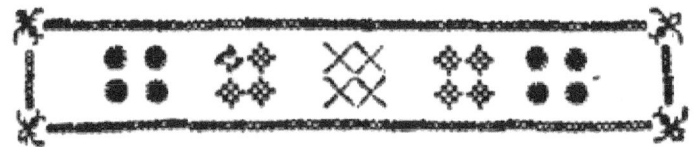

PREFACE.

THERE is certainly no place in the world, where a man may travel with greater pleasure and advantage, than in Italy. One finds something more particular in the face of the country, and more astonishing in the works of nature, than can be met with in any other part of Europe. It is the great school of music and painting, and contains in it all the noblest productions of statuary and architecture, both ancient and modern. It abounds with cabinets of curiosities and vast collections of all kinds of antiquities. No other country in the world has such a variety of governments, that are so different in their constitutions, and so refined in their politics. There is scarce any part of the nation

PREFACE.

nation that is not famous in history, nor so much as a mountain or river, that has not been the scene of some extraordinary action.

As there are few men that have talents and opportunities for examining so copious a subject, one may observe among those who have written on Italy, that different authors have succeeded best on different sorts of curiosities. Some have been more particular in their accounts of pictures, statues, and buildings; some have searched into libraries, cabinets of rarities, and collections of medals; as others have been wholly taken up with inscriptions, ruins and antiquities. Among the authors of our own country, we are obliged to the Bishop of Salisbury, for his masterly and uncommon observations on the religion and governments of Italy: Lassels may be useful in giving us the names of such writers as have treated of the several states through which he passed: Mr. Ray is to be valued for his observations on the natural productions of the place. Monsieur Misson has wrote a more correct account of Italy in general than any

PREFACE.

any before him, as he particularly excels in the plan of the country, which he has given us in true and lively colours.

There are still several of these topics that are far from being exhausted, as there are many new subjects that a traveller may find to employ himself upon. For my own part, as I have taken notice of several places and antiquities that nobody else has spoken of, so, I think, I have mentioned but few things in common with others, that are not either set in a new light, or accompanied with different reflexions. I have taken care particularly to consider the several passages of the ancient Poets, which have any relation to the places or curiosities that I have met with; for before I entered on my voyage I took care to refresh my memory among classic authors, and to make such collections out of them as I might afterwards have occasion for. I must confess it was not one of the least entertainments that I met with in travelling, to examine these several descriptions, as it were upon the spot, and to compare the natural face of the country with the landskips
that

PREFACE.

that the Poets have given us of it. However, to avoid the confusion that might arise from a multitude of quotations, I 'have only cited such verses as have given us some image of the place, or that have something else besides the bare name of it to recommend them.

MO-

MONACO,

GENOA, &c.

ON the twelfth of December, 1699, I set out from Marseilles to Genoa in a tartane, and arrived late at a small French port, called Cassis, where the next morning we were not a little surprised to see the mountains about the town covered with green olive-trees, or laid out in beautiful gardens, which gave us a great variety of pleasing prospects, even in the depth of winter. The most uncultivated of them produce abundance of sweet plants, as wild-thyme, lavender, rosemary, balm, and myrtle. We were here shewn at a distance the deserts, which have been rendered so famous by the penance of Mary Magdalene, who, after her arrival with Lazarus and Joseph of Arimathea at Marseilles, is said to have wept away the rest of her life among these solitary rocks and mountains. It is so romantic a scene, that it has always probably given occasion to

B such

such chimerical relations; for it is perhaps of this place that Claudian speaks, in the following description:

Et locus extremum pandit qua Gallia littus,
Oceans prætentus aquis qua fertur Ulysses
Sanguine libato populum movisse silentum:
Illic umbrarum tenui stridore volantum
Flebilis auditur questus; simulacra coloni
Pallida defunctasque vident migrare figuras, &c.
Claud, in Ruf. lib. 1.

A place there lies on Gallia's utmost bounds,
Where rising seas insult the frontier grounds:
Ulysses here the blood of victims shed,
And rais'd the pale assembly of the dead.
Oft in the winds is heard a plaintive sound
Of melancholy ghosts that hover round:
The lab'ring plow-man oft with horror spies }
Thin airy shapes that o'er the furrows rise, }
(A dreadful scene!) and skim before his eyes. }

I know there is nothing more undetermined among the learned than the voyage of Ulysses; some confining it to the Mediterranean, others extending it to the great ocean, and others ascribing it to a world of the Poet's own making; though his conversations with the dead are generally supposed to have been in the Narbon Gaul.

Incultos adiit læstrigonas antiiphatenque, &c.
Atque hæc seu nostras intersunt cognita terras,
Fabula sive novum dedit his erroribus orbem.
Tibul. Lib. iv. Eleg. i. ver. 59.

Uncertain whether, by the winds convey'd,
On real seas to real shores he stray'd;
Or

Or, by the fable driven from coast to coast,
In new imaginary worlds was lost.

The next day we again set sail, and made the best of our way, until we were forced by contrary winds, into St. Remo, a very pretty town in the Genoese dominions. The front to the sea is not large; but there are a great many houses behind it, built up the side of the mountain to avoid the winds and vapours that came from the sea. We here saw several persons that in the midst of December had nothing over their shoulders but their shirts, without complaining of the cold. It is certainly very lucky for the poorer sort to be born in a place that is free from the greatest inconvenience, to which those of our northern nations are subject; and indeed, without this natural benefit of their climates, the extreme misery and poverty that are in most of the Italian governments would be insupportable. There are at St. Remo many plantations of palm-trees, though they do not grow in other parts of Italy. We sailed from hence directly for Genoa; and had a fair wind that carried us into the middle of the gulph, which is very remarkable for tempests and scarcity of fish. It is probable one may be the cause of the other, whether it be that the fishermen cannot employ their art with so much success in so troubled a sea, or that the fish do not care for inhabiting such stormy waters:

———————————————*Atrum*
Defendens pisces hiemat mare--Hor.Sat.ii. lib.ii.v.16.

While black with storms the ruffled ocean rolls,
And from the fisher's art defends her finny shoals.

We were forced to lie in it two days, and our captain thought his ship in so great danger, that he fell upon his knees, and confessed himself to a capuchin who was on board with us. But at last, taking the advantage of a side-wind, we were driven back in a few hours time as far as Monaco. Lucan has given us a description of the harbour that we found so very welcome to us, after the great danger we had escaped.

Quaque sub Herculeo sacratus nomine portus
Urget rupe cava pelagus: non corus in illum
Jus habet aut zephyrus: Solus sua littora turbat
Circius, & tuta prohibet statione Monœci.
Lib. i. v. 405.

The winding rocks a spacious harbour frame,
That from the great Alcides takes its name:
Fenc'd to the west and to the north it lies;
But when the winds in southern quarters rise,
Ships, from their anchors torn, become their sport,
And sudden tempests rage within the port.

On the promontory, where the town of Monaco now stands, was formerly the temple of Hercules Monæcus, which still gives the name to this small principality.

Aggeribus socer Alpinis atque arce Monæci
Descendens——————————Virg. En. vi. v. 830.

From Alpine heights, and from Monæcus' fane,
The father first descends into the plain.

There are but three towns in the dominions of the prince of Monaco. The chief of them is situate on a rock which runs out into the sea, and is well
fortified

fortified by nature. It was formerly under the protection of the Spaniard, but not many years since drove out the Spanish garrison, and received a French one, which consists at present of five hundred men, paid and officered by the French King. The officer, who shewed me the palace, told me, with a great deal of gravity, that his master and the King of France, amidst all the confusions of Europe, had ever been good friends and allies. The palace has handsome apartments that are many of them hung with pictures of the reigning beauties in the court of France. But the best of the furniture was at Rome, where the prince of Monaco resided at that time ambassador. We here took a little boat to creep along the sea-shore as far as Genoa; but at Savona, finding the sea too rough, we were forced to make the best of our way by land, over very rugged mountains and precipices: For this road is much more difficult than that over mount Cenis.

The Genoese are esteemed extremely cunning, industrious, and inured to hardship above the rest of the Italians; which was likewise the character of the old Ligurians. And indeed it is no wonder, while the barrenness of their country continues, that the manners of the inhabitants do not change: Since there is nothing makes men sharper, and sets their hands and wits more at work, than want. The Italian proverb says of the Genoese, that they have a sea without fish, land without trees, and men without faith. The character the Latin Poets have given of them is not much different.

Assuetumque malo Ligurem. Virg. Georg. ii. v. 168.

The hard Ligurians, a laborious kind.

―― *Pernix Ligur.*   Sil. Ital. El. 8.
The swift Ligurian.

Fallaces Liguras.   Auson. Eid. 12
The deceitful Ligurians.

Apenninicolæ bellator filius auni
Haud Ligorum extremus, dum fallere fata sinebant.
         Virg. Æn. xf. v. 700.

Yet, like a true Ligurian, born to cheat,
(At least whilst fortune favour'd his deceit.) Dryden

Vane Ligur, frustraque animis elate superbis,
Nequicquam patrias tentasti lubricus artes.
         Id. ib. iv. 715.

Vain fool and coward, cries the lofty maid,
Caught in the train which thou thyself hast laid,
On others practise thy Ligurian arts;
Thin stratagems, and tricks of little arts
Are lost on me; nor shalt thou safe retire,
With vaunting lies, to thy fallacious sire. Dryden.

There are a great many beautiful palaces standing along the sea-shore on both sides of Genoa, which make the town appear much longer than it is, to those that sail by it. The city itself makes the noblest show of any in the world. The houses are most of them painted on the outside; so that they look extremely gay and lively; besides that they are esteemed the highest in Europe, and stand very thick together. The new street is a double range of palaces from one end to the other, built with an excellent fancy, and fit for the greatest princes to inhabit. I cannot however be reconciled to their manner

manner of painting several of the Genoese houses. Figures, perspectives, or pieces of history, are certainly very ornamental, as they are drawn on many of the walls, that would otherwise look too naked and uniform without them: But, instead of these, one often sees the front of a palace covered with painted pillars of different orders. If these were so many true columns of marble set in their proper architecture, they would certainly very much adorn the places where they stand; but as they are now, they only shew us that there is something wanting, and that the palace, which without these counterfeit pillars would be beautiful in its kind, might have been more perfect by the addition of such as are real. The front of the Villa Imperiale, at a mile distance from Genoa, without any thing of this paint upon it, consists of a Doric and Corinthian row of pillars, and is much the handsomest of any I saw there. The Duke of Doria's palace has the best outside of any in Genoa, as that of Durazzo is the best furnished within. There is one room in the first, that is hung with tapestry, in which are wrought the figures of great persons that the family has produced; as perhaps there is no house in Europe that can shew a longer line of heroes, that have still acted for the good of their country. Andrew Doria has a statue erected to him at the entrance of the Doge's palace, with the glorious title of Deliverer of the common wealth; and one of his family another, that calls him its preserver. In the Doge's palace are the rooms, where the great and little council, with the two colleges, hold their assemblies; but as the state of Genoa is very poor, though several of its members are extremely rich, so one may observe infinitely more splendor and magnificences in particular persons houses, than in those that belong

belong to the public. But we find in most of the
states of Europe, that the people show the greatest
marks of poverty, where the governors live in the
greatest magnificence. The churches are very fine
particularly that of the Annunciation, which looks
wonderfully beautiful in the inside, all but one corner of it being covered with statues, gilding, and
paint. A man would expect, in so very ancient a
town of Italy, to find some considerable antiquities;
but they have to show of this nature is an old
rostrum of a Roman ship, that stands over the door
of their arsenal. It is not above a foot long, and
perhaps would never have been thought the beak of
a ship, had it not been found in so probable a place
as the haven. It is all of iron, fashioned at the
end like a boar's head; as I have seen it represented
on medals, and on the Columna Rostrata in Rome.
I saw at Genoa signior Micceni's famous collection of
shells, which, as father Buonani the jesuit has since
told me, is one of the best in Italy. I know nothing
more remarkable in the government of Genoa, than
the bank of St. George, made up of such branches
of the revenues, as have been set apart and appropri-
ated to the discharging of several sums, that have
been borrowed from private persons, during the exi-
gences of the common wealth. Whatever inconve-
niencies the state has laboured under, they have never entertained a thought of violating the public
credit, or of alienating any part of these revenues
to other uses, than to what they have been thus
assigned The administration of this bank is for
life, and partly in the hands of the chief citizens,
which gives them a great authority in the state, and
a powerful influence over the common people. This
bank is generally thought the greatest load on the
Genoese, and the managers of it have been represented

as a second kind of senate, that break the uniformity of government, and destroy in some measure the fundamental constitution of the state. It is, however, very certain, that the people reap no small advantages from it, as it distributes the power among more particular members of the republic, and gives the commons a figure: So that it is no small check upon the aristocracy, and may be one reason why the Genoese senate carries it with greater moderation towards their subjects than the Venetian.

It would have been well for the republic of Genoa, if she had followed the example of her sister of Venice, in not permitting her nobles to make any purchase of lands or houses in the dominions of a foreign prince. For at present, the greatest among the Genoese, are in part subject to the monarchy of Spain, by reason of their estates that lie in the kingdom of Naples. The Spaniards tax them very high upon occasion, and are so sensible of the advantage this gives them over the republic, that they will not suffer a Neapolitan to buy the lands of a Genoese, who must find a purchaser among his own countrymen, if he has a mind to sell. For this reason, as well as on account of the great sums of money which the Spaniard owes the Genoese, they are under a necessity, at present, of being in the interest of the French, and would probably continue so though all the other states of Italy entered into a league against them. Genoa is not yet secure from a bombardment, though it is not so exposed as formerly; for, since the insult of the French, they have built a mole, with some little ports, and have provided themselves with long guns and mortars. It is easy for those that are strong at sea to bring them to what terms they please; for having but very little arable land, they are forced to fetch all their corn from Naples, Sicily, and other foreign countries; except what comes to them from Lombardy, which probably goes another way, whilst it furnishes two great armies with provisions. Their fleet, that formerly gained so many victories over the Saracens, Pisans, Venetians, Turks, and Spaniards, that made them masters of Crete, Sardinia, Majorca, Minorca, Negremont, Lesbos, Malta, that settled them in Scio, Smyrna, Achaia, Theodosia, and several towns on the eastern confines of Europe, is now reduced to six gallies. When they had made an addition of but four new ones, the King of France sent his orders to suppress them, telling the republic at the same time, that he knew very well how many they had occasion for. This little fleet serves only to fetch them wine and corn, and to give their ladies an airing in the summer-season. The republic of Genoa has a crown and scepter for its doge, by reason of their conquest of Corsica, where there was formerly a Saracen King. This indeed gives their ambassadors a more honourable reception at some courts, but, at the same time, may teach their people to have a mean notion of their own form of government, and is a tacit acknowledgment that monarchy is the more honourable. The old Romans, on the contrary, made use of a very barbarous kind of politics, to inspire their people with a contempt of Kings, whom they treated with infamy, and dragged at the wheels of their triumphal chariots.

PAVIA,

PAVIA,

MILAN, &c.

FROM Genoa we took chaise for Milan, and by the way stopped at Pavia, that was once the metropolis of a kingdom, but is at present a poor town. We here saw the convent of Austin monks, who about three years ago, pretended to have found out the body of the saint that gives the name to their order. King Luitprand, whose ashes are in the same church, brought hither the corps, and was very industrious to conceal it, lest it might be abused by the barbarous Nations, which at that time ravaged Italy. One would therefore rather wonder that it has not been found out much earlier, than that it is discovered at last. The fathers however do not yet find their account in the discovery they have made; for there are canons regular, who have half the same church in their hands, that will by no means allow it to be the body of the saint, nor is it yet recognized by the Pope. The monks say for themselves, that the very name was written on the urn where the ashes lay, and that, in an old record of the convent, they are said to have been interred between the very wall and the altar where they

they were taken up. They have already too, as the monks told us, begun to juftify themfelves by miracles. At the corner of one the cloyfters of this convent are buried the duke of Suffolk, and the duke of Lorrain, who were both killed in the famous battle of Pavia. Their monument was erected to them by one Charles Parker, an ecclefiaftic, as I learned from the infcription, which I cannot omit tranfcribing, fince I have not feen it printed.

Capto a milite Cæfareo Francifco I. Gallorum rege in agro papienfi Anno 1525. 23. Feb. inter alios proceres, qui ex Juis in prælio occifi funt, occubuerunt duo illuftriffimi princepes, Francifcus dux Lotharingiæ et Richardus de la Poole Anglus dux Suffolciæ a rege tyranno Hen. VIII. pulfus regno. Quorum corpora hoc in cœnobio et ambitu per annos 57. fine honore tumultata funt. Tandem Carolus Parker a Morley, Richardi proximus confanguineus, Regno Angliæ a Regina Elizabetha ob catholicam fidem ejectus beneficentia tamen Philippi Regis Cath. Hifpaniarum Monarchæ invictiffimi in Satu Mediolanenfi fuftentatus, hoc qualecunque monumentum, pro rerum fuarum tenuitate chariffimo propinquo et illuftriffimis principibus pofuit, 5. Sept. 1582. et poft fuum exilium 23. majora et honorificentiora commendans Lotharingicis. Viator precare Quietem.

Francis the firft, King of France, being taken prifoner by the imperialifts, at the battle of Pavia, February the 23d. 1525, among the other noblemen who died in the field, were two moft illuftrious princes, Francis duke of Lorrain, and Richard de la Poole, an Englifhman, duke of Suffolk, who had been banifhed by the Tyrant King Henry the eighth. Their bodies lay buried without honour fifty-

fifty-seven years in this convent. At length, Charles Parker of Morley, a near kinsman of the duke of Suffolk, who had been banished from England by Queen Elizabeth for the catholic faith, and was supported in the Milanese by the bounty of the catholic King Philip, the invincible monarch of Spain, erected this monument, the best his slender abilities could afford, to his most dear kinsman, and these most illustrious princes, recommending a better and more honourable one to the Lorrainers. Passengers, pray for their souls repose.

This pretended duke of Suffolk was Sir Richard de la Poole, brother to the earl of Suffolk, who was put to death by Henry the eighth. In his banishment he took upon him the title of duke of Suffolk, which had been sunk in the family ever since the attainder of the great duke of Suffolk under the reign of Henry the sixth. He fought very bravely in the battle of Pavia, and was magnificently interred by the duke of Bourbon, who, though an enemy, assisted at his funeral in mourning.

Parker himself is buried in the same place, with the following inscription.

D. O. M.

Carolo Parchero a Morley Anglo ex illustrissima clarissima stirpe. Qui Episcopus def. ob fidem Catholicam actus in Exilium. An. XXXI peregrinatus ab Invictiss. Phil. rege Hispan. honestissimis pietatis & constantiæ præmiis ornatus moritur Anno a partu Virginis, M.D.C. XI *Men. Septembris.*

To the memory of Charles Parker of Morley, an Englishman of a most noble and illustrious family; who,

who, a bishop elect, being banished for the catholic faith, and, in the thirty-first year of his exile, honourably rewarded for his piety and constancy by the most invincible Philip King of Spain, died in September 1611.

In Pavia is an university of seven colleges, one of them called the college of Borromee, very large, and neatly built. There is likewise a statue in Brass, of Marcus Antoninus on horseback, which people of the place call Charles the fifth, and some learned men Constantine the great.

Pavia is the Ticinum of the antients, which took its name from the river Ticinus, which runs by it, and is now called the Tesin. This river falls into the Po, and is excessively rapid. The bishop of Salisbury says, that he ran down with the stream thirty miles in an hour, by the help of but one rower. I do not know therefore why Silius Italicus has represented it as so very gentle and still a river, in the beautiful description he has given us of it.

Cæruleus Ticinus aquas et stagna vadosa,
Perspicuus servat, turbari nescia fundo,
Ac nitidum viridi lente trahit amne liquorem;
Vix credas lubi, ripis tam mitis opacis
Argutos inter (volucrum certamina) cantus
Somniferam ducit lucenti gurgite lympham. Lib. iv.

Smooth and untroubled the Ticinus flows,
And through the crystal stream the shining bottom
    shows:
Scarce can the sight discover if it moves;
So wond'rous slow, amidst the shady groves,
And tuneful birds that warble on its sides,
Within its gloomy banks the limpid liquor glides.

A poet

A poet of another nation would not have dwelt so long upon the clearness and transparency of the stream; but in Italy one seldom sees a river that is extremely bright and limpid, most of them falling down from the mountains, that make their waters very troubled and muddy; whereas the Tesin is only an outlet of that vast lake, which the Italians now call the Lago Maggiore.

I saw between Pavia and Milan the convent of Carthusians, which is very spacious and beautiful. Their church is extremely fine, and curiously adorned, but of a gothic structure.

I could not stay long in Milan without going to see the great church that I had heard so much of, but was never more deceived in my expectation than at my first entering: For the front, which was all I had seen of the outside, is not half finished, and the inside is so smutted with dust and the smoke of lamps, that neither the marble, nor the silver, nor brass-work shew themselves to an advantage. This vast Gothic pile of building is all of marble, except the roof, which would have been of the same matter with the rest, had not its weight rendered it improper for that part of the building. But for the reason I have just now mentioned, the outside of the church looks much whiter and fresher than the inside; for where the marble is so often washed with rains, it preserves itself more beautiful and unsullied, than in those parts that are not at all exposed to the weather. That side of the church indeed, which faces the Tramontane wind, is much more unsightly than the rest, by reason of the dust and smoke that are driven against it. This profusion of marble, though astonishing to strangers, is not very wonderful in a country that has so many veins of it within

its

its bowels. But though the stones are cheap, the working of them is very expensive. It is generally said there are eleven thousand statues about the church; but they reckon into the account every particular figure in the history-pieces, and several little images which make up the equipage of those that are larger. There are indeed a great multitude of such as are bigger than the life: I reckoned above two hundred and fifty on the outside of the church, though I only told three sides of it; and these are not half so thick set as they intend them. The statues are all of marble, and generally well cut; but the most valuable one they have is St. Bartholomew, new-flead, with his skin hanging over his shoulders: it is esteemed worth its weight in gold. They have inscribed this verse on the pedestal, to shew the value they have for the workman.

Non me Praxiteles, sed Marcus finxit Agrati.

Left at the sculptor doubtfully you guess,
'Tis Marc Agrati, not Praxiteles.

There is just before the entrance of the quire, a little subterraneous chapel dedicated to St. Charles Borromee, where I saw his body, in episcopal robes lying upon the altar in a shrine of rock crystal. His chapel is adorned with abundance of silver-work: He was but two and twenty years old when he was chosen archbishop of Milan, and forty-six at his death; but made so good use of so short a time, by his works of charity and munificence, that his countrymen bless his memory, which is still fresh among them. He was canonized about a hundred years ago: and indeed if this honour were due to any man, I think such public-
spirited

spirited virtues may lay a juster claim to it, than a sour retreat from mankind, a fiery zeal against heterodoxies, a set of chimerical visions, or of whimsical penances, which are generally the qualifications of Roman saints. Miracles indeed are required of all who aspire to this dignity, because, they say, an hypocrite may imitate a saint in all other particulars, and these they attribute in a great number to him I am speaking of. His merit and the importunity of his countrymen procured his canonization before the ordinary time; for it is the policy of the Roman church not to allow this honour, ordinarily, until fifty years after the death of the person, who is candidate for it; in which time it may be supposed that all his contemporaries will be worn out, who could contradict a pretended miracle, or remember any infirmity of the saint. One would wonder that Roman catholics, who are for this kind of worship, do not generally address themselves to the holy apostles, who have a more unquestionable right to the title of saints than those of a modern date; but these are at present quite out of fashion in Italy, where there is scarce a great town, which does not pay its devotions, in a more particular manner, to some one of their own making. This renders it very suspicious, that the interests of particular families, religious orders, convents or churches, have too great a sway in their canonizations. When I was at Milan I saw a book newly published, that was dedicated to the present head of the Borromean family, and intitled, A discourse on the humility of Jesus Christ, and of St. Charles Borromee.

The great church of Milan has two noble pulpits of brass, each of them running round a large pillar,

pillar, like a gallery, and supported by huge figures of the same metal. The history of our saviour, or rather of the blessed virgin (for it begins with her birth, and ends with her coronation in heaven, that of our saviour coming in by way of episode) is finely cut in marble by Andrew Biffy. This church is very rich in relics, which run up as high as Daniel, Jonas and Abraham. Among the rest they show a fragment of our countryman Becket, as indeed there are very few treasuries of relics in Italy that have not a tooth or a bone of this saint. It would be endless to count up the riches of silver, gold, and precious stones, that are amassed together in this and several other churches of Milan. I was told, that in Milan there are sixty convents of women, eighty of men, and two hundred churches. At the Celestines is a picture in Fresco of the marriage of Cana, very much esteemed; but the painter, whether designedly or not, has put six fingers to the hand of one of the figures. They show the gates of a church that St. Ambrose shut against the emperor Theodosius, as thinking him unfit to assist at divine service, until he had done some extraordinary penance for his barbarous massacring the inhabitants of Thessalonica. That Emperor was however so far from being displeased with the behaviour of the Saint, that at his death he committed to him the education of his children. Several have picked splinters of wood out of the gates for relics. There is a little chapel lately re-edified, where the same Saint baptised St. Austin. An inscription upon the wall of it says, that it was in this chapel, and on this occasion, that he first sung his Te Deum, and that this great convert answered him verse by verse. In one of the churches I saw a pulpit and confessional,

fessional, very finely inlaid with Lapis-Lazuli, and several kinds of marble, by a father of the convent. It is very lucky for a religious, who has so much time on his hands, to be able to amuse himself with works of this nature; and one often finds particular members of convents, who have excellent mechanical genius's, and divert themselves, at leisure hours, with painting, sculpture, architecture, gardening, and several kinds of handicrafts. Since I have mentioned confessionals, I shall set down here some inscriptions that I have seen over them in Roman catholic countries, which are all texts of scripture, and regard either the penitent or the father. *Abi, ostende te ad Sacerdotem*———*Ne taceat pupilla oculi tui*———*Ibo ad Patrem meum & dicam, Pater peccavi*———*Soluta erunt in Cœlis*——— *Redi Anima mea in Requiem tuam*——— ———*Vade, & ne deinceps pecca*———*Qui vos audit, me audit*———*Venite ad me omnes qui fatigati estis & onerati*——— *Corripiet me justus in misericordia*——— *Vide si via iniquitatis in me est, & deduc me in via æterna*——— ———*Ut audiret gemitus campeditorum.* i. e. Go thy way, shew thyself to the priest. Matth. viii 4.———Let not the apple of thine eye cease. Lam. ii. 18———I will go to my father, and will say unto him, father, I have sinned. Luke xv. 18.———Shall be loosed in Heaven. Matth. xvi. 19.———Return unto thy rest, O my Soul. Psal. cxvi. 7.———Go, and sin no more. John viii. 11.——— He that heareth you, heareth me. Luke x. 16.———Come unto me, all ye that labour and are heavy laden. Matth: xi. 28.———See if there be any wicked way in me, and lead me in the way everlasting. Psal. cxxxix. 24.———To hear the groaning of the prisoners, Psal. cii. 20. I saw the Ambrosian library, where,

to

to shew the Italian genius, they have spent more money on pictures than on books. Among the heads of several learned men, I met with no Englishman, except bishop Fisher, whom Henry the eighth put to death for not owning his supremacy. Books are indeed the least part of the furniture that one ordinarily goes to see in an Italian library, which they generally set off with pictures, statues, and other ornaments, where they can afford them after the example of the old Greeks and Romans.

————————*Plena omnia gypso*
Chrysippi invenias : nam perfectissimus horum est,
Si quis, Aristotelem similem vel pittacon emit,
Et jubet archelypos pluteum servare cleanthas.

Juv. Sat. ii. v. 4.

Chrysippus' statue decks thy library.
Who makes his study finest, is most read;
The dolt that with an Aristotle's head,
Carv'd to the life, has once adorn'd his shelf,
Straight sets up for a stagirite himself. Tate.

In an apartment behind the library are several rarities, often described by travellers, as Brugeal's elements, a head of Titian by his own hand, a manuscript in Latin of Josephus, which the Bishop of Salisbury says was written about the age of Theodosius, and another of Leonardus Vincius, which King James the first could not procure though he proffered for it three thousand Spanish pistoles. It consists of designings in mechanism and engineering. I was shewn in it a sketch of bombs and mortars, as they are now used. Canon Settala's cabinet is always shewn to a stranger among

among the curiosities of Milan, which I shall not be particular upon, the printed account of it being common enough. Among its natural curiosities, I took particular notice of a piece of cryftal, that inclofed a couple of drops, which looked like water when they were shaken, though perhaps they are nothing but bubbles of air. It is fuch a rarity as this that I faw at Vendome in France, which they there pretend is a tear that our Saviour fhed over Lazarus, and was gathered up by an angel, who put it in a little chryftal vial, and made a prefent of it to Mary Magdalene. The famous Pere Mabillon is now engaged in the vindication of this tear, which a learned ecclefiaftic, in the neighbourhood of Vendome, would have fuppreffed as a falfe and ridiculous relic, in a book that he has dedicated to his diocefan the Bifhop of Blois. It is in the poffeffion of a Benedictine convent, which raifes a confiderable revenue out of the devotion that is paid to it, and has now retained the moft learned father of their order to write in its defence.

It was fuch a curiofity as this I have mentioned, that Claudian has celebrated in about half a fcore epigrams:

Solibus indomitum glacies Alpina rigorem
  Sumebat, nimio jam preciofa gelu.
Nec potuit toto mentiri corpore gemmam,
  Sed medio manfit proditor orbe latex :
Auctus honor ; liquidi crefcunt miracula faxi,
  Et confervatæ plus meruiftis aquæ.

Deep in the fnowy Alps, a lump of ice
By frofts was harden'd to a mighty price ;

Proof to the sun, it now securely lies,
And the warm dog-star's hottest rage defies:
Yet still, unripen'd in the dewy mines,
Within the ball a trembling water shines,
That through the chrystal darts its spurious rays,
And the proud stone's original betrays:
But common drops, when thus with chrystal mixt,
Are valu'd more, than if in rubies fixt.

As I walked through one of the streets of Milan, I was surprised to read the following inscription, concerning a barber, that had conspired with the commissary of health and others to poison his fellow-citizens. There is a void space where his house stood, and in the midst of it a pillar, superscribed *Colonna Infame*. The story is told in handsome Latin, which I shall set down, as having never seen it transcribed.

Hic, ubi, hæc Area patens est,
Surgebat olim Tonstrina
Jo' Jacobi Moræ :
Qui facta cum Gulielmo Platea publ. Sanit. Commissario,
Et cum aliis Conspiratione,
Dum pestis atrox sæviret,
Lethiferis unguentis huc & illuc aspersio
Plures ad diram mortem compulit.
Hos igitur ambos, hostes patriæ judicatos,
Excelso in plaustro
Candenti prius vellicatos forcipe
Et dextra mulctatos manu
Rota infringi
Rotæque intextos post horas sex jugulari,
Comburi deinde,

Ac,

Ac, ne quid tam fceleſtorum hominum reliqui ſit,
Publicatis bonis
Cineres in flumen projici
Senatus juſſit:
Cujus rei memoria æterna ut ſit,
Hanc domum, Sceleris officinam,
Solo æquari,
Ac nunquam in poſterum refici,
Et erigi Columnam,
Quæ vocatur Infamis,
Idem ordo mandavit.
Procul hinc procul ergo
Boni Cives,
Ne Vos Infelix, Infame ſolum
Commaculet!
M. D. C. xxx. Cal. Auguſti.
Præſide Pub. Sanitatis M. Antonio Montio Senatore
R. Juſtitiæ Cap. Jo. Baptiſta Vicecomit.

In this void ſpace ſtood formerly the barber's ſhop of John James Mora, who, having conſpired with William Platea, the commiſſary of health, and others, during the time of a raging plague, deſtroyed the lives of a great number of citizens by diſperſing poiſonous drugs. The ſenate therefore ordered them both, as enemies of their country, to be broke on the wheel, their fleſh being firſt torn with red-hot pincers, and their right hand cut off; and, after lying ſix hours on the wheel, their throats to be cut, and their bodies burned; and, that there might be no remains of ſuch wicked men, their goods to be plundered, and their aſhes thrown in the river: And, to perpetuate the memory of this tranſaction, the houſe, in which the villainy was contrived, was ordered to be pulled down to the ground, and never to be rebuilt;

and

and a column to be raised on the spot, call'd The Infamous. Fly from hence, good citizens, lest the wretched and infamous soil infect you. Aug. 1, 1630. M. Anthony Monthius, the senator, commissary of health, &c.

The citadel of Milan is thought a strong fort in Italy, and has held out formerly after the conquest of the rest of the dutchy. The governor of it is independent on the governor of Milan; as the Persians used to make the rulers of provinces and fortresses of different conditions and interests, to prevent conspiracies.

At two miles distance from Milan, there stands a building, that would have been a master-piece in its kind, had the architect designed it for an artificial echo. We discharged a pistol, and had the sound returned upon us above fifty-six times, though the air was very foggy. The first repetitions follow one another very thick, but are heard more distinctly in proportion as they decay: There are two parallel walls, which beat the sound back on each other, till the undulation is quite worn out, like the several reverberations of the same image from two opposite looking-glasses. Father Kircher has taken notice of this particular echo, as father Bartolin has done since in his ingenious discourse on sounds. The state of Milan is like a vast garden, surrounded by a noble mound-work of rocks and mountains. Indeed, if a man considers the face of Italy in general, one would think that nature had laid it out into such a variety of states and governments as one finds in it. For as the Alps, at one end, and the long range of Apennines, that passes through the body of it, branch out on all sides into several different divisions; they serve as so many natural

tural boundaries and fortifications to the little territories that lie among them. Accordingly we find the whole country cut into a multitude of particular kingdoms and commonwealths in the oldest accounts we have of it, until the power of the Romans, like a torrent that overflows its banks, bore down all before it, and spread itself into the remotest corners of the nation. But as this exorbitant power became unable to support itself, we find the Government of Italy again broken into such a variety of sub-divisions, as naturally suits with its situation.

In the court of Milan, as in several others of Italy, there are many who fall in with the dress and carriage of the French. One may however observe a kind of awkwardness in the Italians, which easily discovers the airs they give themselves not to be natural. It is indeed very strange there should be such a diversity of manners, where there is so small a difference in the air and climate. The French are always open, familiar, and talkative: The Italians, on the contrary, are still, ceremonious, and reserved. In France every one aims at a gaiety and sprightliness of behaviour, and thinks it an accomplishment to be brisk and lively: The Italians, notwithstanding their natural fieryness of temper, affect always to appear sober and sedate; insomuch that one sometimes meets young men walking the streets with spectacles on their noses, that they might be thought to have impaired their sight by much study, and seem more grave and judicious than their neighbours. This difference of manners proceeds chiefly from difference of education. In France it is usual to bring their children into company, and to cherish in them,

C from

from their infancy, a kind of forwardness and assurance: Besides, that the French apply themselves more universally to their exercises than any other nation in the world, so that one seldom sees a young gentleman in France that does not fence, dance, and ride in some tolerable perfection. These agitations of the body do not only give them a free and easy carriage, but have a kind of mechanical operation on the mind, by keeping the animal spirits always awake and in motion. But what contributes most to this light airy humour of the French, is the free conversation that is allowed them with their women, which does not only communicate to them a certain vivacity of temper, but makes them endeavour after such a behaviour as is most taking with the sex.

The Italians, on the contrary, who are excluded from making their court this way, are for recommending themselves to those they converse with by their gravity and wisdom. In Spain therefore, where there are fewer liberties of this nature allowed, there is something still more serious and composed in the manner of the inhabitants. But as mirth is more apt to make proselytes than melancholy, it is observed that the Italians have many of them for these late years given very far into the modes and freedoms of the French; which prevail more or less in the courts of Italy, as they lie at a smaller or greater distance from France. It may be here worth while to consider how it comes to pass, that the common people of Italy have in general have so great an aversion to the French, which every traveller cannot but be sensible of, that has passed through the country. The most

obvious

obvious reason is certainly the great difference that there is in the humours and manners of the two nations, which always works more in the meaner sort, who are not able to vanquish the prejudices of education, than with the nobility. Besides, that the French humour, in regard of the liberties they take in female conversations, and their great ambition to excel in all companies, is in a more particular manner very shocking to the Italians, who are naturally jealous, and value themselves upon their great wisdom. At the same time, the common people of Italy, who run more into news and politicks than those of other countries, have all of them something to exasperate them against the King of France. The Savoyards, notwithstanding the present inclinations of their court, cannot forbear resenting the infinite mischiefs he did them in the last war. The Milanese and Neapolitans remember the many insults he has offered to the house of Austria, and particularly to their deceased King, for whom they still retain a natural kind of honour and affection. The Genoese cannot forget his treatment of their Doge, and his bombarding their city. The Venetians will tell you of his leagues with the Turks; and the Romans, of his threats to pope Innocent the eleventh, whose memory they adore. It is true, that interest of state, and change of circumstances, may have sweetened these reflections to the politer sort; but impressions are not so easily worn out of the minds of the vulgar. That however, which I take to be the principal motive among most of the Italians, for their favouring the Germans above the French, is this, that they are entirely persuaded it is for the interest of Italy, to have Milan and Naples rather in the hands of the first, than of the other. One may generally observe, that the body of a people has juster views for the public good, and pursues them with greater uprightness than the nobility and gentry, who have so many private expectations and particular interests, which hang like a false bias upon their judgments, and may possibly dispose them to sacrifice the good of their country to the advancement of their own fortunes; whereas the gross of the people can have no other prospect in changes and revolutions than of public blessings, that are to diffuse themselves through the whole state in general.

To return to Milan, I shall here set down the description Ausonius has given of it, among the rest of his great cities.

Et Mediolani mira omnia, copia rerum:
Innumeræ cultæque domus, facunda virorum
Ingenia, et mores læti: Tum duplice muro
Amplificata loci species, populique voluptas
Circus, et inclusi moles cuneata Theatri:
Templa, palatinæque arces, opulensque Moneta,
Et regio Herculei celebris ab honore lavacri,
Cunctaque marmoreis ornata peristyle signis,
Omnia quæ magnis operum velut æmula formis
Excellunt; nec juncta premit vicinia Romæ.

Milan with plenty and with wealth o'erflows,
And num'rous streets and cleanly dwelling shows.
The people, bless'd with nature's happy force,
Are eloquent and chearful in discourse;
A Circus and a theatre invites
Th' unruly mob to races and to fights;

Moneta

Moneta confecrated buildings grace,
And the whole town redoubled walls embrace:
Here fpacious baths and palaces are feen,
And intermingled temples rife between;
Here circling Colonnades the ground inclofe,
And here the marble ftatues breathe in rows:
Profufely grac'd the happy town appears,
Nor Rome itfelf, her beauteous neighbour, fears.

BRESCIA,

VERONA,

PADUA.

FROM Milan we travelled through a very pleasant country to Brescia, and by the way crossed the river Adda, that falls into the Lago di Como, which Virgil calls the Lake Larius, and running out at the other end loses itself at last in the Po, which is the great receptacle of all the rivers of this country. The town and province of Brescia, have freer access to the senate of Venice, and a quicker redress of injuries, than any other part of their dominions. They have always a mild and prudent governor, and live much more happily than their fellow-subjects; for as they were once a part of the Milanese, and are now on their frontiers, the Venetians dare not exasperate them, by the loads they lay on other provinces, for fear of a revolt; and are forced to treat them with more indulgence than the Spaniards do their neighbours, that they may have no temptation to it. Brescia is famous for its iron-works. A small day's journey

ney more brought us to Verona. We saw the lake Benacus in our way, which the Italians now call Lago di Garda: It was so rough with tempests when we passed by it, that it brought into my mind Virgil's noble description of it.

Adde lacus tantos, te Lari maxime, teque
Fluctibus et fremitu assurgens, Benace, marino.
Georg. ii. v. 159.

Here vex'd by winter storms Benacus raves,
Confus'd with working sands and rolling waves;
Rough and tumultuous like a sea it lies,
So loud the tempest roars, so high the billows rise.

This lake perfectly resembles a sea, when it is worked up by storms. It is thirty-five miles in length, and twelve in breadth. At the lower end of it we crossed the Mincio.

——*Tardis ingens ubi flexibus errat*
Mincius, et tenerâ prætexit arundine ripas.
Virg. Georg. iii. v. 14.

Where the slow Mincius thro' the valley strays:
Where cooling streams invite the flocks to drink,
And reeds defend the winding waters brink.
Dryden.

The river Adige runs through Verona; so much is the situation of the town changed from what it was in Silius Italicus his time.

——*Venora Athesi circumflua.*   Lib. viii.

Verona by the circling Adige bound.

This is the only great river in Lombardy that does not fall into the Po; which it must have done, had it run but a little further before its entring the Adriatic. The rivers are all of them mentioned by Claudian.

> ——*Venetosque erectior amnes*
> *Magnâ voce ciet. Frondentibus humida ripis*
> *Colla levant, pulcher Ticinus, et Addua visu*
> *Cæruleus, velox Athesis, tardusque meatu*
> *Mincius, inque novem consurgens ora Timavus.*
>
> Sexto Conf. Hon.

Venetia's rivers, summon'd all around,
Hear the loud call, and answer to the sound;
Her dropping locks the silver Tesin rears;
The blue transparent Adda next appears;
The rapid Adige then erects her head;
And Mincio rising slowly from his bed:
And last Timavus, that with eager force
From nine wide mouths comes gushing to its course.

His Larius is doubtless an imitation of Virgil's Benacus.

> ——*Umbrosâ vestit quâ littus Olivâ*
> *Larius, et dulci mentitur Nerea fluctu.* Del Bel. Get.

The Larius here with groves of olives crown'd,
An ocean of fresh water spreads around.

I saw at Verona the famous amphitheatre, that with a few modern reparations has all the seats entire. There is something very noble in it, though the high wall and corridors that went round it are almost entirely ruined, and the area is quite filled up to the lower feat, which was formerly deep enough to let the spectators fee in safety the combats of the wild beasts and gladiators. Since I have Claudian before me, I cannot forbear setting down the beautiful description he has made of a wild beast newly brought from the woods, and making its first appearance in a full amphitheatre.

Ut fera quæ nuper montes amisit avitos,
Altorumque exul nemorum, damnatur arenæ
Muneribus, commota ruit: vir murmure contra
Hortatur, nixusque genu venabula tendit;
Illa pavit strepitus, cuneosque erecta Theatri
Despicit, et tanti miratur sibila vulgi. In Ruf. lib. ii.

So rushes on his foe the grisly bear,
That banish'd from the hills and brushy brakes,
His old hereditary haunts forsakes.
Condemn'd the cruel rabble to delight,
His angry keeper goads him to the fight.
Bent on his knee, the savage glares around,
Scar'd with the mighty crowd's promiscuous sound;
Then rearing on his hinder paws retires,
And the vast hissing multitude admires.

There are some other antiquities in Verona, of which the principal is the ruin of a triumphal arch erected to Flaminius, where one sees old Doric pillars without any pedestal or basis, as Vitruvius has described them. I have not yet seen any gardens in Italy worth taking notice of. The Italians fall as far short of the French in this particular, as they excel them in their palaces. It must however be said, to the honour of the Italians, that the French took from them the first plans of their gardens, as well of their water-works; so that their surpassing of them at present is to be attributed rather to the greatness of their riches, than the excellence of their taste. I saw the terrace-garden of Verona, that travellers generally mention. Among the churches of Verona, that of St. George is the handsomest: Its chief ornament is the martyrdom of the saint, done by Paul Veronese; as there are many other pictures about the town by the same hand. A stranger is always shewn the tomb of pope Lucius, who lies buried in the dome. I saw in the same church a monument erected by the public to one of their Bishops: The inscription says, that there was between him and his maker, *Summa Necessitudo, Summa Similitudo*. The Italian epitaphs are often more extravagant than those of other countries, as the nation is more given to compliment and hyperbole. From Verona to Padua we travelled through a very pleasant country: It is planted thick with rows of white mulberry-trees, that furnish food for great quantities of silk-worms with their leaves, as the swine and poultry consume the fruit. The trees themselves serve at the same time, as so many stays for their vines, which hang all along like garlands from tree to tree. Between the several ranges lie fields of corn, which in these warm countries ripens much better among the mulberry shades, than if it were exposed to the open sun. This was one reason why the inhabitants of this country, when I passed through it, were extremely apprehensive of seeing Lombardy the seat of war, which must have made miserable havock among their plantations; for it is not here as in the corn fields of Flanders, where the whole product of the place rises from year to year. We arrived so late at Vicenza, that we had not time to take a full sight

of

of the place. The next day brought us to Padua. St. Anthony, who lived about five hundred years ago, is the great faint to whom they here pay their devotions. He lies buried in the church that is dedicated to him at prefent, though it was formerly confecrated to the bleffed Virgin. It is extremely magnificent, and very richly adorned. There are narrow clifts in the monument that ftands over him, where good catholics rub their beads, and fmell his bones, which they fay have in them a natural perfume, though very like apoplectic balfam ; and what would make one fufpect that they rub the marble with it, it is obferved that the fcent is ftronger in the morning than at night. There are abundance of infcriptions and pictures hung up by his votaries in feveral parts of the church: For it is the way of thofe that are in fignal danger to implore his aid, and if they come off fafe they call their deliverance a miracle, and perhaps hang up the picture or defcription of it in the church. This cuftom fpoils the beauty of feveral Roman catholic churches, and often covers the walls with wretched daubings, impertinent infcriptions, hands, legs, and arms of wax, with a thoufand idle offerings of the fame nature.

They fell at Padua the life of Anthony, which is read with great devotion; the moft remarkable part of it is his difcourfe to an affembly of fifh. As the audience and fermon are both very extraordinary, I will fet down the whole paffage at length.

Non curando gli Heretici il fuo parlare, egli fi come era alla riva del mare, dove fbocca il fiume Marcethia, chiamò da parte di Dio li pefci, che veniffero à fentir la fua fanta parola. Et ecco che di fubito fopra l' acque nuotando gran moltitudine di varii, & diverfi pefci, pesci, e del mare, e del fiume, si unirono tutti, secondo le specie loro, e con bell'ordine, quasi che di ragion capaci stati fossero, attenti, e cheti con gratioso spettacolo s'accommodaro per sentir la parola di Dio. Ciò veduto il santo entro al cuor suo di dolcezza stillandosi, & per altre tanta maraviglia inarcando le ciglia, della obedientia di queste irragionevoli creature così cominciò loro à parlare. Se bene in tutto le cose create (cari, & amati pesci) si scuopere la potenza, & providenza infinita di Dio, como nel Cielo, nel Sole, nella Luna, nelle Stelle, in questo mondo inferiore, nel huomo, e nelle altre creature perfette, nondimeno in Voi particolarmente lampeggia e risplende la bontà della maestà divina; perche se bene siete chiamati Rettili, mezzi frà pietre, e bruti, confinati nelli profondi abissi delle ondeggiante acque: agitati sempre da flutti: mossi sempre da procelle: sordi al' udire, mutoli al parlare, & horridi al vedere; con tutto cio in Voi maravigliosamente si scorge la Divina grandezza; e da voi si cavano la maggiori misterii della bonta di Dio, ne mai si parla di voi nella Scrittura Sacra, che non vi sia ascosto qualche profondo Sacramento; Credete voi, che sia senza grandissimo misterio, che il primo dono fatto dall' omnipotente Iddio all' huomo fosse di voi Peschi? Credete voi che non sia misterio in questo, che di tutte le creature, e di tutti gl' animali si sien fatti sacrificii, eccetto, che di voi Pesci? Credete, che non vi sia qualche secreto in questo, che Christo nostro salvatore dall' agnelo pasquale in poi, si compiaque tanto del cibo di voi pesci? Credete, che sia à caso questo, che dovendo il Redentor del mondo, pagar, come huomo, il censo à Cesare la volesse trovare nella bocca di un pesce? Tutti, tutti sono misteri e Sacramenti: perciò siete particolarmente obligati a lodare il vostro Creatore: amati pesci di Dio havete ricevuto l' essere, la vita, il moto, e'l senso; per stanza vi hà dato il liquido

do clemento dell' Acqua, secondo che alla vostra naturale inclinatione conviene: ivi hà fatti amplissimi alberghi stanze, caverne, grotte, e secreti luoghi à voi più che sale Regie, e regal Palazzi, cari, e grati; & per propria sede havete l' acqua, elemento diasano, transparente, e sempre lucido quasi cristallo, e verro; & dalle più basse e profonde vostre stanze scorgete ciò che sopra acqua ò si fa, ò nuota; havete gli occhi quasi di Lince, ò di Argo, & da causa non errante guidati, seguite ciò che vi giova, & aggrada; & fuggite ciò che vi nuoce, havete natural desio di conservarvi secondo le spetie vostre, fase, oprate & caminate ove natura vi detta senza contrasto alcuno; nè algor d' inverno, nè calor di state vi offende, ò nuoce: siasi per sereno, ò turbato il cielo, che alli vostri humidi alberghi nè frutto, nè danno apporta; siasi pure abbondevole de suoi tesori, ò scarsa de suo frutti la terra, che a voi nulla giova; piova, tuoni, saette, lampaggi, è subissi il mondo, che avoi ciò poco importa; ver deggi primavera, scaldi la state fruttifichi l' Autunno, & assideri li inverno, questo non vi rileva punto: ne trappassar del' hore, nè correr de giorni, nè volar de mesi, nè fuggir d' anni, nè mutar de tempi, nè cangiar de stagioni vi dan pensiero alcuno ma sempre sicura, & tranquilla vita liatamente vivere: O quanto, o quanto grande la Maestà di Dio in voi si scuopre, O quanto mirabile la potenza sua; O quanto stupenda, & maravigliosa sa sua providenza; poi che frà tutte le creature dell' universo voi solo non sentisti il diluvio universale dell' acque; nè provasti i danni, che egli face al mondo; e tutto questo ch' io ho detto dovrebbe muovervi à lodar Dio, à ringratiare sua divina maestà di tante e cosi singolari beneficii, che vi ha fatti; di tante gratie, che vi ha conferite; ai tanti favori, di che vi ha fatti degna; per tanto, se non potete snodar la lingua à ringratiar
il

il vostro Benefattore, & non sapete con parole esprimer le sue lodi, fatele segno di riverenza almeno; chinatevi al suo nome; mostrate nell modo che potete sembiante di gratitudine; rendetevi benevoli alla bontà sua, in quel miglior modo che potete; O sapete, non siate sconoscenti de suoi beneficii, & non siate ingrati de suoi favori. A questo dire, O maraviglia grande, come si quelli pesci havessero havuto humano intelletto, e discorso, con gesti di profonda Humiltà, con riverenti sembianti di religione, chinarono la testa, blandiro co'l corpo, quasi approvando ciò che detto havea il benedetto padre St. Antonio.

'When the heretics would not regard his
'preaching, he betook himself to the sea-shore,
'where the river Marecchia disembogues itself
'into the Adriatic. He here called the fish toge-
'ther in the name of God, that they might hear
'his holy word. The fish came swimming to-
'wards him in such vast shoals, both from the
'sea and from the river, that the surface of the
'water was quite covered with their multitudes.
'They quickly ranged themselves, according to
'their several species, into a very beautiful con-
'gregation, and, like so many rational creatures,
'presented themselves before him to hear the
'word of God. St. Antonio was so struck with
'the miraculous obedience and submission of these
'poor animals, that he found a secret sweetness
'distilling upon his soul, and at last addressed
'himself to them in the following words.

'Although the infinite power and providence of
'God (my dearly beloved fish) discovers itself in
'all the works of his creation, as in the heavens,
'in the sun, in the moon, and in the stars, in
'this lower world, in man, and in other perfect
'creatures; nevertheless the goodness of the di-
'vine

'vine majesty shines out in you more eminently,
'and appears after a more particular manner,
'than in any other created beings. For notwith-
'standing you are comprehended under the name
'of Reptiles, partaking of a middle nature be-
'tween stones and beasts, and imprisoned in the
'deep abyss of waters; notwithstanding you are
'tost among billows, thrown up and down by
'tempests, deaf to hearing, dumb to speech,
'and terrible to behold: notwithstanding, I say,
'these natural disadvantages, the divine greatness
'shows itself in you after a very wonderful man-
'ner. In you are seen the mighty mysteries of
'an infinite goodness. The holy scripture has
'always made use of you, as the types and sha-
'dows of some profound sacrament.

'Do you think that, without a mystery, the
'first present that God almighty made to man,
'was of you, O ye fishes? do you think that,
'without a mystery, among all creatures and ani-
'mals which were appointed for sacrifices, you on-
'ly were excepted, O ye fishes? do you think
'there was nothing meant by our Saviour Christ,
'that next to the paschal lamb he took so much
'pleasure in the food of you, O ye fishes? do
'you think it was by mere chance, that, when,
'the Redeemer of the world was to pay a tribute
'to Cæsar, he thought fit to find it in the mouth
'of a fish? These are all of them so many my-
'steries and sacraments, that oblige you in a more
'particular manner to the praises of your Creator.

'It is from God, my beloved fish, that you have
'received being, life, motion, and sense. It is
'he that has given you, in compliance with your
'natural inclinations, the whole world of waters
'for your habitation. It is he that has furnished

'it

' it with lodgings, chambers, caverns, grottoes,
' and such magnificent retirements as are not to be
' met with in the seats of Kings, or in the palaces
' of Princes. You have the water for your dwell-
' ing, a clear transparent element, brighter than
' crystal; you can see from its deepest bottom
' every thing that passes on its surface; you have
' the eyes of a Lynx, or of an Argus; you are
' guided by a secret and unerring principle,
' delighting in every thing that may be be-
' neficial to you, and avoiding every thing that
' may be hurtful; you are carried on by a hid-
' den instinct to preserve yourselves, and to pro-
' pagate your species; you obey, in all your ac-
' tions, works and motions, the dictates and sug-
' gestions of nature, without the least repugnan-
' cy or contradiction.

' The colds of winter, and the heats of sum-
' mer, are equally incapable of molesting you. A
' serene or a clouded sky are indifferent to you.
' Let the earth abound in fruits, or be cursed with
' scarcity, it has no influence on your welfare.
' You live secure in rains and thunders, light-
' nings and earthquakes; you have no concern in
' the blossoms of spring, or in the glowings of
' summer, in the fruits of autumn, or in the frosts
' of winter. You are not solicitous about hours
' or days, months or years; the variableness of
' the weather, or the change of seasons.

' In what dreadful majesty, in what wonder-
' ful power, in what amazing providence, did
' God Almighty distinguish you among all the
' species of creatures that perished in the univer-
' sal deluge! You only were insensible of the
' mischief that had laid waste the whole world.

' An

'All this, as I have already told you, ought to inspire you with gratitude and praise towards the divine majesty, that has done so great things for you, granted you such particular graces and privileges, and heaped upon you so many distinguishing favours. And since for all this you cannot employ your tongues in the praises of your benefactor, and are not provided with words to express your gratitude; make at least some sign of reverence; bow yourselves at his name; give some show of gratitude, according to the best of your capacities; express your thanks in the most becoming manner that you are able, and be not unmindful of all the benefits he has bestowed upon you.

'He had no sooner done speaking, but, behold a miracle! The fish, as though they had been endued with reason, bowed down their heads with all the marks of a profound humility and devotion, moving their bodies up and down with a kind of fondness, as approving what had been spoken by the blessed father, St. Antonio. The legend adds, that after many heretics, who were present at the miracle, had been converted by it, the saint gave his benediction to the fish, and dismissed them.'

Several other the like stories of St. Anthony are represented about his monument in a very fine Basso Relievo.

I could not forbear setting down the titles given to St. Anthony in one of the tables that hangs up to him, as a token of gratitude from a poor peasant, who fancied the saint had saved him from breaking his neck.

*Sacratissimi pusionis Bethlehemitici
Lilio candidiori Delicio,
Seraphidum soli fulgidissimo,
Celsissimo sacræ sapientiæ tholo,
Prodigiorum putratori potentissimo,
Mortis, Erronis, Calamitatis, Lepræ, Dæmonis,
Dispensatori, correctori, liberatori, curatori, fugatori,
Sancto, sapienti, pio, potenti, tremendo,
Ægrotorum & Naufragantium Salvatori
Præsentissimo, tutissimo
Membrorum restitutori, vinculorum confractori,
Rerum perditarum Inventori stupendo,
Periculorum omnium profligatori
Magno, Mirabili,
Ter Sancto
Antonio Paduano,
Pientissimo post Deum ejusque Virgineam matrem
Protectori & Sospitatori suo,* &c.

To the thrice holy Anthony of Padua, delight (whiter than the lily) of the most holy child of Bethlehem, brightest son of the seraphs, highest roof of sacred wisdom, most powerful worker of miracles, holy dispenser of death, wise corrector of error, pious deliverer from calamity, powerful curer of leprosy, tremendous driver-away of devils, most ready and most trusty preserver of the sick and ship-wrecked, restorer of limbs, breaker of bonds, stupendous discoverer of lost things, great and wonderful defender from all dangers, his most pious (next to God and his virgin mother) protector and safe-guard, &c.

The custom of hanging up limbs in wax, as well as pictures, is certainly derived from the old heathens who used, upon their recovery, to make an offering in wood, metal or clay, of the part that had been afflicted

afflicted with a diftemper, to the deity that delivered them. I have feen, I believe, every limb of a human body figured in iron or clay, which were formerly made on this occafion, among the feveral collections of antiquities that have been fhewn me in Italy. The church of St. Juftina, defigned by Palladio, is the moft handfome, luminous, difencumbered building in the infide that I have ever feen, and is efteemed by many artifts one of the fineft works in Italy. The long nef confifts of a row of five cupolas; the crofs one has on each fide a fingle cupola deeper and broader than the others. The martyrdom of St. Juftina hangs over the altar, and is a piece of Paul Veronefe. In the great townhall of Padua ftands a ftone fuperfcribed Lapis Vituperii. Any debtor that will fwear himfelf not worth five pound, and is fet by the bailiffs thrice with his bare buttocks on this ftone in a full hall, clears himfelf of any farther profecution from his creditors; but this is a punifhment that no body has fubmitted to thefe four-and-twenty years. The univerfity of Padua is of late much more regular than it was formerly, though it is not yet fafe walking the ftreets after fun-fet. There is at Padua a manufacture of cloth, which has brought very great revenues into the republic. At prefent the Englifh have not only gained upon the Venetians in the Levant, which ufed chiefly to be fupplied from this manufacture, but have great quantities of their cloth in Venice itfelf; few of the nobility wearing any other fort, notwithftanding the magiftrate of the pomps is obliged by his office to fee that no body wears the cloth of a foreign country. Our merchants indeed are forced to make ufe of fome artifice to get thefe prohibited goods into port. What they here fhow for the afhes of Livy and

and Atenor is disregarded by the best of their own antiquaries.

The pretended tomb of Antenor put me in mind of the latter part of Virgil's description, which gives us the original of Padua.

Antenor potuit mediis elapsus Achivis
Illyricos penetrare sinus, atque intima tutus
Regna Liburnorum, & fontem superare Timavi:
Unde per ora novem vasto cum murmure montis
It mare præruptum, & pelago premit arva sonanti;
Hic tamen ille urbem Patavi, sedesque locavit
Teucrorum, et genti nomen dedit, armaque fixit
Troïa: nunc placidâ compostus pace quiescit.
Æn. i. v. 246.

Antenor, from the midst of Grecian hosts,
Could pass secure, and pierce th' Illyrian coasts;
Where rolling down the steep Timavus raves,
And through nine channels disembogues his waves.
At length he founded Padua's happy seat,
And gave his Trojans a secure retreat; (names:
There fix'd their arms, and there renew'd their
And there in quiet lies.————   Dryden.

From Padua I went down the river Brent in the ordinary ferry, which brought me in a day's time to Venice.

VENICE.

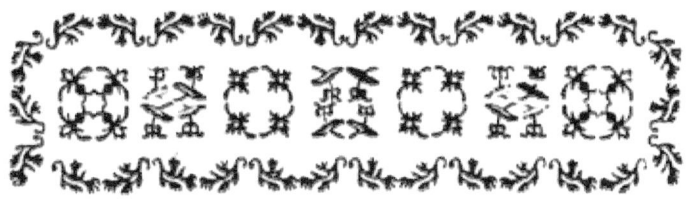

VENICE.

HAVING often heard Venice reprefented as one of the moft defenfible cities in the world, I took care to inform myfelf of the particulars in which its ftrength confifts. And thefe I find are chiefly owing to its advantageous fituation; for it has neither rocks nor fortifications near it, and yet is, perhaps, the moft impregnable Town in Europe. It ftands at leaft four miles from any part of the *Terra firma*; nor are the fhallows that lie about it ever frozen hard enough to bring over an army from the land fide; the conftant flux and reflux of the fea, or the natural mildnefs of the climate, hindering the ice from gathering to any thicknefs; which is an advantage the Hollanders want, when they have laid all their country under water. On the fide that is expofed to the Adriatic, the entrance is fo difficult to hit, that they have marked it out with feveral ftakes driven into the ground, which they would not fail to cut upon the firft approach of an enemy's fleet. For this reafon they have not fortified the little iflands, that lie at the entrance, to the beft advantage, which might otherwife very eafily command all the paffes that lead to the city from the Adriatic. Nor could an ordinary fleet with bomb-veffels, hope to fucceed againft a place that has always in its arfenal a confiderable number of gallies and men of war ready to put to

fea

sea on a very short warning. If we could therefore suppose them blocked up on all sides, by a power too strong for them, both by sea and land, they would be able to defend themselves against every thing but famine; and this would not be a little mitigated by the great quantities of fish that their seas abound with, and that may be taken up in the midst of their very streets; which is such a natural magazine as few other places can boast of.

Our voyage-writers will needs have this city in great danger of being left, within an age or two, on the *Terra firma*; and represent it in such a manner, as if the sea was insensibly shrinking from it, and retiring into its channel. I asked several, and among the rest father Coronelli, the state's geographer of the truth of this particular, and they all assured me that the sea rises as high as ever, though the great heaps of dirt it brings along with it are apt to choak up the shallows; but that they are in no danger of losing the benefit of their situation, so long as they are at the charge of removing these banks of mud and sand. One may see abundance of them above the surface of the water, scattered up and down like so many little islands, when the tide is low; and they are these that make the entrance for ships difficult to such as are not used to them; for the deep canals run between them, which the Venetians are at a great expence to keep free and open.

This city stands very convenient for commerce. It has several navigable rivers that run up into the body of Italy, by which they might supply a great many countries with fish and other commodities; not to mention their opportunities for the Levant, and each side of the Adriatic. But notwithstanding these conveniencies, their trade is far from being in a flourishing condition for many reasons. The duties are great that are laid on merchandises. Their nobles think it below their quality to engage in traffic. Their merchants who are grown rich, and able to manage great dealings, buy their nobility, and generally give over trade. Their manufactures of cloth, glass, and silk, formerly the best in Europe, are now excelled by those of other countries. They are tenacious of old laws and customs to their great prejudice, whereas a trading nation must be still for new changes and expedients, as different junctures and emergencies arise. The state is at present very sensible of this decay in their trade, and, as a noble Venetian, who is still a merchant, told me, they will speedily find out some method to redress it; possibly by making a free port, for they look with an evil eye upon Leghorn, which draws to it most of the vessels bound for Italy. They have hitherto been so negligent in this particular, that many think the great Duke's gold has had no small influence in their councils.

Venice has several particulars, which are not to be found in other cities, and is therefore very entertaining to a traveller. It looks at a distance, like a great town half floated by a deluge. There are canals every where crossing it, so that one may go to most houses either by land or water. This is a very great convenience to the inhabitants; for a Gondola with two oars at Venice, is as magnificent as a coach and six horses with a large equipage, in another country; besides that it makes all other carriages extremely cheap. The streets are generally paved with brick or freestone, and always kept very neat; for there is no carriage, not so much as a chair, that passes through them. There
is

is an innumerable multitude of very handsome bridges, all of a single arch, and without any fence on either side, which would be a great inconvenience to a city less sober than Venice. One would indeed wonder that drinking is so little in vogue among the Venetians, who are in a moist air and a moderate climate, and have no such diversions as bowling, hunting, walking, riding, and the like exercises to employ them without doors. But as the nobles are not to converse too much with strangers, they are in no danger of learning it; and they are generally too distrustful of one another for the freedoms that are used in such kind of conversations. There are many noble palaces in Venice. Their furniture is not commonly very rich, if we except the pictures, which are here in greater plenty than any other place in Europe, from the hands of the best masters of the Lombard school; as Titian, Paul Veronese, and Tintoret. The last of these is in greater esteem at Venice than in other parts of Italy. The rooms are generally hung with gilt leather, which they cover on extraordinary occasions with Tapestry, and hangings of greater value. The flooring is a kind of red plaister made of brick ground to powder, and afterwards worked into mortar. It is rubbed with oil, and makes a smooth, shining, and beautiful surface. These particularities are chiefly owing to the moisture of the air, which would have an ill effect on other kinds of furniture, as it shows itself too visibly in many of their finest pictures. Though the Venetians are extremely jealous of any great fame or merit in a living member of their commonwealth, they never fail of giving a man his due praises, when they are in no danger of suffering from his ambition. For this reason, though there are

are a great many monuments erected to such as have been benefactors to the republic, they are generally put up after their deaths. Among the many elogiums that are given to the Doge, Pisauro, who had been ambassador in England, his epitaph, says, *In Anglia Jacobi Regis obitum mira calliditate celatum mira sagacitate rimatus priscam benevolentiam firmavit.* ' In England, having with wonderful sagacity discovered the death of King James, which was kept secret with wonderful art, he confirmed the ancient friendship.' The particular palaces, churches, and pictures of Venice, are enumerated in several little books that may be bought on the place, and have been faithfully transcribed by many voyage-writers. When I was at Venice, they were putting out very curious stamps of the several edifices which are most famous for their beauty or magnificence. The Arsenal of Venice is an island of about three miles round. It contains all the stores and provisions for war, that are not actually employed. There are docks for their gallies and men of war, most of them full, as well as workhouses for all land and naval preparations. That part of it, where the arms are laid, makes a great shew, and was indeed very extraordinary about a hundred years ago; but at present a great part of its furniture is grown useless. There seem to be almost as many suits of armour as there are guns. The swords are old fashioned and unwieldy in a very great number, and the fire-arms fitted with locks of little convenience in comparison of those that are now in use. The Venetians pretend they could set out, in case of great necessity, thirty men of war, a hundred gallies, and ten galeasses, though I cannot conceive how they cou'd man a fleet of half the number. It was certainly a mighty error

error in this state to effect so many conquests on the Terra firma, which has only served to raise the jealousy of the christian Princes, and about three hundred years ago had like to have ended in the utter extirpation of the commonwealth; whereas, had they applied themselves, with the same politics and industry, to the increase of their strength by sea, they might perhaps have had all the islands of the Archipelago in their hands, and, by consequence the greatest fleet, and the most seamen of any other state in Europe. Besides, that this would have given no jealousy to the Princes their neighbours, who would have enjoyed their own dominions in peace, and have been very well contented to have seen so strong a bulwark against all the forces and invasions of the Ottoman empire.

This republic has been much more powerful than it is at present, as it is still likelier to sink than increase in its dominions. It is not impossible but the Spaniard may, some time or other, demand of them Creme, Brescia, and Bergame, which have been torn from the Milanese; and in case a war should arise upon it, and the Venetians lose a single battle, they might be beaten off the continent in a single summer, for their fortifications are very inconsiderable. On the other side the Venetians are in continual apprehensions from the Turk, who will certainly endeavour at the recovery of the Morea, as soon as the Ottoman empire has recruited a little of its ancient strength. They are very sensible that they had better have pushed their conquests on the other side of the Adriatic into Albania; for then their territories would have lain together, and have been nearer the fountain-head to have received succours on occasion; but the Venetians are under articles with the Emperor, to resign into his hands
what-

VENICE.

whatever they conquer of the Turkish dominions, that has been formerly dismembered from the empire. And having already very much dissatisfy'd him in the Frioul and Dalmatia, they dare not think of exasperating him further. The Pope disputes with them their pretensions to the Polesin, as the Duke of Savoy lays an equal claim to the kingdom of Cyprus. 'Tis surprising to consider with what heats these two powers have contested their title to a kingdom that is in the hands of the Turk.

Among all these difficulties the republic will still maintain itself, if policy can prevail over force; for it is certain the Venetian senate is one of the wisest councils in the world, though at the same time, if we believe the reports of several that have been well versed in their constitution, a great part of their politics is founded on maxims, which others do not think consistent with their honour to put in practice. The preservation of the republic is that to which all other considerations submit. To encourage idleness and luxury in the nobility, to cherish ignorance and licentiousness in the clergy, to keep alive a continual faction in the common people, to connive at the viciousness and debauchery of convents, to breed dissensions among the nobles of the Terra firma, to treat a brave man with scorn and infamy, in short to stick at nothing for the publick interest, are represented as the refined parts of the Venetian wisdom.

Among all the instances of their politics, there is none more admirable than the great secrecy that reigns in their public councils. The senate is generally as numerous as our house of commons, if we only reckon the sitting members, and yet carries its resolutions so privately, that they are seldom known 'till they discover themselves in the

execution.

execution. It is not many years since they had before them a great debate concerning the punishment of one of their admirals, which lasted a month together, and concluded in his condemnation; yet was there none of his friends, nor of those who had engaged warmly in his defence, that gave him the least intimation of what was passing against him, until he was actually seized, and in the hands of justice.

The noble Venetians think themselves equal at least to the electors of the empire, and but one degree below Kings; for which reason they seldom travel into foreign countries, where they must undergo the mortification of being treated like private gentlemen: Yet it is observed of them, that they discharge themselves with a great deal of dexterity in such embassies and treaties as are laid on them by the republic; for their whole lives are employed in intrigues of state, and they naturally give themselves airs of Kings and Princes, of which the ministers of other nations are only the representatives. Monsieur Amelot, reckons in his time, two thousand five hundred nobles that had voices in the great council; but at present, I am told, there are not at most fifteen hundred, notwithstanding the addition of many new families since that time. It is very strange, that with this advantage they are not able to keep up their number, considering that the nobility spreads equally through all the brothers, and that so very few of them are destroyed by the wars of the republic. Whether this may be imputed to the luxury of the Venetians, or to the ordinary celibacy of the younger brothers, or to the last plague which swept away many of them, I know not. They generally thrust the females of their families into convents, the better

to

to preserve their estates. This makes the Venetian nuns famous for the liberties they allow themselves. They have operas within their own walls, and often go out of their bounds to meet their admirers, or they are very much misrepresented. They have many of them their lovers, that converse with them daily at the grate; and are very free to admit a visit from a stranger. There is indeed one of the Cornara's, that not long ago refused to see any under the degree of a prince.

The carnival of Venice is every where talked of. The great diversion of the place at that time, as well as on all other high occasions, is masking. The Venetians, who are naturally grave, love to give into the follies and entertainments of such seasons, when disguised in a false personage. They are indeed under a necessity of finding out diversions that may agree with the nature of the place, and make some amends for the loss of several pleasures which may be met with on the continent. These disguises give occasion to abundance of love-adventures; for there is something more intriguing in the amours of Venice, than in those of other countries; and I question not but the secret history of a carnival would make a collection of very diverting novels. Operas are another great entertainment of this season. The poetry of them is generally as exquisitely ill, as the music is good. The arguments are often taken from some celebrated action of the ancient Greeks or Romans, which sometimes looks ridiculous enough; for who can endure to hear one of the rough old Romans, squeaking through the mouth of an eunuch, especially when they may choose a subject out of courts where eunuchs are really actors, or represent by them any of the soft Asiatic monarchs? the opera that was most in vogue during my stay at Venice, was built on the following subject. Cæsar and Scipio are rivals for Cato's daughter. Cæsar's first words bid his soldiers fly, for the enemies are upon them: *Si leva Cæsare, e dice a Soldati, A' la fugga, A' la scampo.* The daughter gives the preference to Cæsar, which is made the occasion of Cato's death. Before he kills himself, you see him withdrawn into his library, where, among his books, I observed the titles of Plutarch and Tasso. After a short soliloquy, he strikes himself with the dagger that he holds in his hand; but, being interrupted by one of his friends, he stabs him for his pains, and by the violence of the blow unluckily breaks the dagger on one of his ribs, so that he is forced to dispatch himself by tearing up his first wound. This last circumstance puts me in mind of a contrivance in the opera of St. Angelo, that was acted at the same time. The King of the play endeavours at a rape; but the Poet being resolved to save his heroine's honour, has so ordered it, that the King always acts with a great case-knife stuck in his girdle, which the lady snatches from him in the struggle, and so defends herself.

The Italian Poets, besides the celebrated smoothness of their tongue, have a particular advantage, above the writers of other nations, in the difference of their poetical and prose language. There are indeed sets of phrases that in all countries are peculiar to the Poets; but among the Italians there are not only sentences, but a multitude of particular words, that never enter into common discourse. They have such a different turn and polishing for poetical use, that they drop several of their letters and appear in another form, when they come to be ranged in verse. For this reason, the Italian opera

seldom

seldom sinks into a poorness of language, but, amidst all the meanness and familiarity of the thoughts has something beautiful and sonorous in the expression. Without this natural advantage of the tongue, their present poetry would appear wretchedly low and vulgar, notwithstanding the many strained allegories that are so much in use among the writers of this nation. The English and French, who always use the same words in verse as in ordinary conversation, are forced to raise their language with metaphors and figures, or, by the pompousness of the whole phrase, to wear off any littleness that appears in the particular parts that compose it. This makes our blank verse, where there is no rhyme to support the expression, extremely difficult to such as are not masters in the tongue, especially when they write on low subjects; and it is probably for this reason that Milton has made use of such frequent transpositions, latinisms, antiquated words and phrases, that he might the better deviate from vulgar and ordinary expressions.

The comedies that I saw at Venice, or indeed in any other part of Italy, are very indifferent, and more lewd than those of other countries. Their Poets have no notion of genteel comedy, and fall into the most filthy double meanings imaginable, when they have a mind to make their audience merry. There is no part generally so wretched as that of the fine gentleman, especially when he converses with his mistress; for then the whole dialogue is an insipid mixture of pedantry and romance. But it is no wonder that the Poets of so jealous and reserved a nation fail in such conversations on the stage, as they have no patterns of in nature. There are four standing characters which enter into every piece that

that comes on the stage, the Doctor, Harlequin, Pantalone, and Coviello. The Doctor's character comprehends the whole extent of a pedant, that, with a deep voice, and a magisterial air, breaks in upon conversation, and drives down all before him: Every thing he says is backed with quotations out of Galen, Hippocrates, Plato, Virgil, or any other author that rises uppermost, and all answers from his companions are looked upon as impertinencies or interruptions. Harlequin's part is made up of blunders and absurdities: He is to mistake one name for another, to forget his errands, to stumble over Queens, and to run his head against every post that stands in his way. This is all attended with something so comical in the voice and gestures, that a man, who is sensible of the folly of the part, can hardly forbear being pleased with it. Pantalone is generally an old cully, and Coviello a sharper.

I have seen a translation of the Cid acted at Bolonia, which would never have taken, had they not found a place in it for these buffoons. All four of them appear in masks that are made like the old Roman personæ, as I shall have occasion to observe in another place. The French and Italians have probably derived this custom, of shewing some of their characters in masks, from the Greek and Roman theatre. The old Vatican Terence has, at the head of every scene, the figures of all the persons that are concerned in it, with the particular disguises in which they acted; I remember to have seen in the Villa Mattheio an antique statue masked, which was perhaps designed for Gnatho in the eunuch; for it agrees exactly with the figure he makes in the Vatican manuscript. One would wonder indeed how so polite a people as the ancient Romans and Athenians should not look on these borrowed faces as unnatural.

tural. They might do very well for a cyclops, or a satyr that can have no resemblance in human features; but for a flatterer, a miser, or the like characters, which abound in our own species, nothing is more ridiculous than to represent their looks by a painted vizard. In persons of this nature the turns and motions of the face are often as agreeable as any part of the action. Could we suppose that a mask represented ever so naturally the general humour of a character, it can never suit with the variety of passions that are incident to every single person in the whole course of a play. The grimace may be proper on some occasions, but is too steady to agree with all. The rabble indeed are generally pleased at the first entry of a disguise; but the jest grows cold even with them too when it comes on the stage in a second scene.

Since I am on this subject, I cannot forbear mentioning a custom at Venice, which they tell me is particular to the common people of this country, of singing stanzas out of Tasso. They are set to a pretty solemn tune, and when one begins in any part of the Poet, it is odds but he will be answered by some body else that overhears him: So that sometimes you have ten or a dozen in the neighbourhood of one another, taking verse after verse, and running on with the poem as far as their memories will carry them.

On Holy Thursday, among the several shows that are yearly exhibited, I saw one that is odd enough, and particular to the Venetians. There is a set of artisans, who, by the help of several poles, which they lay across each others shoulders, build themselves up into a kind of pyramid; so that you see a pile of men in the air of four or five rows rising one above another. The weight is so equally distributed,

buted, that every man is very well able to bear his Part of it, the stories, if I may so call them, growing less and less as they advance higher and higher. A little boy represents the point of the pyramid, who, after a short space, leaps off with a great deal of dexterity, into the arms of one that catches him at the bottom. In the same manner the whole building falls to pieces. I have been the more particular on this, because it explains the following verses of Claudian, which show that the Venetians are not the inventors of this trick.

Vel qui more avium sese jaculantur in auras,
Corporaque ædificant, celeri crescentia nexu,
Quorum compositam puer augmentatus in arcem
Emicat, et vinctus plantæ, vel cruribus hærens.
Pendula librato figit vestigia saltu.
Claud. de Pr. & Olyb. Conf.

Men, pil'd on men, with active leaps arise,
And build the breathing fabric to the skies;
A sprightly youth above the topmost row
Points the tall pyramid, and crowns the show.

Though we meet with the Veneti in the old Poets the city of Venice is too modern to find a place among them. Sannazarius's epigram is too well known to be inserted. The same Poet has celebrated this city in two other places of his poems.

————— Quis Venetæ miracula proferat urbis,
   Una instar magni quæ simul orbis habet?
Salva Italum Regina, altæ pulcherrima Romæ
   Æmula, quæ terris, quæ dominaris aquis!
Tu tibi vel Reges cives facis, O Decus, O Lux,
   Ausoniæ, per quam libera turba sumus,
Per

VENICE.

*Per quam Barbaries nobis non imperat, et Sol
Exoriens nostro clarius orbe nitet!* Lib. iii. Eleg. 1.

Venetia stands with endless beauties crown'd,
And as a world within herself is found.
Hail Queen of Italy! for years to come
The mighty rival of immortal Rome!
Nations and seas are in thy states enroll'd,
And Kings among thy citizens are told.
Ausonia's brightest ornament! by thee
She sits a sov'reign unenslav'd and free;
By thee the rude barbarian chas'd away,
The rising sun chears with a purer ray
Our western world, and doubly gilds the day.

*Nec Tu semper eris, quæ septem amplecteris arces,
Nec Tu, quæ mediis æmula surgis aquis.*
Lib. ii. Eleg. 1.

Thou too shalt fall by time or barb'rous foes,
Whose circling walls the sev'n fam'd hills inclose;
And thou, whose rival tow'rs invade the skies,
And, from amidst the waves, with equal glory rise

FERRARA, RAVENNA, RIMINI,

AT Venice I took a bark for Ferrara, and in my way thither saw several mouths of the Po, by which it empties itself into the Adriatic.

——————*Quo non alius per pinguia culta*
In mare purpureum violentior influit amnis.
Virg. Georg. iv. v. 372.

which is true, if understood only of the rivers of Italy.

Lucan's description of the Po would have been very beautiful, had he known when to have given over.

Quoque magis nullum tellus se solvit in amnem
Eridanus, fractasque evolvit in æquora sylvas,
Hesperiamque exhaurit aquis: hunc fabula primum
Populea fluvium ripas umbrasse corona:
Cumque diem pronum transverso limite ducens
Succendit Phaeton flagrantibus æthera loris;
Gurgitibu

Gurgitibus raptis, penitus tellure perusta,
Hunc habuisse pares Phœbeis ignibus undas.
Lib. ii. v. 408.

The Po, that, rushing with uncommon force,
O'erfets whole woods in its tumultuous courfe,
And, rifing from Hefperia's watry veins,
Th' exhaufted land of all its moifture drains.
The Po, as fings the fable, firft convey'd
Its wand'ring current through a poplar fhade:
For when young Phaëton miftook his way,
Loft and confounded in the blaze of day,
This river, with furviving ftreams fupply'd,
When all the reft of the whole earth were dry'd,
And nature's felf lay ready to expire,
Quench'd the dire flame that fet the world on fire.

The Poet's reflections follow.

Nec minor hic Nilo, si non per plana jacentis
Ægypti Libycas Nilus stagnaret arenas.
Non minor hic Istro, nisi quod dum permeat orbem
Ister, casuros in quælibet æquora fontes
Accipit & Scythicas exit non solus in undas.
Ib. v. 416.

Nor would the Nile more watry ftores contain,
But that he ftagnates on his Lybian plain:
Nor would the Danube run with greater force,
But that he gathers in his tedious courfe
Ten thoufand ftreams, and, fwelling as he flows,
In Scythian feas the glut of rivers throws.

That is, fays Scaliger, the Eridanus would be bigger than the Nile and Danube, if the Nile and Danube were not bigger than the Eridanus. What makes the Poet's remark the more improper, the very reason why the Danube is greater than the Po, as he assigns it, is that which really makes the Po as great as it is; for before its fall into the gulf, it receives into its channel the most considerable rivers of Piedmont, Milan, and the rest of Lombardy.

From Venice to Ancona the tide comes in very sensibly at its stated periods, but rises more or less in proportion as it advances nearer the head of the gulf. Lucan has run out of his way to describe the Phænomenon, which is indeed very extraordinary to those who lie out of the neighbourhood of the great ocean, and, according to his usual custom, lets his poem stand still that he may give way to his own reflections.

Quaque jacet littus dubium, quod terra fretumque
Vendicat alternis vicibus, cum funditor ingens
Oceanus vel cum refugis se fluctibus aufert.
Ventus ab extremo pelagus sic axe volutet
Destituatque ferens: an sidere mota secundo
Tethyos unda vagæ Lunaribus æstuet horis:
Flammiger an Titan, ut alentes hauriat undas
Erigat Oceanum, fluctusque ad sidera tollat;
Quærite quos agitat mundi labor: at mihi semper
Tu quæcunque moves tam crebros causa meatus,
Ut superi voluere, lates. ⸻

Lib. i. v. 409.

Wash'd with successive seas, the doubtful strand
By turns is ocean, and by turns is land:
Whether the winds in distant regions blow,
Moving the world of waters to and fro;
Or waining moons their settled periods keep
To swell the billows, and ferment the deep;

Or

Or the tir'd sun, his vigour to supply,
Raises the floating mountains to the sky,
And slakes his thirst within the mighty tide,
Do you who study nature's works decide:
Whilst I the dark mysterious cause admire,
Nor, into what the gods conceal, presumptuously inquire.

At Ferrara I met nothing extraordinary. The town is very large, but extremely thin of people. It has a citadel, and something like a fortification running round it, but so large that it requires more soldiers to defend it, than the pope has in his whole dominions. The streets are as beautiful as any I have seen, in their length breadth, and regularity. The Benedictines have the finest convent of the place. They shewed us in the church Aristo's monument: His epitaph says he was, *Nobilitate Generis atque Animi clarus, in rebus publicis administrandis in regendis populis, in gravissimis et summis Pontificio legationibus prudentia, consilio, eloquentia præstantissimus.* i. e. Noble both in birth and mind, and most conspicuous for prudence, counsel, and eloquence, in administering the affairs of the public, and discharging the most important embassies from the Pope.

I came down a branch of the Po, as far as Alberto, within ten miles of Ravenna. All this space lies miserably uncultivated until you come near Ravenna, where the soil is made extremely fruitful, and shows what much of the rest might be, were there hands enough to manage it to the best advantage. It is now on both sides the road very marshy, and generally overgrown with rushes which made me fancy it was once floated by the sea, that lies within four miles of it. Nor could I in the least doubt it when
I saw

I saw Ravenna, that is now almost at the same distance from the Adriatic, though it was formerly the most famous of all the Roman ports.

One may guess at its ancient situation from Martial's

Meliusque Ranæ garriant Ravennates. Lib. iii. Epigr.

Ravenna's frogs in better music croak.

And the description that Silius Italicus has given us of it.

Quaque gravi remo limosis segnitur unda
Lenta paludosæ perscindunt stagna Ravennæ. Lib. viii.

Incumber'd in the mud, their oars divide
With heavy strokes the thick unwieldy tide.

Accordingly the old geographers represent it as situated among marshes and shallows. The place, which is shown for the haven, is on a level with the town, and has probably been stopped up by the great heaps of dirt that the sea has thrown into it; for all the soil on that side of Ravenna has been left there insensibly by the sea's discharging itself upon it for so many ages. The ground must have been formerly much lower, for otherwise the town would have lain under water. The remains of the Pharos that stand about three miles from the sea, and two from the town, have their foundations covered with earth for some yards, as they told me, which notwithstanding are upon a level with the fields that lie about them, though it is probable they took the advantage of a rising ground to set it upon. It was a square tower, of about twelve yards in breadth, as appears by that part of it which yet remains entire; so that its height must have been very considerable to have preserved a proportion. It is made in the form of the Venetian Campanello, and is probably the high tower mentioned by Pliny, Lib. 36. cap. 12.

On the side of the town, where the sea is supposed to have laid formerly, there is now a little church called the Rotonda. At the entrance of it are two stones, the one with an inscription in Gothic characters, that has nothing in it remarkable; the other is a square piece of marble, that by the inscription appears ancient, and by the ornaments about it shows itself to have been a little pagan monument of two persons who were shipwrecked, perhaps in the place where now their monument stands. The first line and a half, that tells their names and families in prose, is not legible; the rest run thus:

―――*Raniæ domus bos produxit alumnos,*
Libertatis opus contulit una dies.
Naufraga mors pariter rapuit quos junxerat ante,
Et duplices luctus mors periniqua dedit

Both with the same indulgent master bless'd,
On the same day their liberty possess'd:
A shipwreck slew whom it had join'd before,
And left their common friends their fun'rals to deplore.

There is a turn in the third verse, that we lose by not knowing the circumstances of their story. It was the *Naufraga mors* which destroyed them, as it had formerly united them; what this union

union was is expressed in the preceding verse, by their both having been made free-men on the same day. If therefore we suppose they had been formerly shipwrecked with their master, and that he made them free at the time time, the Epigram is unriddled. Nor is this interpretation perhaps so forced as it may seem at first sight, since it was the custom of the masters, a little before their death, to give their slaves their freedom, if they had deserved it at their hands; and it is natural enough to suppose one, involved in a common shipwreck, would give such of his slaves their liberty, as should have the good luck to save themselves. The chancel of this church is vaulted with a single stone of four foot in thickness, and a hundred and fourteen in circumference. There stood, on the outside of this little cupola, a great tomb of Porphyry, and the statues of the twelve apostles; but in the war that Louis the twelfth made on Italy, the tomb was broken in pieces by a cannon ball. It was, perhaps, the same blow that made the flaw in the cupola, though the inhabitants say it was cracked by thunder, that destroyed a son of one of their Gothic Princes, who had taken shelter under it, as having been foretold what kind of death he was to die. I asked an abbot, that was in the church, what was the name of this Gothic Prince, who, after a little recollection, answered me, that he could not tell precisely, but that he thought it was one Julius Cæsar. There is a convent of Theatins, where they show a little window in the church, through which the Holy Ghost is said to have entered in the shape of a dove, and to have settled on one of the candidates for the bishoprick. The dove is represented

sented in the window, and in several places of the church, and is in great reputation all over Italy. I should not indeed think it impossible for a pigeon to fly in accidentally through the roof, where they still keep the hole open, and by its fluttering over such a particular place, to give so superstitious an assembly an occasion of favouring a competitor, especially if he had many friends among the electors that would make a politic use of such an accident: But they pretend the miracle has happened more than once. Among the pictures of several famous men of their order, there is one with this inscription. *P. D. Thomas Gouldvellus Ep. Asis Tridno consilio contra Hæreticos, & in Anglia contra Elisabeth. Fidei Confessor conspicuus.* The statue of Alexander the seventh stands in the large square of the town; it is cast in brass, and has the posture that is always given the figure of a Pope; an arm extended, and blessing the people. In another square on a high pillar is set the statue of the blessed Virgin, arrayed like a Queen, with a scepter in her hand, and a crown upon her head, for having delivered the town from a raging pestilence. The custom of crowning the Holy Virgin is so much in vogue among the Italians, that one often sees in their churches a little tinsel crown, or perhaps a circle of stars glued to the canvas over the head of the figure, which sometimes spoils a good picture. In the convent of Benedictines, I saw three huge chests of marble, with no inscription on them that I could find, though they are said to contain the ashes of Valentinian, Honorius, and his sister Placidia. From Ravenna I came to Rimini, having passed the Rubicon by the way. This river is not so very contemptible as it
is.

is generally represented, and was much increased by the melting of the snows when Cæsar passed it, according to Lucan.

Fonte cadit modico parvisque impellitur undis
Puniceus Rubicon, cum fervida canduit æstas ;
Perque imas serpit valles, & Gallica certus
Limes ab Ausoniis disterminat arva colonis:
Tunc vires præbebat hyems, atque auxerat undas
Tertia jam gravido pluvialis Cynthia cornu,
Et madidis Euri resolutæ flatibus Alpes. Lib. i. v. 213.

While summer lasts, the streams of Rubicon
From their spent source in a small current run ;
Hid in the winding vales they gently glide,
And Italy from neighb'ring Gaul divide ;
But now, with winter storms increas'd, they rose,
By watry moons produc'd, and Alpine snows,
That melting on the hoary mountains lay,
And in warm eastern winds dissolv'd away.

This river is now called Pisatello.

Rimini has nothing modern to boast of. Its antiquities are as follow: A marble bridge of five arches, built by Augustus and Tiberius, for the inscription is still legible, though not rightly transcribed by Gruter. A triumphal arch raised by Augustus, which makes a noble gate to the town, though part of it is ruined. The ruins of an amphitheatre. The Suggestum, on which it is said that Julius Cæsar harangued his army after having passed the Rubicon. I must confess I can by no means look on this last as authentic: It is built of an hewn stone, like the pedestal of a pillar, but something higher than ordinary, and is but just broad enough for one man to stand upon it. On the contrary, the ancient Suggestums, as I have often observed on medals, as well as on Constantine's arch, were made of wood like a little kind of stage; for the heads of the nails are sometimes represented, that are supposed to have fastened the boards together. We often see on them the Emperor, and two or three general officers, sometimes sitting, and sometimes standing, as they made speeches, or distributed a congiary to the soldiers or people. They were probably always in readiness, and carried among the baggage of the army, whereas this at Rimini must have been built on the place, and required some time before it could be finished.

If the observation I have here made is just, it may serve as a confirmation of the learned Fabretti's conjecture on Trajan's pillar; who suppoſes, I think, with a great deal of reaſon, that the camps, intrenchments, and other works of
the

the same nature, which are cut out as if they had been made of brick or hewn stone, were in reality only of earth, turf, or the like materials; for there are on the pillar some of these Suggestums, which are figured like those on medals, with only this difference, that they seem built with brick or free-stone. At twelve miles distance from Rimini stands the little republic of St. Marino, which I could not forbear visiting, though it lies out of the common tour of travellers, and has excessively bad ways to it. I shall here give a particular account of it, because I know of no body else that has done it. One may, at least, have the pleasure of seeing in it something more singular than can be found in great governments, and from it an idea of Venice in its first beginnings, when it had only a few heaps of earth for its dominions, or of Rome it self, when it had as yet covered but one of its seven hills.

THE REPUBLIC OF St. MARINO.

THE town and republic of St. Marino ſtands on the top of a very high and craggy mountain. It is generally hid among the clouds, and lay under ſnow when I ſaw it, though it was clear and warm weather in all the country about it. There is not a ſpring or fountain, that I could hear of in the whole dominions, but they are always well provided with huge ciſterns and reſervoirs of rain and ſnow-water. The wine that grows on the ſide of the mountain is extraordinary good, and I think much better than any I met with on the cold ſide of the Appennines. This puts me in mind of their cellars, which have moſt of them a natural advantage that renders them extremely cool in the hotteſt ſeaſons; for they have generally in the ſides of them deep holes that run into the hollows of the hill, from whence there conſtantly iſſues a breathing kind of vapour, ſo very chilling in the ſummer-time, that a man can ſcarce ſuffer his hand in the wind of it.

This

This mountain, and a few neighbouring hillocks that lie scattered about the bottom of it, is the whole circuit of these dominions. They have, what they call, three castles, three convents, and five churches, and reckon about five thousand souls in their community. The inhabitants, as well as the historians, who mention this little republic, give the following account of its original. St. Marino was its founder, a Dalmatian by birth, and by trade a mason. He was employed above thirteen hundred years ago in the reparation of Rimini, and, after he had finished his work, retired to this solitary mountain, as finding it very proper for the life of a hermit which he led in the greatest rigours and austerities of religion. He had not been long here before he wrought a reputed miracle, which, joined with his extraordinary sanctity, gained him so great an esteem, that the Princess of the country made him a present of the mountain to dispose of it at his own discretion. His reputation quickly peopled it, and gave rise to the republic which calls itself after his name. So that the commonwealth of Marino may boast at least of a nobler original than that of Rome, the one having been at first an Asylum for robbers and murderers, and the other a resort of persons eminent for their piety and devotion. The best of their churches is dedicated to the saint, and holds his ashes. His statue stands over the high altar with the figure of a mountain in its hands, crowned with three castles, which is likewise the arms of the commonwealth. They attribute to his protection the long duration of their state, and look on him as the greatest saint next the blessed Virgin. I saw in their statute-book a law against such as speak disrespectfully of him, who are to be punished in the same manner as those who are convicted of blasphemy.

This petty republic has now lasted thirteen hundred years, while all the other states of Italy have several times changed their masters and forms of government. Their whole history is comprised in two purchases, which they made of a neighbouring Prince, and in a war in which they assisted the Pope against a Lord of Rimini. In the year 1100 they bought a castle in the neighbourhood as they did another in the year 1170. The papers of the conditions are preserved in their archieves, where it is very remarkable that the name of the agent for the commonwealth, of the seller, of the notary, and the witnesses, are the same in both the instruments, though drawn up at seventy years distance from each other. Nor can it be any mistake in the date, because the Popes and Emperors names, with the year of their respective reigns are both punctually set down. About two hundred and ninety years after this, they assisted Pope Pius the second against one of the Malstatea's, who was then Lord of Rimini; and when they had helped to conquer him, received from the Pope, as a reward for their assistance, four little castles. This they represent as the flourishing time of the commonwealth, when their dominions reached half way up a neighbouring hill ; but at present they are reduced to their old extent. They would probably sell their liberty as dear as they could to any that attacked them ; for there is but one road by which to climb up to them, and they have a very severe law against any of their own body that enters the town by another path, lest any new one should be worn on the sides of their mountain. All that are capable of bearing arms are exercised, and ready at a moment's call.

The sovereign power of the republic was lodged originally in what they call the Arengo, a great council

council in which every house had its representative. But because they found too much confusion in such a multitude of statesmen, they devolved their whole authority into the hands of the council of sixty. The Arengo however is still called together in cases of extraordinary importance; and if, after due summons, any member absents himself, he is to be fined to the value of about a penny English, which the statute says he shall pay, *Sine aliqua diminutione aut gratia. i. e.* Without any abatement or favour. In the ordinary course of government, the council of sixty (which, notwithstanding the name, consists but of forty persons) has in its hands the administration of affairs, and is made up half out of the noble families, and half out of the Plebeian. They decide all by balloting, are not admitted until five and twenty years old, and choose the officers of the commonwealth.

Thus far they agree with the great council of Venice; but their power is much more extended; for no sentence can stand that is not confirmed by two thirds of this council. Besides, that no son can be admitted into it during the life of his father, nor two be in it of the same family, nor any enter but by election. The chief officers of the commonwealth are the two Capitaneos, who have such a power as the old Roman consuls had, but are chosen every six months. I talked with some that had been Capitaneos six or seven times, though the office is never to be continued to the same persons twice successively. The third officer is the commissary, who judges in all civil and criminal matters. But because the many alliances, friendships, and intermarriages, as well as the personals feuds and animosities that happen among so small a people, might obstruct the course of justice, if one of their own number had the diftribution of it, they have always a foreigner for this employ, whom they choofe for three years, and maintain out of the public ftock. He muft be a doctor of law, and a man of known integrity. He is joined in commiffion with the Capitaneos, and acts fomething like the recorder of London under the lord mayor. The commonwealth of Genoa was forced to make ufe of a foreign judge for many years, whilft their republic was torn into the divifions of Guelphs and Gibelines. The fourth man in the ftate is the phyfician, who muft likewife be a ftranger, and is maintained by a public falary. He is obliged to keep a horfe, to vifit the fick, and to infpect all drugs that are imported. He muft be at leaft thirtyfive years old, a doctor of the faculty, and eminent for his religion and honefty; that his rafhnefs or ignorance may not unpeople the commonwealth. And that they may not fuffer long under any bad choice, he is elected only for three years. The prefent phyfician is a very underftanding man, and well read in our countrymen, Harvey Willis, Sydenham, &c. He has been continued for fome time among them, and they fay the commonwealth thrives under his hands. Another Perfon, who makes no ordinary figure in the republic, is the fchool-mafter. I fcarce met with any in the place that had not fome tincture of learning. I had the perufal of a latin book in Folio, intitled, *Statuta Illuftriffimæ Reipublicæ Sancti Marini*, printed at Rimini by order of the commonwealth. The chapter on the public minifters fays, that when an ambaffador is difpatched from the republic to any foreign ftate, he fhall be allowed, out of the treafury, to the value of a fhilling a day. The people are efteemed very honeft and rigorous in the execution of juftice, and feem to live more happy and contented

among

among their rocks and snows, than others of the Italians do in the pleasantest valleys of the world. Nothing indeed can be a greater instance of the natural love that mankind has for liberty, and of their aversion to arbitrary government, than such a savage mountain covered with people, and the Campania of Rome, which lies in the same country, almost destitute of inhabitants.

PESARO, FANO, SENIGALLIA,

ANCONA, LORETTO, &c.

To ROME.

FROM Rimini to Loretto the towns of note are Pesaro, Fano, Senigallia, and Ancona. Fano received ts name from the fane or temple of fortune that stood in it. One may still see the triumphal arch erected there to Augustus: It is indeed very much defaced by time; but the plan of it, as it stood intire with all its inscriptions, is neatly cut upon the wall of a neighbouring building. In each of these towns is a beautiful marble fountain, where the water runs continually through several little spouts, which looks very refreshing in these hot countries, and gives a great coolness to the air about them. That of Pesaro is handsomely designed. Ancona is much the most considerable of these towns. It stands on a promontory, and looks more beautiful at a distance than when you are in it. The port was made by Trajan, for which he has a triumphal arch erected to him by the sea-side. The marble of this arch looks very white and fresh, as being exposed to the winds and salt sea-vapours, that by continually fretting it preserves itself from

that

that mouldy colour, which others of the same materials have contracted. Though the Italians and voyagewriters call these of Rimini, Fano, and Ancona, triumphal arches, there was probably some distinction made among the Romans between such honorary arches erected to Emperors, and those that were raised to them on account of a victory, which are properly triumphal arches. This at Ancona was an instance of gratitude to Trajan for the port he had made there, as the two others I have mentioned were probably for some reason of the same nature. One may, however, observe the wisdom of the ancient Romans, who, to encourage their Emperors in their inclination of doing good to their country, gave the same honours to the great actions of peace which turned to the advantage of the public, as to those of war. This is very remarkable in the medals that were stamped on the same occasions. I remember to have seen one of Galba's with a triumphal arch on the reverse, that was made by the senate's order for his having remitted a tax. *R. XXXX. REMISSA. S. C.* The medal, which was made for Trajan, in remembrance of his beneficence to Ancona, is very common. The reverse has on it a port with a chain running across it, and betwixt them both a boat, with this inscription, *S. P. Q. R. OPTIMO PRINCIPI. S. C*

I know, Fabretti would fain aſcribe this medal to another occaſion ; but Bellorio, in his additions to Angeloni, has ſufficiently refuted all he ſays on that ſubject.

At Loretto I enquired for the Engliſh jeſuits lodgings, and on the ſtair-caſe that leads to them I ſaw ſeveral pictures of ſuch as had been executed

cuted in England, as the two Garnets, Old-Corn, and others to the number of thirty. Whatever were their crimes, the inscription says they suffered for their religion, and some of them are represented lying under such tortures as are not in use among us. The martyrs of 1679 are set by themselves, with a knife stuck in the bosom of each figure, to signify that they were quartered.

The riches in the holy house and treasury are surprisingly great, and as much surpassed my expectation as other sights have generally fallen short of it. Silver can scarce find an admission, and gold itself looks but poorly among such an incredible number of precious stones. There will be, in a few ages more, the jewels of the greatest value in Europe, if the devotion of its Princes continues in its present fervour. The last offering was made by the Queen Dowager of Poland, and cost her 18000 crowns. Some have wondered that the Turk never attacks this treasury, since it lies so near the seashore, and is so weakly guarded. But besides that he has attempted it formerly with no success, it is certain the Venetians keep too watchful an eye over his motions at present, and would never suffer him to enter the Adriatic. It would indeed be an easy thing for a christian Prince to surprise it, who has ships still passing to and fro without suspicion, especially if he had a party in the town, disguised like pilgrims to secure a gate for him; for there have been sometimes to the number of 100000 in a day's time, as it is generally reported. But it is probable the veneration for the holy house, and the horror of an action that would be resented by all the catholic Princes of Europe, will be as great a security to the place as the strongest fortification. It is indeed an amazing thing to see such a prodigious quantity of riches lie dead, and untouched in the midst of so much poverty and misery as reign on all sides of them. There is no question, however, but the Pope would make use of these treasures in case of any great calamity that should endanger the holy see; as an unfortunate war with the Turk, or a powerful league among the protestants. For I cannot but look on these vast heaps of wealth, that are amassed together in so many religious places of Italy as the hidden reserves and magazines of the church, that she would open on any pressing occasion for her last defence and preservation. If these riches were all turned into current coin, and employed in commerce, they would make Italy the most flourishing country in Europe. The case of the holy house is nobly designed, and executed by the great masters of Italy that flourished about an hundred years ago. The statues of the Sibyls are very finely wrought each of them in a different air and posture, as are likewise those of the prophets underneath them. The roof of the treasury is painted with the same kind of device. There stands at the upper end of it a large crucifix very much esteemed, the figure of our Saviour, represents him in his last agonies of death, and amidst all the ghastliness of the visage has something in it very amiable. The gates of the church are said to be of Corinthian brass, with many scripture stories rising on them in Basso Relievo. The Pope's statue, and the fountain by it, would make a noble show in a place less beautified with so many other productions of art. The spicery, the cella and its furniture, the great revenues of the convent, with the story of the holy house, are too well known to be here insisted upon.

Whoever were the first inventors of this imposture they seem to have taken the hint of it from the veneration

neration that the old Romans paid to the cottage o Romulus, which stood on mount Capitol, and was repaired from time to time as it fell to decay. Virgil has given a pretty image of this little thatch'd palace, that represents it standing in Manlius's time, 327 years after the death of Romulus.

In summo custos Tarpeiæ Manlius arcis
Stabat pro templo, & Capitolia celsa tenebat:
Romuleoque recens horrebat Regia culmo.
Æn. Lib. viii. v. 652.

High on a rock heroic Manlius stood
To guard the temple, and the temple's god:
Then Rome was poor, and there you might behold
The palace thatch'd with straw.   Dryden.

From Loretto, in my way to Rome, I passed thro' Recanati, Macerata, Tolentino, and Poligni. In the last there is a convent of nuns called la Contessa, that has in the church an incomparable Madonna of Raphael. At Spoletto, the next town on the road, are some antiquities. The most remarkable is an aqueduct of a Gothick structure, that conveys the water from mount St. Francis to Spoletto, which is not to be equall'd for its height by any other in Europe. They reckon from the foundation of the lowest arch to the top of it 230 yards. In my way hence to Terni I saw the river Clitumnus, celebrated by so many of the Poets for a particular quality in its waters of making cattle white that drink of it. The inhabitants of that country have still the same opinion of it, as I found upon inquiry, and have a great many oxen of a whitish colour to confirm them in it. It is probable this breed was first settled in the country, and continuing still the same species, has made the inhabitants impute it to a wrong cause;
though

though they may as well fancy their hogs turn black for some reason of the same nature, because there are none in Italy of any other breed. The river Clitumnus, and Mevania that stood on the banks of it, are famous for the herds of victims with which they furnished all Italy.

Qua formosa suo Clitumnus flumina luco
Integit, & niveos abluit unda boves.
Prop. Lib. ii. Eleg. 19. v. 25.

Shaded with trees, Clitumnus' waters glide,
And milk-white oxen drink its beauteous tide.

Hinc Albi, Clitumne, greges, & maxima Tauri
Victima, sæpe tuo perfusi flumine sacro,
Romanos ad Templa Deum duxere triumphos.
Virg. Georg. ii. v. 146.

There flows Clitumnus thro' the flow'ry plain;
Whose waves, for triumphs after prosp'rous war,
The victim ox, and snowy sheep prepare.

———— *Patulis Clitumnus in Arvis*
Candentes gelido perfundit flumine Tauros.
Sil. Ital. Lib. ii.

Its cooling stream Clitumnus pours along,
To wash the snowy kine, that on its borders throng.

———— *Tauriferis ubi se Mevania campis*
Explicat ————
Luc. Lib. i. v. 468.

Where cattle graze in fair Mevania's fields.

————*Atque urbe latis*
Projecta in campis nebulas exhalta inertes,
Et

Et sedet ingentem pascens Mevania taurum,
Dona Jovi———————— Id.

Here fair Mevania's pleasant fields extend,
Whence rising vapours sluggishly ascend;
Where, 'midst the herd that in the meadows rove
Feeds the large bull, a sacrifice to Jove.

———*Nec si vacuet Mevania valles,*
Aut præstent niveos Clitumna novalia tauros,
Sufficiam——————— Stat. Syl. iv. Lib. i.

Tho' fair Mevania should exhaust her field,
Or his white kine the swift Clitumnus yield,
Still I were poor———————

Pinguior Hispulla traheretur taurus et ipsa
Mole piger, non finitima nutritus in herba,
Læta sed ostendens Clitumni pascua sanguis
Iret, et a grandi cervix ferienda Ministro.
Juv. Sat. xii. ver. 11.

A bull high-fed should fall the sacrifice,
One of Hispulla's huge prodigious size:
Not one of those our neighb'ring pastures feed,
But of Clitumnus' whitest sacred breed;
The lively tincture of whose gushing blood
Should clearly prove the richness of his Food:
A neck so strong, so large, as would command
The speeding blow of some uncommon hand.
Congreve.

I shall afterwards have occasion to quote Claudian.

Terni is the next town in course, formerly called Interamna, for the same reason that a part of Asia was named Mesopotamia. We enter at the gate of

98   Pesaro, Fano, Senigallia,

the three monuments, so called, because there stood near it a monument erected to Tacitus the historian, with two others to the Emperors Tacitus and Florianus, all of them natives of the place. These were a few years ago demolished by thunder, and the fragments of them are in the hands of some gentlemen of the town. Near the dome I was shown a square marble, inserted in the wall, with the following inscription.

Saluti perpetuæ Augustæ
Libertatique Publicæ Populi Romani
　　　　　　Genio municipi Anno post
　　　　　　Interamnam Conditam
　　　　　　D. CC. IV.
　　　　　　Ad Cneium Domitium
Ahenobarbum.　　——————————
—————————— *Coss. providentiæ Ti. Cæsaris Augusti nati ad Æternitatem Romani nominis sublato hoste perniciosissimo P. R. Faustus Titius Liberalis* VI. *vir iterum P. S. F. C.* that is, *pecunia sua fieri curavit.*

　　This stone was probably set up on occasion of the fall of Sejanus. After the name of Ahenobarbus there is a little furrow in the marble, but so smooth and well polished, that I should not have taken notice of it had not I seen Coss. at the end of it, by which it is plain there was once the name of another consul, which has been industriously razed out. Lucius Aruncius Camillus Scribonianus was consul, under the reign of * Tiberius, and was afterwards put to death for a conspiracy that he had formed against the Emperor Claudius; at

* Vid. Fast. Consul. Sicul.
　　　　　　　　　　　　which

which time it was ordered that his name and consulate should be effaced out of all public registers and incriptions. It is not therefore improbable, that it was this long name which filled up the gap I am now mentioning. There are near this monument the ruins of an ancient theatre, with some of the caves intire. I saw among the ruins an old heathen altar, with this particularity in it, that it is hollow'd, like a dish, at one end; but it was not this end on which the sacrifice was laid, as one may guess from the make of the festoon, that runs round the altar, and is inverted when the hollow stands uppermost. In the same yard, among the rubbish of the theatre, lie two pillars, the one of granate, and the other of a very beautiful marble. I went out of my way to see the famous Cascade about three miles from Terni. It is formed by the fall of the river Velino, which Virgil mentions in the seventh Æneid——*Rosea rura Velini.*

The channel of this river lies very high, and is shaded on all sides by a green forest, made up of several kinds of trees, that preserve their verdure all the year. The neighbouring mountains are covered with them, and by reason of their height are more exposed to the dews and drizzling rains than any of the adjacent parts, which gives occasion to Virgil's *rosea rura* (dewy countries). The river runs extremely rapid before its fall, and rushes down a precipice of a hundred yards high. It throws itself into the hollow of a rock, which has probably been worn by such a constant fall of water. It is impossible to see the bottom on which it breaks, for the thickness of the mist that rises from it, which looks at a distance like clouds of smoke ascending from some vast furnace, and distils in
perpetual

perpetual rains on all the places that lie near it. I think there is something more astonishing in this Cascade, than in all the water-works of Versailles, and could not but wonder when I first saw it, that I had never met with it in any of the old Poets, especially in Claudian, who makes his Emperor Honorious go out of his way to see the river Nar, which runs just below it, and yet does not mention what would have been so great an embellishment to his poem. But at present I do not in the least question, notwithstanding the opinion of some learned men to the contrary, that this is the gulf through which Virgil's Alecto shoots herself into hell: for the very place, the great reputation of it, the fall of waters, the woods that encompass it, with the smoke and noise that arise from it, are all pointed at in the description. Perhaps he would not mention the name of the river, because he has done it in the verses that precede. We may add to this, that the Cascade is not far off that part of Italy which has been called *Italiæ Meditullium*.

Est locus Italiæ medio, sub montibus altis,
Nobilis, et fama multis memoratus in oris,
Amsancti valles; densis hunc frondibus atrum
Urget utrinque latus nemoris, medioque fragosus
Dat sonitum saxis et torto vortice torrens
Hic specus horrendum, & sævi spiracula Ditis
Monstrantur, ruptoque ingens Acheronte vorago
Pestiferas aperit fauces, queis condita Erinnys,
Invisum Numen, terras cælumque levabat.

Æn. vii. v. 563.

In midst of Italy, well known to fame,
There lies a vale, Amsanctus is the name,

Below

Ancona, Loretto, &c. to Rome.

Below the lofty mount: On either side
Thick forests the forbidden entrance hide:
Full in the center of the sacred wood
An arm ariseth of the Stygian flood:
Which falling from on high, with bellowing sound
Whirls the black waves and rattling stones around.
Here Pluto pants for breath from out his cell,
And opens wide the grinning jaws of hell.
To this infernal gate the fury flies,
Here hides her hated head, and frees the lab'ring
    skies.   Dryden.

It was indeed the most proper place in the world for a fury to make her *Exit*, after she had filled a nation with distractions and alarms; and I believe every reader's imagination is pleased, when he sees the angry goddess thus sinking, as it were, in a tempest, and plunging herself into hell, amidst such a scene of horror and confusion.

The river Velino, after having found its way out from among the rocks where it falls, runs into the Nera. The channel of this last river is white with rocks, and the surface of it for a long space, covered with froth and bubbles; for it runs all along upon the fret, and is still breaking against the stones that oppose its passage: So that for these reasons, as well as for the mixture of sulphur in its waters, it is very well described by Virgil, in that verse which mentions these two rivers in their old Roman names.

Tartaream intendit vocem, qua protinus omne
Contremuit nemus, et sylvæ intonuere profundæ,
Audiit et longe Triviæ lacus, audiit amnis
Sulfurea Nar albus aqua, fontesque Velini.
                      Æn. vii. v. 514.

The sacred lake of Trivia from afar,
The Veline fountains, and sulphureous Nar,
Shake at the baleful blast, the signal of the war.

          Drden.

He makes the sound of the fury's trumpet run up the Nera to the very sources of Velino, which agrees extremely well with the situation of these rivers. When Virgil has marked any particular quality in a river, the other Poets seldom fail of copying after him.

———— *Sulphureus Nar.*   Auson.

———— The sulphureous Nar.

———— *Narque albescentibus undis*
In Tibrim properans ————   Sil. Ital. Lib. viii.
———— *Et Nar vitiatus odoro*
Sulfure ————   Claud. de Pr. & Olyb. Conf.

———— The hoary Nar
Corrupted with the stench of sulphur flows,
And into Tiber's streams th' infected current throws.

From this river our next town on the road receives the name of Narni. I saw hereabouts nothing remarkable except Augustus's bridge, that stands half a mile from the town, and is one of the stateliest ruins in Italy. It has no cement, and looks as firm as one intire stone. There is an arch of it unbroken, the broadest that I have ever seen, though by reason of its great height it does not appear so. The middle one was still much broader. They join together to the mountains, and belonged, without doubt, to the bridge that Martial mentions,

tions, though Mr. Ray takes them to be the remains of an aqueduct.

Sed jam parce mihi, nec abutere Narnia Quinto:
Perpetuo liceat sic tibi ponte frui!

Preserve my better part, and spare my friend;
So, Narni, may thy bridge for ever stand.

From Narni I went to Otricoli, a very mean little village, that stands where the castle of Ocriculum did formerly. I turned about half a mile out of the road, to see the ruins of the old Ocriculum that lie near the banks of the Tiber. There are still scattered pillars and pedestals, huge pieces of marble, half buried in the earth, fragments of towers, subterraneous vaults, bathing-places, and the like marks of its ancient magnificence.

In my way to Rome, seeing a high hill standing by itself in the Campania, I did not question but it had a Classic name, and upon enquiry found it to be mount Soracte. The Italians at present call it, because its name begins with an S, St. Oreste.

The fatigue of our crossing the Appennines, and of our whole journey from Loretto to Rome, was very agreeably relieved by the variety of scenes we passed through. For not to mention the rude prospect of rocks rising one above another, of the deep gutters worn in the side of them by torrents of rain and snow-water, or the long channels of sand winding about their bottoms, that are sometimes filled with so many rivers; we saw, in six days travelling, the several seasons of the year in their beauty and perfection. We were sometimes shiver-
ing

ing on the top of a bleak mountain, and a little while after basking in a warm valley, covered with violets, and almond-trees in blossom, the bees already swarming over them, though but in the month of February. Sometimes our road led us through groves of olives, or by gardens of oranges, or into several hollow appartments among the rocks and mountains, that look like so many natural green houses; as being always shaded with a great variety of trees and shrubs that never lose their verdure.

I shall say nothing of the *Via Flaminia*, which has been spoken of by most of the voyage-writers that have passed it, but shall set down Claudian's account of the journey that Honorius made from Ravenna to Rome, which lies most of it in the same road that I have been describing.

————Antiquæ muros egressa Ravennæ
Signa movet,, jamque ora Padi portusque relinquit
Fluminees, certis ubi legibus advena Nereus
Æstuat, et pronas puppes nunc amne secundo,
Nunc redeunte vehit, nudataque littora fluctu
Deserit, Oceani Lunaribus æmula damnis ;
Lætior hinc Fano recipit Fortuna vetusto
Despiciturque vagus prærupta valle Metaurus,
* *Qua mons arte patens vivo se perforat Arcu,*
Admisitque viam sectæ per viscera rupis.
Exuperans delubra Jovis, saxoque minantes
Appenninigenis cultas pastoribus aras :
Quin et Clitumni sacras victoribus undas,
Candida quæ Latiis præbent armenta triumphis,

* An highway made by Vespasian, like the *Grotto Obscuro* near Naples.

Visere

Ancona, Loretto, &c. to Rome. 105

Visere cura fuit. Nec te miracula Fontis *
Prætereunt: tacito paſſu quem ſi quis adiret,
Lentus erat; ſi voce gradum majore citaſſet,
Commiſtis fervebat aquis: cumque omnibus una
Sit natura vadis, ſimiles ut corporis umbras
Oſtendant, hæc ſola novam jactantia ſortem
Humanos properant imitari flumina mores.
Celſa dehinc patulum proſpectans Narnia campum
Regali calcatur equo, rarique coloris
Non procul amnis adeſt urbi, qui nominis auctor
Ilice ſub denſa ſylvis arctatus opacis
Inter utrumque jugum tortis anfractibus albet.
Inde ſalutato libatis Tibride Nymphis,
Excipiunt arcus, operoſaque ſemita, vaſtis
Molibus, & quicquid tantæ præmittitur urbi.
                                De ſexto Conſ. Hon.

They leave Ravenna, and the mouths of Po,
That all the borders of the town o'erflow;
And ſpreading round in one continu'd lake,
A ſpacious hoſpitable harbour make.
Hither the ſeas at ſtated times reſort,
And ſhove the loaden veſſels into port;
Then with a gentle ebb retire again,
And render back their cargo to the main.
So the pale moon the reſtleſs ocean guides,
Driv'n to and fro by ſuch ſubmiſſive tides
Fair Fortune next with looks ſerene and kind,
Receives 'em, in her ancient fane enſhrin'd;
Then the high hills they croſs, and from below
In diſtant murmurs hear Metaurus flow,
'Till to Clitumno's ſacred ſtreams they come,
That ſend white victims to almighty Rome;

* The fountain not known.

When

When her triumphant sons in war succeed,
And slaughter'd hecatombs around 'em bleed.
At Narni's lofty seats arriv'd, from far
They view the windings of the hoary Nar;
Through rocks and woods impetuously he glides,
While froth and foam the fretting surface hides.
And now the royal guest, all dangers pass'd,
Old Tyber and his nymphs salutes at last;
The long laborious pavement here he treads,
That to proud Rome the admiring nation leads;
While stately vaults and tow'ring piles appear,
And show the world's metroplis is near.

 Silius Italicus, who has taken more pains on the geography of Italy than any other of the Latin Poets, has given a catalogue of most of the rivers that I saw in Umbria, or in the borders of it. He has avoided a fault (if it be really such) which Macrobius has objected to Virgil, of passing from one place to another, without regarding their regular and natural situation, in which Homer's catalogues are observed to be much more methodical and exact than Virgil's.

———Cavis venientes montibus Umbri,
Hos Æsis Sapisque lavant, rapidasque sonanti
Vortice contorquens undas per saxa Metaurus:
E. lavat ingentem perfundens flumine sacro
Clitumnus taurum, Narque albescentibus undis
In Tibrim properans, Tiniæque inglorius humor,
Et Clanis, et Rubico, et Senonum de nomine Senon.
Sed pater ingenti medios illabitur amne
Albula, et immota perstringit mœnia ripa,
His urbes, Arva, et latis Mevania pratis,
Hispellum, et duro monti per saxa recumbens
Narnia, &c.———   Sil. Ital. Lib. viii.

The Umbri, that from hollow mountains came:
These Æsis and the stream of Sapis laves;
And swift Metaurus, that with rapid waves
O'er beds of stone its noisy current pours:
Clitumnus, that presents its sacred stores,
To wash the bull: the Nar's infected tide,
Whose sulph'rous waters into Tiber glide;
Tinia's small stream, that runs inglorious on
The Clanis, Senon, and the Rubicon:
With larger waters, and superior sway,
Amidst the rest, the hoary Albula
Thro' fields and towns pursues his watry way.

Since I am got among the Poets, I shall end this chapter with two or three passages out of them, that I have omitted inserting in their proper places.

Sit Cisterna mi bi quam Vinea malo Ravennæ,
Cum possim multo vendere pluris Aquam.
Mart. Lib. iii. Epigr. 56.

Lodg'd at Ravenna, (water sells so dear)
A cistern to a vineyard I prefer.

Callidus imposuit nuper mibi Caupo Ravennæ:
Cum peterem mixtum, vendidit ille merum.
Id. ib. Epigr. 57.

By a Ravenna vintner once betray'd,
So much for wine and water mix'd I paid;
But when I thought the purchas'd liquor mine,
'The rascal fobb'd me off with only wine.
Stat

108 Pesaro, Fano, Senigallia, &c.

Stas fucare colus, nec Sidone vilior Ancon,
Murice nec Tyrio——   Sil. Ital. Lib. viii.

The wool, when shaded with Ancona's dye,
May with the proudest Tyrian purple vie.

Fountain water is still very scarce at Ravenna, and was probably much more so, when the sea was within its neighbourhood.

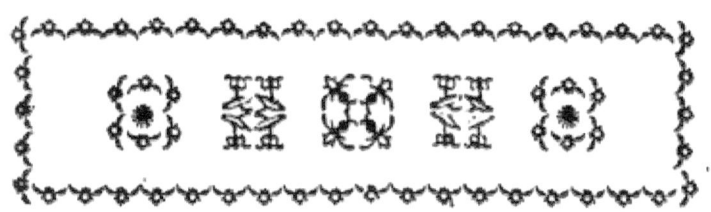

FROM ROME TO NAPLES.

UPON my arrival at Rome I took a view of St. Peter's, and the Rotunda, leaving the rest until my return from Naples, when I should have time and leisure enough to consider what I saw. St. Peter's seldom answers expectation at first entering it, but enlarges itself on all sides insensibly, and mends upon the eye every moment. The proportions are so very well observed, that nothing appears to an advantage, or distinguishes itself above the rest. It seems neither extremely high, nor long nor broad, because it is all of them in a just equality. As on the contrary, in our Gothic cathedrals, the narrowness of the arch makes it rise in height, or run out in length; the lowness often opens it in breadth, or the defectiveness of some other particular makes any single part appear in great perfection. Though every thing in this church is admirable, the most astonishing part of it is the cupola. Upon my going to the top of it, I was surprised to find that the dome, which we see in the church, is not the same that one looks upon without doors, the laſt of them being a kind of caſe to the other, and the ſtairs lying betwixt them both, by which one aſcends into the ball. Had there been only the outward dome, it would not have ſhewn itſelf to an advantage to thoſe that are in the church; or had there only been the inward one, it would ſcarce have been ſeen by thoſe that are without; had they both been one ſolid dome of ſo great a thickneſs, the pillars would have been too weak to have ſupported it. After having ſurveyed this dome, I went to ſee the Rotunda, which is generally ſaid to have been the model of it. This church is at preſent ſo much changed from the ancient Pantheon, as Pliny has deſcribed it, that ſome have been inclined to think it is not the ſame temple; but the cavalier Fontana has abundantly ſatisfied the world in this particular, and ſhewn how the ancient figure, and ornaments of the Pantheon, have been changed into what they are at preſent This author, who is now eſteemed the beſt of the Roman architects, has lately written a treatiſe on Veſpaſian,s amphitheatre, which is not yet printed.

After having ſeen theſe two maſter-pieces of modern and ancient architecture, I have often conſidered with myſelf, whether the ordinary figure of the heathen, or that of the chriſtian temples be the moſt beautiful, and the moſt capable of magnificence, and cannot forbear thinking the croſs figure more proper for ſuch ſpacious buildings than the Rotund I muſt confeſs the eye is much better filled at firſt entering the Rotund, and takes in the whole beauty and magnificence of
the

the temple at one view. But such as are built in the form of a cross give us a greater variety of noble prospects. Nor is it easy to conceive a more glorious show in architecture, that what a man meets with in St. Peter's, when he stands under the dome. If he looks upward, he is astonished at the spacious hollow of the cupola, and has a vault on every side of him, that makes one of the beautifullest Vistas that the eye can possibly pass through. I know that such as are professed admirers of the ancients will find abundance of chimerical beauties the architects themselves never thought of; as one of the most famous of the moderns in that art tells us, the hole in the roof of the Rotunda is so admirably contrived, that it makes those who are in the temple look like angels, by diffusing the light equally on all sides of them.

In all the old highways that lead from Rome, one sees several little ruins on each side of them, that were formerly so many sepulchres; for the ancient Romans generally buried their dead near the great roads.

Quorum Flaminia tegitur cinis atque Latina.
Juv. Sat. i. v. ult.

———————————Whose ashes lay
Under the Latin and Flaminian way.

None but some few of a very extraordinary quality, having been interred within the walls of the city.

Our christian epitaphs, that are to be seen only in churches, or churchyards, begin often with a *Siste Viator*; *Viator precare salutem*, &c. probably in imitation of the old Roman inscriptions, that generally addressed themselves to the travellers;

as it was impossible for them to enter the city or to go out of it, without passing through one of these melancholy roads, which for a great length was nothing else but a street of funeral monuments.

In my way from Rome to Naples I found nothing so remarkable as the beauty of the country, and the extreme poverty of its inhabitants. It is indeed an amazing thing to see the present desolation of Italy, when one considers what incredible multitudes of people it abounded with during the reigns of the Roman emperors: And notwithstanding the removal of the imperial seat, the irruptions of the barbarous nations, the civil wars of this country, with the hardships of its several governments, one can scarce imagine how so plentiful a soil should become so miserably unpeopled in comparison of what it once was. We may reckon, by a very moderate computation, more inhabitants in the Campania of old Rome, than are now in all Italy. And if we could number up those prodigious swarms that had settled themselves in every part of this delightful country, I question not but that they would amount to more than can be found at present, in any six parts of Europe of the same extent. This desolation appears no where greater than in the pope's territories; and yet there are several reasons would make a man expect to see these dominions the best regulated, and most flourishing of any other in Europe. Their prince is generally a man of learning and virtue, mature in years and experience, who has seldom any vanity or pleasure to gratify at his people's expence, and is neither encumbered with wife, children, or mistresses; not to mention the supposed sanctity of his character, which obliges him in a more particular manner to consult the good and happiness of mankind.

kind. The direction of church and state are lodged intirely in his own hands, so that government is naturally free from those principles of faction and division, which are mixed in the very composition of most others. His subjects are always ready to fall in with his designs, and are more at his disposal than any others of the most absolute government, as they have a greater veneration for his person, and not only court his favour but his blessing. His country is extremely fruitful, and has good havens both for the Adriatic and Mediterranean, which is an advantage peculiar to himself, and the Neapolitans, above the rest of the Italians. There is still a benefit the pope enjoys above all other sovereigns, in drawing great sums out of Spain, Germany, and other countries that belong to foreign princes, which one would fancy might be no small ease to his own subjects. We may here add, that there is no place in Europe so much frequented by strangers, whether they are such as come out of curiosity, or such who are obliged to attend the court of Rome on several occasions, as are many of the cardinals and prelates, that bring considerable sums into the pope's dominions. But notwithstanding all these promising circumstances, and the long peace that has reigned so many years in Italy, there is not a more miserable people in Europe than the pope's subjects. His state is thin of inhabitants, and a great part of his soil uncultivated. His subjects are wretchedly poor and idle, and have neither sufficient manufactures nor traffic to employ them. These ill effects may arise, in a great measure, out of the arbitrariness of the government; but I think they are chiefly to be ascribed to the very genius of the Roman catholic religion, which here shews itself in its perfection. It is not strange to find a country half unpeopled, where so great a proportion of the inhabitants of both sexes is tied under such vows of chastity, and where at the same time an inquisition forbids all recruits out of any other religion. Nor is it less easy to account for the great poverty and want that are to be met with in a country, which invites into it such swarms of vagabonds, under the title of pilgrims, and shuts up in cloisters such an incredible multitude of young and lusty beggars who, instead of increasing the common stock by their labour and industry, lie as a dead weight on their fellow-subjects, and consume the charity that ought to support the sickly, old and decrepid. The many hospitals that are every where erected, serve rather to encourage idleness in the people, than to set them at work; not to mention the great riches which lie useless in churches and religious houses, with the multitude of festivals that must never be violated by trade or business. To speak truly, they are here so wholly taken up with mens souls, that they neglect the good of their bodies; and when, to these natural evils in the government and religion, there arises among them an avaricious pope, who is for making a family, it is no wonder if the people sink under such a complication of distempers. Yet it is to this humour of nepotism that Rome owes its present splendor and magnificence; for it would have been impossible to have furnished out so many glorious palaces with such a profusion of pictures, statues, and the like ornaments, had not the riches of the people at several times fallen into the hands of many different families, and of particular persons; as we may observe, though the bulk of the Roman people was more rich and happy in the times of the

com-

commonwealth, the city of Rome received all its beauties and embellishments under the emperors. It is probable the Campania of Rome, as well as other parts of the pope's territories, would be cultivated much better than it is, were there not such an exorbitant tax on corn, which makes them plow up only such spots of ground as turn to the moſt advantage: Whereas were the money to be raiſed on lands, with an exception to ſome of the more barren parts, that might be tax-free for a certain term of years, every one would turn his ground to the beſt account, and in a little time perhaps bring more money into the pope's treaſury.

 The greateſt pleaſure I took in my journey from Rome to Naples was in ſeeing the fields, towns, and rivers, that have been deſcribed by ſo many claſſic authors, and have been the ſcenes of ſo many great actions; for this whole road is extremely barren of curioſities. It is worth while to have an eye on Horace's voyage to Brundiſi, when one paſſes this way; for by comparing his ſeveral ſtages, and the road he took, with thoſe that are obſerved at preſent, we may have ſome idea of the changes that have been made in the face of this country ſince his time. If we may gueſs at the common travelling of perſons of quality, among the ancient Romans, from this poet's deſcription of his voyage, we may conclude they ſeldom went above fourteen miles a day over the Appian way, which was more uſed by the noble Romans than any other in Italy, as it led to Naples, Baiæ, and the moſt delightful parts of the nation. It is indeed very diſagreeable to be carried in haſte over this pavement.

F 4   *Minus*

Minus est gravis Appia tardis.

Hor. Sat. 5. l. i. v. 6.

For to quick trav'lers, 'tis a tedious road ;
But if you walk but flow, 'tis pretty good. Creech.

Lucan has defcribed the very road from Anxur to Rome, that Horace took from Rome to Anxur. It is not indeed the ordinary way at prefent, nor is it marked out by the fame places in both Poets.

*Jamque et præcipites fuperaverat Anxuris arces,
Et qua* * *Pontinas via dividit uda paludes ;
Qua fublime nemus, fcythicæ qua regna Dianæ ;
Quæque iter eft Latiis ad fummam fafcibus Albam:
Excelfa de rupe procul jam confpicit urbem.*

Lib. iii. v. 84.

He now had conquer'd Anxur's fteep afcent,
And to Pontina's wat'ry marfhes went ;
A long canal the muddy fen divides,
And with a clear unfully'd current glides ;
Diana's woody realms he next invades,
And croffing through the confecrated fhades,
Afcends high Alba, whence with new delight
He fees the city rifing to his fight.

In my way to Naples I croffed the two moft confiderable rivers of the Campania Felice, that were formerly called the Liris and Vulturnus, and are at prefent the Garigliano and Vulturno. The firft of thefe rivers has been defervedly celebrated by the Latin poets for the gentlenefs of its courfe, as the other for its rapidity and noife.

* A canal, the marks of it ftill feen.

—— *Rura*

———*Rura quæ Liris quieta*
Mordet aqua taciturnus amnis.
Hor. Lib. i. Od. 31. v. 37.

Liris———qui fonte quieto
Dissimulat cursum, et nullo mutabilis imbre
Perstringit tacitas gemmanti gurgite ripas.
Sil. Ital. Lib. iv.

———*Miscentem flumina Lirim*
Sulfureum, tacitisque vadis ad littora lapsum
Accolit Arpinas———
Id. Lib. viii.

Where the smooth streams of Liris stray
And steal insensibly away,
The warlike Arpine borders on the sides
Of the slow Liris, that in silence glides,
And in its tainted stream the working sulphur hides

Vulturnusque rapax—   Cl. de Pr. & Olyb. Conf.
Vulturnusque celer———   Luc. Lib. ii. 28.
———*Fluctuque sonorum*
Vulturnum———
Sil. Ital. Lib. viii.

The rough Vulturnus, furious in its course,
With rapid streams divides the fruitful grounds,
And from afar in hollow murmurs sounds.

   The ruins of Anxur and old Capua mark out the pleasant situation in which those towns formerly stood. The first of them was planted on the mountain where we now see Terracina, and by reason of the breezes that came off the sea, and the height of its situation, was one of the summer retirements of the antient Romans.

O nemus, O fontes! solidumque madentis arenæ
  Littus, et æquoreis splendidus Anxur aquis!
Mar. Lib. x. Epigr. 51.

Ye warbling fountains, and ye shady trees,
Where Anxur feels the cool refreshing breeze
Blown off the sea, and all the dewy strand
Lies cover'd with a smooth unsinking sand.

Anxuris æquorei placidos, frontine, recessus,
  Et propius Baias littoreamque domum.
Et quod inhumanæ cancro fervente cicadæ
  Non novere, nemus flumineosque lacus,
Dum colui, &c. —————   Id. ib. Epigr. 58

On the cool shore, near Baia's gentle seats,
I lay retir'd in Anxur's soft retreats;
Where silver lakes, with verdant shadows crown'd,
Disperse a grateful chilness all around;
The grashopper avoids th' untainted air,
Nor in the midst of summer, ventures there.

Impositum Saxis late candentibus Anxur.
                    Hor. Lib. i. Sat. 5. v. 26.
Monte præcelloso murranum miserat Anxur.
                             Sil. Ital. Lib. iv.
————*Scopulosi verticis Anxur.*   ibid.
  Capuæ luxum viae apud.   Sil. Ital. Lib. xi

Murranus came from Anxur's show'ry height,
With ragged rocks, and stony quarries white;
Seated on hills———

I do not know whether it be worth while to take notice that the figures which are cut in the rock near Terracina, increase still in a decimal proportion as they come nearer the bottom. If one of our voyage-writers, who passed this way more than once, had observed the situation of these figures, he
                                        would

would not have troubled himself with the differtation that he has made upon them. Silius Italicus has given us the names of several towns and rivers in the Campania Felice.

Jam vero quos opum, quos dives avorum
Et toto dabat ad bellum Campania tractu;
Ductorum adventum vicinis sedibus Osci
Servabant; sinuessa tepens, fluctuque sonorum
Vulturnum, quasque evertere silentia, Amyclæ,
Fundique et regnata Lamo Cajeta, domusque
Antiphate compressa freto, stagnisque palustre
Linternum, et quondam fatorum conscia Cumæ;
Illic Nuceriæ, et Gaurus navalibus apta,
Prole Dicharchæa multo cum milite Graia;
Illic Parthenope, et Pœno non pervia Nola,
Alliphe, et Clanio contentæ semper Acerræ;
Sarrastes etiam populos totasque videres
Sarni mitis opes: illic quos sulphure pingues
Phlegræi legere sinus, Misenus et ardens
Ore gigantæo sedes Ithacesia, Bajæ,
Non Prochyte, non ardentem sortita Typhœa
Inarime, non antiqui saxosa Telonis
Insula, nec parvis aberat Calatia muris,
Surrentum, et pauper sulci Cerealis Avella;
In primis Capua, heu rebus servare secundis
Inconsulta modum, et pravo pertura tumore. Lib. viii.

Now rich Campania sends forth all her sons,
And drains her populous cities for the war:
The Osci, first, in arms their leaders wait:
Warm Sinuessa comes; Vulturnum too,
Whose walls are deafen'd by the sounding main;
And fair Amyclæ, to the foe betray'd
Thro' fatal silence: Fundi too was there;
And Cajeta by antient Lamus ruled;

Anti-

Antiphata, wash'd by the rolling sea;
And moist Linternum on its marshy soil:
Cumæ, the Sybil's ancient seat was there;
Nuceriæ too, and woody Gaurus, came:
There was Parthenope, and Nola there,
Nola, impervious to the Punic arms;
Alliphe, and Acerræ still o'erflow'd
By the swift Clanius: there you might behold
Sarraste's manly sons, and all the wealth
Of gentle Sarnus; those whom Phlegra sent
Streaming with sulphur: Thither Baiæ came,
Built by Ulysses' friend; Misenus too;
Nor Prochyte was absent, nor the fam'd
Inarime, where huge Typhœus lies
Transfix'd with thunder; nor the stony isle
Of Telon, nor Calatia's humble walls;
Surrentum, and Avella's barren soil:
But chiefly Capua, Capua, doom'd, alas!
By her own pride and insolence to fall.

NAPLES.

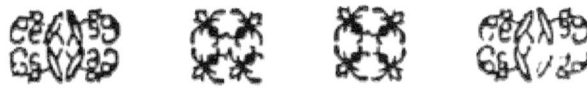

NAPLES.

MY first days at Naples were taken up with the sight of processions, which are always very magnificent in the holy-week. It would be tedious to give an account of the several representations of our Saviour's death and resurrection, of the figures of himself, the blessed virgin and the apostles, which were carried up and down on this occasion, with the cruel penances that several inflict on themselves, and the multitude of ceremonies that attend these solemnities. I saw, at the same time, a very splendid procession for the accession of the Duke of Anjou to the crown of Spain, in which the Vice-Roy bore his part at the left hand of Cardinal Cantelmi. To grace the parade, they exposed, at the same time, the blood of St. Januarius, which liquify'd at the approach of the saint's head, though as they say, it was hard congealed before. I had twice an opportunity of seeing the operation of this pretended miracle, and must confess I think it so far from being a real miracle, that I look upon it as one of the most bungling tricks that I ever saw: Yet it is this that makes as great a noise as any in the Roman church, and that Monsieur Paschal has hinted at among the rest, in his marks of the true religion. The modern Neapolitans seem to have copied it out from one, which was shewn in a town of the

the kingdom of Naples, as long ago as in Horace's time.

―――*Debine Gnatia lymphis*
Iratis extructa dedit, risusque jocosque,
Dum, flamma sine, thura liquescere limine sacro
Persuadere cupit: credat Judæus Apella,
Non ego.――― Lib. i. Sat. 5. v. 97.

At Gnatia next arriv'd, we laugh'd to see
The superstitious crowd's simplicity,
That in the sacred temple needs would try
Without a Fire th' unheated gums to fry;
Believe who will the solemn sham, not I.

One may see at least that the heathen priesthood had the same kind of secret among them, of which the Roman catholics are now masters.

I must confess, though I had lived above a year in a Roman catholic country, I was surprised to see many ceremonies and superstitions in Naples, that are not so much as thought of in France. But as it is certain there has been a kind of secret reformation made, though not publicly owned, in the Roman catholic church, since the spreading of the protestant religion, so we find the several nations are recovered out of their ignorance, in proportion as they converse more or less with those of the reformed churches. For this reason the French are much more enlightened than the Spaniards or Italians, on occasion of their frequent controversies with the Huguenots; we find many of the Roman catholic gentlemen of our own country, who will not stick to laugh at the superstitions they sometimes meet with in other nations.

I shall

I shall not be particular in describing the grandeur of the city of Naples, the beauty of its pavement, the regularity of its buildings, the magnificence of its churches and convents, the multitude of its inhabitants, or the delightfulness of its situation, which so many others have done with a great deal of leisure and exactness. If a war should break out the town has reason to apprehend the exacting of a large contribution, or a bombardment. It has but seven gallies, a mole, and two little castles, which are capable of hindering an enemy's approaches. Besides that the sea which lies near it is not subject to storms, has no sensible flux and reflux, and is so deep that a vessel of burden may come up to the very mole. The houses are flat-roofed to walk upon, so that every bomb that fell on them would take effect.

Pictures, statues, and pieces of antiquity are not so common at Naples as one might expect in so great and antient a city of Italy; for the Vice-Roys take care to send into Spain every thing that is valuable of this nature. Two of their finest modern statues are those of Apollo and Minerva, placed on each side of Sannazarius's tomb. On the face of this monument, which is all of marble, and very neatly wrought, is represented, in Bas Relief, Neptune among the satyrs, to shew that this poet was the inventor of piscatory eclogues. I remember Hugo Grotius describes himself, in one of his poems as the first that brought the muses to the sea-side; but he must be understood only of the poets of his own country. I here saw the temple that Sannazarius mentions in his invocation of the blessed virgin, at the beginning of his *De partu virginis,* which was all raised at his own expence.

—*Niveis*

———Niveis tibi si solemnia templis
Serta damus; si mansuras tibi ponimus aras
Excisa in scopulo, fluctus unde aurea canos
Despiciens celso de culmine Mirgelline
Attollit, nautisque procul venientibus offert;
Tu vatem ignarumque viæ insuetumque labori
Diva mone———   Lib. i.

Thou bright celestial goddess, if to thee
An acceptable temple I erect,
With fairest flow'rs and freshest garlands deck'd,
On tow'ring rocks, whence Mergelline spies
The ruffled deep in storms and tempests rise:
Guide thou the pious poet, nor refuse
Thine own propitious aid to his unpractis'd muse.

There are several very delightful prospects about Naples, especially from some of the religious houses; for one seldom finds in Italy a spot of ground more agreeable than ordinary, that is not covered with a convent. The cupolas of this city, though there are many of them, do not appear to the best advantage when one surveys them at a distance, as being generally too high and narrow. The Marquis of Medina Sidonia, in his Vice-Royalty, made the shell of a house, which he had not time to finish, that commands a view of the whole bay, and would have been a very noble building, had he brought it to perfection. It stands so on the side of a mountain, that it would have had a garden to every story, by the help of a bridge, which was to have been laid over each garden.

The bay of Naples is the most delightful one that I ever saw. It lies in almost a round figure of about thirty miles in the diameter. Three parts of it are sheltered with a noble circuit of woods

woods and mountains. The high promontory of Surrentum divides it from the bay of Salernum. Between the utmost point of this promontory, and the isle of Caprea, the sea enters by a strait of about three miles wide. This island stands as a vast mole, which seems to have been planted there on purpose to break the violence of the waves that run into the bay. It lies longways, almost in a parallel line to Naples. The excessive height of its rocks secures a great part of the bay from winds and waves, which enter again between the other end of this island and the promontory of Miseno. The bay of Naples is called the Crater by the old geographers, probably from this its resemblance to a round bowl half filled with liquor. Perhaps Virgil, who composed here a great part of his Æneids, took from hence the plan of that beautiful harbour, which he has made in his first book; for the Libyan port is but the Neapolitan bay in little.

Est in secessu longo locus: Insula portum
Efficit objectu laterum, quibus omnis ab alto
Frangitur, inque sinus scindit sese unda reductos:
Hinc atque hinc vastæ rupes geminique minantur
In cœlum scopuli, quorum sub vertice late
Æquora tuta silent; tum Silvis scena coruscis
Desuper, horrentique atrum nemus imminet umbra.
Æn. i. v. 163.

Within a long recess there lies a bay;
An island shades it from the rolling sea,
And forms a port secure for ships to ride:
Broke by the jutting land on either side,
In double streams the briny waters glide
Between two rows of rocks. a Silvan scene
Appears above, and groves for ever green. Dryden.

Naples ſtands in the boſom of this bay, and has the pleaſanteſt ſituation in the world, though, by reaſon of its weſtern mountains, it wants an advantage Vitruvius would have to the front of his palace, of ſeeing the ſetting ſun.

One would wonder how the Spaniards, who have but very few forces in the kingdom of Naples, ſhould be able to keep a people from revolting, that has been famous for its mutinies and ſeditions in former ages. But they have ſo well contrived it, that, though the ſubjects are miſerably harraſſed and oppreſſed, the greateſt of their oppreſſors are thoſe of their own body. I ſhall not mention any thing of the clergy, who are ſufficiently reproached in moſt itineraries for the univerſal poverty that one meets with in this noble and plentiful kingdom. A great part of the people is in a ſtate of vaſſalage to the Barons, who are the harſheſt tyrants in the world to thoſe that are under them. The vaſſals indeed are allowed, and invited to bring in their complaints and appeals to the Vice-Roy, who, to foment diviſions, and gain the hearts of the populace, does not ſtick at impriſoning and chaſtiſing their maſters very ſeverely on occaſion. The ſubjects of the crown are notwithſtanding much more rich and happy than the vaſſals of the Barons. Inſomuch that when the King has been upon the point of ſelling a town to one of his Barons, the inhabitants have raiſed the ſum upon themſelves, and preſented it to the King, that they might keep out of ſo inſupportable a ſlavery. Another way the Spaniards have taken to grind the Neapolitans, and yet to take off the odium from themſelves, has been by erecting ſeveral courts of juſtice, with a very ſmall penſion for ſuch as ſit at the head of them, ſo that they are tempted to take bribes, keep cauſes undecided,

decided, encourage law-suits, and do all they can to fleece the people, that they may have wherewithal to support their own dignity. It is incredible how great a multitude of retainers to the law there are at Naples. It is commonly said, that when Innocent the eleventh had desired the Marquis of Carpio to furnish him with thirty thousand head of swine, the Marquis answered him, that for his swine he could not spare them, but if his holiness had occasion for thirty thousand lawyers, he had them at his service. These gentlemen find a continual employ for the fiery temper of the Neapolitans, and hinder them from uniting in such common friendships and alliances as might endanger the safety of the government. There are very few persons of consideration who have not a cause depending; for when a Neapolitan cavalier has nothing else to do, he gravely shuts himself up in his closet, and falls a tumbling over his papers, to see if he can start a law-suit, and plague any of his neighbours. So much is the genius of the people changed since Statius's time.

Nulla foro rabies, aut strictæ jurgia legis ;
Morum jura viris, solum et sine fascibus æquum.
Sylv. 1. Lib. iii. v. 87.

By love of right and native justice led,
In the straight paths of equity they tread;
Nor know the bar, nor fear the judge's frown,
Unpractis'd in the wranglings of the gown.

There is another circumstance, which makes the Neapolitans, in a very particular manner, the oppressors of each other. The gabels of Naples are

are very high on oil, wine, tobacco, and indeed on almost every thing that can be eaten, drank, or worn. There would have been one on fruit, had not Massianello's rebellion abolished it, as it has probably put a stop to many others. What makes these imposts more intolerable to the poorer sort, they are laid on butchers meat, while at the same time the fowl and gibbier are tax free. Besides all meat being taxed equally by the pound, it happens that the duty lies heaviest on the coarser sorts, which are most likely to fall to the share of the common people, so that beef perhaps pays a third, and veal a tenth of its price to the government, a pound of either sort having the same tax fixed on it. These gabels are most of them at present in the hands of private men; for as the King of Spain has had occasion for money, he has borrowed it of the rich Neapolitans, on condition that they should receive the interest out of such or such gabels until he could repay them the principal.

This he has repeated so often that at present there is scarce a single gabel unmortgaged; so that there is no place in Europe which pays greater taxes, and at the same time no Prince who draws less advantage from them. In other countries the people have the satisfaction of seeing the money they give spent in the necessities, defence, or ornament of their state, or at least, in the vanity or pleasures of their Prince: but here most of it goes to the enriching of their fellow-subjects. If there was not so great a plenty of every thing in Naples the people could not bear it. The Spaniard however reaps this advantage from the present posture of affairs, that the murmurs of the people are turned upon their own countrymen, and what is more considerable,

able, that almoſt all the perſons, of the greateſt wealth and power in Naples, are engaged by their own intereſts to pay theſe impoſitions chearfully, and to ſupport the government which has laid them on. For this reaſon, though the poorer ſort are for the Emperor, few of the perſons of conſequence can endure to think of a change in their preſent eſtabliſhment; though there is no queſtion but the King of Spain will reform moſt of theſe abuſes, by breaking or retrenching the power of the barons, by cancelling ſeveral unneceſſary employs, or by ranſoming or taking the gabels into his own hands. I have been told too there is a law of Charles the fifth, ſomething like our ſtatute of mormain, which has laid dormant ever ſince his time, and will probably have new life put into it under the reign of an active prince. The inhabitants of Naples have been always very notorious for leading a life of laziness and pleaſure, which I take to ariſe partly out of the wonderful plenty of their country, that does not make labour ſo neceſſary to them, and partly out of the temper of their climate, that relaxes the fibres of their bodies, and diſpoſes the people to ſuch an idle indolent humour. Whatever it proceeds from, we find they were formerly as famous for it as they are at preſent.

This was perhaps the reaſon that the ancients tell us one of the Sirens was buried in this city, which thence received the name of Parthenope.

———*Improbria Siren*
Deſidia———   Hor. Sat. iii. Lib. ii. v. 14.

Sloth, the deluding Siren of the mind.

———*Et*

NAPLES.

>———*Et in Otia natam*
>*Parthenopen*——— Ovid. Met. Lib. xv. v. 11.

>———*Otiosa Neapolis.* Hor. Epod. 5. v. 43.

Parthenope, for idle hours defign'd,
To luxury and eafe unbends the mind.

>*Parthenope non dives opum, non spreta vigoris:*
>*Nam molles Urbi ritus, atque hospita Musis*
>*Otia, et exemptum curis gravioribus ævum.*
>*Sirenum dedit una suum et memorabile nomen*
>*Parthenope muris Acheloias, æquore cujus*
>*Regnavere diu cantus, cum dulce per undas*
>*Exitium miseris caneret non prospera Nautis.*
>
>Sil. Ital. Lib. xii.

Here wanton Naples crowns the happy fhore,
Nor vainly rich, nor defpicably poor;
The town in foft folemnities delights,
And gentle poets to her arms invites;
The people, free from cares, ferene and gay,
Pafs all their mild untroubled hours away.
Parthenope the rifing city nam'd
A Siren, for her fongs and beauty fam'd,
That oft had drown'd among the neighb'ring feas
The lift'ning wretch, and made deftruction pleafe.

>*Has ego te sedes (nam nec mihi barbara Thrace*
>*Nec Libye natale solum) transferre laboro:*
>*Quas et mollis hyems et frigida temperat æstas,*
>*Quas imbelle fretum torpentibus alluit undis:*
>*Pax secura locis, et desidia Otia vitæ.*
>*Et nunquam turbata quies somnique peracti:*
>*Nulla foro rabies,* &c. Stat. Sylv. v. Lib. iii. v. 81.

Thefe

These are the gentle seats that I propose,
For not cold Scythia's undissolving snows,
Nor the parch'd Lybian lands thy husband bore,
But mild Parthenope's delightful shore;
Where hush'd in calms the bord'ring ocean laves
Her silent coast, and rolls in languid waves;
Refreshing winds the summer's heat assuage;
And kindly warmth disarms the winter's rage;
Remov'd from noise and the tumultuous war,
Soft sleep and downy ease inhabit there,
And dreams unbroken with intruding care.

THE ANTIQUITIES

AND

Natural Curiosities

That lie near the

CITY of NAPLES.

AT about eight miles diſtance from Naples lies a very noble Scene of antiquities. What they call Virgil's tomb is the firſt that one meets with on the way thither. It is certain this Poet was buried at Naples; but I think it is almoſt as certain, that his tomb ſtood on the other ſide of the town, which looks towards Veſuvio. By this tomb is the entry into the grotto of Pauſilypo. The common people of Naples believe it to have been wrought by magic, and that Virgil was the magician; who is in greater repute among the Neapolitans for having made the grotto than the Æneid.

If

If a man would form to himself a just idea of this place, he must fancy a vast rock undermined from one end to the other, and a highway running through it, near as long and as broad as the mall in St. James's park. This subterraneous passage is much mended since Seneca gave so bad a character of it. The entry at both ends is higher than the middle parts of it, and sinks by degrees to fling in more light upon the rest. Towards the middle are two large funnels, bored through the roof of the grotto, to let in light and fresh air.

There are no where about the mountain any vast heaps of stones, though it is certain the great quantities of them that are dug out of the rock could not easily conceal themselves, had they not probably been consumed in the moles and buildings of Naples. This confirmed me in a conjecture, which I made at the first sight of the subterraneous passage, that it was not at first designed so much for a high-way as a quarry of stone, but that the inhabitants, finding a double advantage in it, hewed it into the form we now see. Perhaps the same design gave the original to the Sibyl's grotto, considering the prodigious multitude of palaces that stood in its neighbourhood.

I remember when I was at Chateaudun in France, I met with a very curious person, a member of one of the German universities. He had stay'd a day or two in the town longer than ordinary, to take the measures of several empty spaces that had been cut in the sides of a neighbouring mountain. Some of them were supported with pillars formed out of the rock; some were made in the fashion of galleries, and some not unlike amphitheatres. The

G gentle-

gentleman had made himself several ingenious hypotheses concerning the use of these subterraneous apartments, and from thence collected the vast magnificence and luxury of the ancient Chateaudunois. But upon communicating his thoughts on this subject to one of the most learned of the place, he was not a little surprised to hear, that these stupendous works of art were only so many quarries of free-stone, that had been wrought into different figures, according as the veins of it directed the workmen.

About five miles from the grotto of Pausilypo, the remains of Puteoli and Baiæ, in a soft air and a delicious situation.

The country about them, by reason of its vast caverns and subterraneous fires has been miserably torn in pieces by earthquakes, so that the whole face of it is quite changed from what it was formerly. The sea has overwhelmed a multitude of palaces, which may be seen at the bottom of the water in a calm day.

The Lucrine lake is but a puddle in comparison of what it once was, its springs having been sunk in an earthquake, or stopped up by mountains that have fallen upon them. The lake of Avernus, formerly so famous for its streams of poison, is now plentifully stocked with fish and fowl. Mount Gaurus, from one of the fruitfullest parts in Italy, is become one of the most barren. Several fields, which were laid out in beautiful groves and gardens, are now naked plains, smoking with sulphur, or incumbered with hills that have been thrown up by eruptions of fire. The works of art lie in no less disorder than those of nature; for that which was once the most beautiful spot of
Italy,

Italy, covered with temples and palaces, adorned by the greateſt of the Roman commonwealth, embelliſhed by many of the Roman Emperors, and celebrated by the beſt of their Poets, has now nothing to ſhew but the ruins of its ancient ſplendor, and a great magnificence in confuſion.

The mole of Puteoli has been miſtaken by ſeveral authors for Caligula's bridge. They have all been led into this error from the make of it, becauſe it ſtands on arches. But to paſs over the many arguments that may be brought againſt this opinion, I ſhall here take away the foundation of it, by ſetting down an inſcription mentioned by Julius Capitolinus in the life of Antoninus Pius, who was the repairer of this mole. *Imp. Cæſari, Divi Hadriani filio, Divi Trajani, Parthici, Nepoti, Divi Nervæ pronepoti, T. Æl. Hadriano Antonino Aug. Pio, &c. quod ſuper cætera beneficia ad hujus etiam tutelam portûs,* Pilarum *viginti* molem *cum ſumptu* fornicum *reliquo ex Ærario ſuo largitus eſt.* i. e. To the Emperor Adrian Antoninus Pius, ſon of the Emperor Adrian, grandſon of the Emperor Trajan ſirnamed Parthicus, great-grandſon of the Emperor Nerva, &c. who, beſides other benefactions, built at his own expence, a mole of twenty piles, for the ſecurity of this haven.

It would have been very difficult to have made ſuch a mole as this of Puteoli, in a place where they had not ſo natural a commodity as the earth of Puzzuola, which immediately hardens in the water, and after a little lying in it looks rather like ſtone than mortar. It was this that gave the ancient Romans an opportunity of making ſo many incroachments on the ſea, and of laying the foundations of their villas and palaces within the very borders of it, as * Horace has elegantly described at more than once.

About four years ago they dug up a great piece of marble near Puzzuola, with several figures and letters engraven round it, which have given occasion to some disputes among the antiquaries §. But they all agree that it is the pedestal of a statue erected to Tiberius by the fourteen cities of Asia, which were flung down by an earthquake; the same that, according to the opinion of many learned men, happened at our Saviour's crucifixion. They have found in the letters, which are still legible, the names of the several cities, and discover in each figure something peculiar to the city, of which it represents the genius. There are two medals of Tiberius stamped on the same occasion, with this inscription to one of them, *Civitatibus Asiæ Restitutis.* The Emperor is represented in both sitting, with a Patera in one hand, and a spear in the other.

* Lib. 2. Od. 18. Lib. 3. Od. 1. Lib. 3. Od. 24. Epist. Lib. 1. § Vid. Gronovium, Fabretti, Buison, &c.

It is probable this might have been the posture of the statue, which in all likelihood does not lie far from the place where they took up the pedestal; for they say there were other great pieces of marble near it, and several of them inscribed, but that no body would be at the charge of bringing them to light. The pedestal itself lay neglected in an open field when I saw it. I shall not be particular on the ruins of the amphitheatre, the ancient reservoirs of water, the Sibyl's grotto, the Centum Cameræ, the sepulchre of Agrippina, Nero's mother, with several other antiquities of less note, that lie in the neighbourhood of this bay, and have been often described by many others. I must confess, after having surveyed the antiquities about Naples and Rome, I cannot but think that our admiration of them does not so much arise out of their greatness as uncommonness.

There are indeed many extraordinary ruins; but I believe a traveller would not be so much asto-

nished at them, did he find any works of the same kind in his own country. Amphitheatres, triumphal arches, baths, grottoes, catacombs, rotunda's, highways paved for so great a length, bridges of such an amazing height, subterraneous buildings for the reception of rain and snow-water, are most of them at present out of fashion, and only to be met with among the antiquities of Italy. We are therefore immediately surprised when we see any considerable sums laid out in any thing of this nature, though at the same time there is many a Gothic cathedral in England, that has cost more pains and money than several of these celebrated works. Among the ruins of the old heathen temples they shewed me what they call the chamber of Venus, which stands a little behind her temple. It is wholly dark, and has several figures on the cieling wrought in Stucco, that seem to represent lust and strength by the emblems of naked Jupiters and Gladiators, Tritons, and Centaurs, &c. so that one would guess it has formerly been the scene of many lewd mysteries. On the other side of Naples are the catacombs. These must have been full of stench and loathsomeness, if the dead bodies that lay in them were left to rot in open niches, as an eminent author of our own country imagines. But upon examining them I find they were each of them stopped up; without doubt as soon as the corps was laid in it. For at the mouth of the nich one always finds the rock cut into little channels, to fasten the board or marble that was to close it up; and I think I did not see one which had not still some mortar sticking in it. In some I found pieces of tiles that exactly tallied with the channel, and in others a little wall of bricks, that sometimes stopped up above a quarter of the nich, the rest
hav-

having been broken down. St. Proculus's sepulchre seems to have a kind of mosaic work on its covering; for I observed at one end of it several little pieces of marble ranged together after that manner. It is probable they were adorn'd, more or less, according to the quality of the dead. One would indeed wonder to find such a multitude of niches unstopped, and I cannot imagine any body should take the pains to do it, who was not in quest of some supposed treasure.

Baiæ was the winter retreat of the old Romans, that being the proper season to enjoy the *Baiani Soles*, and the *Mollis Lucrinus*; as on the contrary; Tiber, Tusculum, Preneste, Alba, Cajeta, Mons Circeius, Anxur, and the like airy mountains and promontories, were their retirements during the heats of summer.

Dum nos blanda tenent jucundi Stagna Lucrini,
   Et quæ pumiceis fontibus antra calent,
Tu colis Argivi regnum, Faustine, coloni *,
   Quò te bis decimus ducit ab urbe lapis.
Horrida sed fervent Nemeæi pectora monstri:
   Nec satis est Baias igne calere suo.
Ergo Sacri fontes, & littora Sacra valete,
   Nympharum pariter, Nereidumque domus.
Herculeos colles gelidâ vos vincite brumâ,
   Nunc Tiburtinus cedite frigoribus.
Mart. Lib. iv. Epigr. 57.

While near the Lucrine lake consum'd to death
I draw the sultry air, and gasp for breath,
Where streams of sulphur raise a stifling heat,
And thro' the pores of the warm pumice sweat;

* Vid. Hor. Lib. ii. Od. 6.

You taste the cooling breeze, where nearer home
The twentieth pillar marks the mile from Rome:
And now the sun to the bright lion turns,
And Baia with redoubled fury burns;
Then briny seas and tasteless springs farewel,
Where fountain nymphs confus'd with Nereids
    dwell;
In winter you may all the world despise,
But now 'tis Tivoli that bears the prize.

  The natural curiosities about Naples are as numerous and extraordinary as the artificial. I shall set them down as I have done the other, without any regard to their situation. The grotto del Cani is famous for the poisonous streams which float within a foot of its surface. The sides of the grotto are marked with green as high as the malignity of the vapour reaches. The common experiments are as follow. A dog, that has his nose held in the vapour, loses all signs of life in a very little time; but if carried into the open air, or thrown into a neighbouring lake, he immediately recovers, if he is not quite gone. A torch, snuff and all, goes out in a moment, when dipped into the vapour. A pistol cannot take fire in it. I split a reed, and laid in the channel of it a train of gun-powder, so that one end of the reed was above the vapour, and the other at the bottom of it; and I found though the steam was strong enough to hinder a pistol from taking fire in it, and to quench a lighted torch, that it could not intercept the train of fire when it had once began flashing, nor hinder it from running to the very end. This experiment I repeated twice or thrice, to see if I could quite dissipate the vapour, which I did in so great a measure, that one might easily let off a pistol in it. I observed how long a
                                                          dog

dog was in expiring the first time, and after his recovery, and found no sensible difference. A viper bore it nine minutes the first time we put him in, and ten the second. When we brought it out after the first trial, it took such a vast quantity of air into its lungs, that it swelled almost twice as big as before; and it was perhaps on this stock of air that it lived a minute longer the second time. Doctor Connor made a discourse in one of the Academies at Rome upon the subject of this grotto, which he has since printed in England. He attributes the death of animals, and the extinction of lights, to a great rarefaction of the air, caused by the heat and eruption of the steams. But how is it possible for these steams, though in ever so great quantity, to resist the pressure of the whole atmosphere? and as for the heat, it is but very inconsiderable. However, to satisfy myself, I placed a thin vial, well stopped up with wax, within the smoke of the vapour, which would certainly have burst in an air rarified enough to kill a dog, or quench a torch, but nothing followed upon it. However, to take away all further doubt, I borrowed a weather-glass, and so fixed it in the grotto, that the Stagnum was wholly covered with the vapour; but I could not perceive the quicksilver sunk after half an hour's standing in it. This vapour is generally supposed to be sulphureous, though I can see no reason for such a supposition. He that dips his hand in it finds no smell that it leaves upon it; and though I put a whole bundle of lighted brimstone matches to the smoke, they all went out in an instant, as if immersed in water. Whatever is the composition of the vapour, let it have but one quality of being very glewy or viscous, and I believe it will mechanically solve all the Phænomena of the grotto. Its unctuousness will

will make it heavy and unfit for mounting higher than it does, unless the heat of the earth, which is just strong enough to agitate and bear it up at a little distance from the surface, were much greater than it is to rarify and scatter it. It will be too gross and thick to keep the lungs in play for any time, so that animals will die in it sooner or later, as their blood circulates slower or faster. Fire will live in it no longer than in water, because it wraps itself in the same manner about the flame, and by its continuity hinders any quantity of air and nitre from coming to its succour. The parts of it however are not so compact as those of liquors, nor therefore tenacious enough to intercept the fire that has once caught a train of gun-powder; for which reason they may be quite broken and dispersed by the repetition of this experiment. There is an unctuous clammy vapour that arises from the stum of grapes, when they lie mashed together in the vat, which puts out a light when dipped into it, and perhaps would take away the breath of weaker animals, were it put to the trial.

It would be endless to reckon up the different baths, to be met with in a country that so much abounds in sulphur. There is scarce a disease which has not one adapted to it. A stranger is generally led into that they call Cicero's bath, and several voyage-writers pretend there is a cold vapour arising from the bottom of it, which refreshes those who stoop into it. It is true the heat is much more supportable to one that stoops, than to one that stands upright, because the steams of sulphur gather in the hollow of the arch about a man's head, and are therefore much thicker and warmer in that part than at the bottom. The three lakes of Agnano, A-vernus, and the Lucrine, have now nothing in them particular.

particular. The Monte Novo was thrown out by an eruption of fire that happened in the place where the mountain now stands. The Sulfatara is very surprising to one who has not seen mount Vesuvio. But there is nothing about Naples, nor indeed in any part of Italy, which deserves our admiration so much as this mountain. I must confess the idea I had of it did not answer the real image of the place when I came to see it; I shall therefore give the description of it as it then lay.

This mountain stands at about six English miles distance from Naples, though, by reason of its height, it seems much nearer to those that survey it from the town. In our way to it we passed by what was one of those rivers of burning matter, that ran from it in a late eruption. This looks at a distance like new-plowed land; but as you come near it, you see nothing but a long heap of heavy disjointed clods lying upon one another. There are innumerable cavities and interstices among the several pieces, so that the surface is all broken and irregular. Sometimes a great fragment stands like a rock above the rest; sometimes the whole heap lies in a kind of channel, and in other places has nothing like banks to confine it, but rises four or five or feet high in the open air, without spreading abroad on either side. This, I think, is a plain demonstration that these rivers were not, as they are usually represented, so many streams of running matter; for how could a liquid, that lay hardening by degrees, settle in such a furrowed compact surface? were the river a confusion of never so many different bodies, if they had been all actually dissolved, they would at least have formed one continued crust, as we see the Scorium of metals always gathers into a solid piece, let it be compounded of a thousand heterogeneous parts. I am am apt to think therefore that these huge unwieldy lumps that now lie upon one another, as if thrown together by accident, remained in the melted matter rigid and unliquified, floating in it like cakes of ice in a river, and that, as the fire and ferment gradually abated, they adjusted themselves together as well as their irregular figures would permit, and by this means fell into such an interrupted disorderly heap as we now find it. What was the melted matter lies at the bottom out of sight. After having quitted the side of this long heap, which was once a stream of fire, we came to the roots of the mountain, and had a very troublesome march to gain the top of it. It is covered on all sides with a kind of burnt earth, very dry, and crumbled into powder, as if it had been artificially sifted. It is very hot under the feet, and mixed with several burnt stones and cakes of cinders, which have been thrown out at different times. A man sinks almost a foot in the earth, and generally loses half a step by sliding backwards. When we had climbed this mountain, we discovered the top of it to be a wide naked plain, smoking with sulphur in several places, and probably undermined with fire; for we concluded it to be hollow by the sound it made under our feet. In the midst of this plain stands a high hill in the shape of a sugar-loaf, so very steep, that there would be no mounting or descending it, were it not made up of such a loose crumbled earth as I have before described. The air of this place must be very much impregnated with salt-petre, as appears by the specks of it on the sides of the mountain, where one can scarce find a stone that has not the top white with it. After we had, with much ado conquered this hill, we saw in the midst of it the present mouth of Vesuvio, that goes shelving

ving down on all sides, until above a hundred yards deep, as near as we could guess, and has about three or four hundred in the diameter, for it seems a perfect round. This vast hollow is generally filled with smoke: but, by the advantage of a wind that blew for us, we had a very clear and distinct sight of it. The sides appear all over stained with mixtures of white, green, red, and yellow, and have several rocks standing out of them that look like pure brimstone. The bottom was entirely covered, and though we looked very narrowly we could see nothing like a hole in it; the smoke breaking through several imperceptible cracks in many places. The very middle was firm ground when we saw it, as we concluded from the stones we flung upon it, and I question not but one might then have crossed the bottom, and have gone up on the other side of it with very little danger, unless from some accidental breath of wind. In the late eruptions this great hollow was like a vast chaldron filled with glowing and melted matter, which, as it boiled over in any part, ran down the sides of the mountain, and made five such rivers as that before-mentioned. In proportion as the heat slackened, this burning matter must have subsided within the bowels of the mountain, and as it sunk very leisurely had time to cake together, and form the bottom which covers the mouth of that dreadful vault that lies underneath it. The next eruption or earthquake will probably break in pieces this false bottom, and quite change the present face of things.

This whole mountain, shaped like a sugar-loaf, has been made at several times, by the prodigious quantities of earth and cinders, which have been flung up out of the mouth that lies in the midst of them; so that it increases in the bulk at every
eruption,

eruption, the afhes ftill falling down the fides of it, like the fand in an hour glafs. A gentleman of Naples told me, that in his memory it had gained twenty feet in thicknefs, and I queftion not but in length of time it will cover the whole plain, and make one mountain with that on which it now ftands.

In thofe parts of the fea, that are not far from the roots of this mountain, they find fometimes a very fragrant oil, which is fold dear, and makes a rich perfume. The furface of the fea is, for a little fpace, covered with its bubbles, during the time that it rifes, which they fkim off into their boats, and afterwards fet a feparating in pots and jars. They fay its fources never run but in calm warm weather. The agitations of the water perhaps hinder them from difcovering it at other times.

Among the natural curiofities of Naples, I cannot forbear mentioning their manner of furnifhing the town with fnow, which they here ufe inftead of ice, becaufe, as they fay, it cools or congeals any liquor fooner. There is a great quantity of it confumed yearly; for they drink very few liquors, not fo much as water, that have not lain in Frefco; and every body, from the higheft to the loweft, makes ufe of it, infomuch that a fcarcity of fnow would raife a mutiny at Naples, as much as a dearth of corn or provifions in another country. To prevent this the King has fold the monopoly of it to certain perfons, who are obliged to furnifh the city with it all the year at fo much the pound. They have a high mountain at about eighteen miles from the town, which has feveral pits dug into it. Here they employ many poor people at fuch a feafon of the year to roll in vaft balls of fnow, which they ram together, and cover from the

the sunshine. Out of these reservoirs of snow they cut several lumps, as they have occasion for them, and send them on asses to the sea-side, where they are carried off in boats, and distributed to several shops at a settled price, that from time to time supply the whole city of Naples. While the Banditti continued their disorders in this kingdom, they often put the snow-merchants under contribution, and threatened them, if they appeared tardy in payments, to destroy their magazines, which they say might easily have been affected by the infusion of some barrels of oil.

It would have been tedious to have put down the many descriptions that the Latin Poets have made of several of the places mentioned in this chapter: I shall therefore conclude it with the general map which Silius Italicus has given us of this great bay of Naples. Most of the places he mentions lie within the same prospect; and if I have passed over any of them, it is because I shall take them in my way by sea, from Naples to Rome.

Stagna inter celebrem nunc mitia monstrat Avernum;
Tum tristi nemore atque umbris nigrantibus horrens,
Et formidatus volucri, lethale vomebat
Suffuso virus cælo, Stygiáque per urbes
Religione sacer, sævum retinebat honorem.
Hinc vicina palus, fama est Acherontis ad undas
Pandere iter, cæcas stagnante voragine fauces
Laxat, et horrendos aperit telluris hiatus,
Interdumque novo perturbat lumine manes.
Juxta caligante situ, longumque per ævum
Infernis pressas nebulis, pallente sub umbrâ
Cimmerias jacuisse domos, noctemque profundam
Tartareæ narrant urbis: tum sulfure et igni
Semper anhelantes, coctoque bitumine campos
Ostentant: tellus atro exundante vapore
Suspirans, ustisque diu calefacta medullis

Æstuat, et Stygios exhalat in aëra status:
Parturit, et tremulis metuendum exsibilat antris,
Interdumque cavas luctatus rumpere sedes,
Aut exire foras, sonitu lugubre minaci
Mulciber immugit, lacerataque viscera terræ
Mandit, et exesos labefactat murmure montes.
Tradunt Herculeâ prostratos mole Gigantes
Tellurem injectam quatere, et spiramine anhelo
Torreri latè campos, quotiesque minantur
Rumpere compagem impositam, expallescere cœlum.
Apparet procul Inarime, quæ turbine nigro
Fumantem premit Iapetum, flammasque rebelli
Ore ejectantem, et siquando evadere detur
Bella Jovi rursus superisque iterare volentem.
Monstrantur Veseva juga, atque in vertice summo
Depasti flammis scopuli, fractusque ruinâ
Mons circûm, atque Ætnæ fatis certantia Saxa.
Nec non Misenum servantem Idæa sepulcro
Nomina, et Herculeos videt ipso in littore Baulos.
         Lib. xii.

Averno next he show'd his wond'ring guest,
Averno now with milder virtues bless'd;
Black with surrounding forests then it stood,
That hung above, and darken'd all the flood:
Clouds of unwholsome vapours, rais'd on high,
The flutt'ring bird entangled in the sky,
Whilst all around the gloomy prospect spread
An awful horror, and religious dread.
Hence to the borders of the marsh they go,
That mingles with the baleful streams below,
And sometimes with a mighty yawn, 'tis said,
Opens a dismal passage to the dead,
Who pale with fear the rending earth survey,
And startle at the sudden flash of day.
The dark Cimmerian grotto then he paints,
Describing all its old inhabitants.
           That

That in the deep infernal city dwell'd,
And lay in everlasting night conceal'd.
Advancing still, the spacious fields he show'd,
That with the smother'd heat of brimstone glow'd:
Through frequent cracks the streaming sulphur broke,
And cover'd all the blasted plain with smoke:
Imprison'd fires, in the close dungeons pent,
Roar to get loose, and struggle for a vent,
Eating their way, and undermining all,
'Till with a mighty burst whole mountains fall.
Here, as 'tis said, the rebel giants lie,
And, when to move th' incumbent load they try,
Ascending vapours on the day prevail,
The sun looks sickly, and the skies grow pale.
Next to the distant isle his sight he turns,
That o'er the thunderstruck Tiphœus burns:
Enrag'd his wide-extended jaws expire
In angry whirlwinds, blasphemies and fire,
Threat'ning, if loosen'd from his dire abodes,
Again to challenge Jove, and fight the gods.
On mount Vesuvio next he fixt his eyes,
And saw the smoking tops confus'dly rise;
(A hideous ruin!) that with earthquakes rent
A second Ætna to the view present.
Miseno's cape and Bauli last he view'd,
That on the sea's extremest borders stood.

Silius Italicus here takes notice, that the poisonous vapours, which arose from the lake Averno in Hannibal's time, were quite dispersed at the time when he wrote his poem; because Agrippa, who lived between Hannibal and Silius, had cut down the woods, that inclosed the lake, and hindered these noxious steams from dissipating, which were immediately scattered as soon as the winds and fresh air were let in among them. THE

THE
ISLE of CAPREA.

Having staid longer at Naples than I at first designed, I could not dispense with myself from making a little voyage to the isle of Caprea, as being very desirous to see a place, which had been the retirement of Augustus for some time, and the residence of Tiberius for several years. The island lies four miles in length from east to west, and about one in breadth. The western part, for about two miles in length, is a continued rock vastly high, and inaccessible on the sea-side. It has however the greatest town in the island that goes under the name of Ano-Caprea, and is in several places covered with a very fruitful soil. The eastern end of the isle rises up in precipices very near as high, though not quite so long as the western. Between these eastern and western mountains lies a slip of lower ground, which runs across the island, and is one of the pleasantest spots I have seen. It is hid with vines, figs, oranges, almonds, olives, myrtles, and fields of corn, which look extremely fresh and beautiful, and make up the most delightful little landskip imaginable, when they are surveyed from the tops of the neighbouring mountains. Here stands the town of Caprea, the Bishop's palace, and two or three convents.

convents. In the midst of this fruitful tract of land rises a hill, that was probably covered with buildings in Tiberius's time. There are still several ruins on the sides of it, and about the top are found two or three dark galleries, low built, and covered with masons work, tho' at present they appear overgrown with grass. I entered one of them that is a hundred paces in length. I observed, as some of my countrymen were digging into the sides of the mountain, that what I took for solid earth was only heaps of brick, stone, and other rubbish, skinned over with a covering of vegetables. But the most considerable ruin is that which stands on the very extremity of the eastern promontory, where are still some apartments left, very high and arched at top. I have not indeed seen the remains of any ancient Roman buildings, that have not been roofed with either vaults or arches. The rooms I am mentioning stand deep in the earth, and have nothing like windows or chimnies, which makes me think they were formerly either bathing-places or reservoirs of water. An old hermit lives at present among the ruins of this palace, who lost his companion a few years ago by a fall from the precipice. He told me they had often found medals and pipes of lead, as they dug among the rubbish, that not many years ago they discovered a paved road running under ground from the top of the mountain to the sea-side, which was afterwards confirmed to me by a gentleman of the island. There is a very noble prospect from the place. On the one side lies a vast extent of seas, that runs abroad further than the eye can reach. Just opposite stands the green promontory of Surrentum, and on the other side the whole circuit of the bay of Naples. This prospect,

according

according to Tacitus, was more agreeable before the burning of Vesuvio. That mountain probably, which after the first eruption looked like a great pile of ashes, was in Tiberius's time shaded with woods and vineyards; but I think Martial's epigram may serve here as a comment to Tacitus.

Hic est pampineis viridis Vesuvius umbris,
  Presserat hic madidos nobilis uva lacus.
Hæc juga, quàm Nisæ colles, plùs Bacchus amavit:
  Hoc nuper Satyri monte dedere choros.
Hæc Veneris sedes, Lacidæmone gratior illi;
  Hic locus Herculeo nomine clarus erat.
Cuncta jacent flammis et tristi mersa favillâ:
  Nec superi vellent hoc licuisse sibi.

Lib. ii. Epigr. 105.

Vesuvio, cover'd with a fruitful Vine,
Here flourish'd once, and ran with floods of wine;
Here Bacchus oft to the cool shades retir'd,
And his own native Nisa less admir'd;
Oft to the mountain's airy tops advanc'd,
The frisking satyrs on the summits danc'd;
Alcides here, here Venus grac'd the shore,
Nor lov'd her fav'rite Lacedæmon more:
Now piles of ashes, spreading all around,
In undistinguish'd heaps deform the ground.
The gods themselves the ruin'd seats bemoan,
And blame the mischiefs that themselves have done.

This view must still have been more pleasant, when the whole bay was encompassed with so long a range of buildings, that it appeared to those, who looked on it at a distance, but as one continued city. On both the shores of that fruitful bottom, which I have before-mentioned, are still to be seen the marks of ancient edifices; particularly on that which looks towards the south there is a little kind of mole, which seems to have been the foundation of a palace; unless we may suppose that the Pharos of Caprea stood there, which Statius takes notice of in his poem that invites his wife to Naples, and is, I think, the most natural among the Sylvæ.

Nec desunt variæ circùm oblectamina vitæ;
Sive vaporiferas, blandissima littora, Baias,
Enthea fatidicæ seu visere tecta Sibyllæ
Dulce sit, Iliacoque jugum memorabile remo:
Seu tibi Bacchei vineta madentia Gauri,
Teleboumque domos, trepidis ubi dulcia nautis
Lumina noctivagæ tollit Pharus æmula Lunæ,
Caraque non molli juga Surrentina Lyæo.
                    Sylv. 5. Lib. iii. v. 95.

The blissful seats with endless pleasures flow,
Whether to Baia's sunny shores you go,
And view the sulphur to the baths convey'd,
Or the dark grot of the prophetic maid,
Or steep Miseno from the Trojan nam'd,
Or Gaurus for its flowing vintage fam'd,
Or Caprea, where the lanthorn fix'd on high
Shines like a moon through the benighted sky,
While by its beams the wary sailor steers;
Or where Surrentum, clad in vines, appears.

They found in Ano Caprea, some years ago, a statue and a rich pavement under ground, as they had occasion to turn up the earth that lay upon them. One still sees, on the bendings of these mountains, the marks of several ancient scales of stairs, by which they used to ascend them. The whole island is so unequal that there were but few
                                              diversions

diversions to be found in it without doors; but what recommended it most to Tiberius was its wholsome air, which is warm in winter and cool in summer, and its inaccessible coasts, which are generally so very steep, that a handful of men might defend them against a powerful army.

We need not doubt but Tiberius had his different residencies, according as the seasons of the year, and his different sets of pleasure required. Suetonius says, *Duodecim Villas totidem nominibus ornavit.* i. e. He distinguished twelve towns by as many names. The whole island was probably cut into several easy ascents, planted with variety of palaces, and adorned with as great a multitude of groves and gardens as the situation of the place would suffer. The works under ground were however more extraordinary than those above it; for the rocks were all undermined with highways, grottoes, galleries, bagnios, and several subterraneous retirements, that suited with the brutal pleasures of the Emperor. One would indeed very much wonder to see such small appearances of the many works of art, that were formerly to be met with in this island, were we not told that the Romans, after the death of Tiberius, sent hither an army of pioneers on purpose to demolish the buildings, and deface the beauties of the island.

In sailing round Caprea we were entertained with many rude prospects of rocks and precipices, that rise in several places half a mile high in perpendicular. At the bottom of them are caves and grottoes formed by the continual breaking of the waves upon them. I entered one which the inhabitants call Grotto Obscuro, and, after the light of the sun was a little worn off my eyes, could see all the parts of of it distinctly, by a glimmering reflection that played upon them from the surface of the water. The mouth is low and narrow; but after having entered pretty far in, the grotto opens itself on both sides in an oval figure of an hundred yards from one extremity to the other, as we are told, for it would not have been safe measuring of it. The roof is vaulted, and distils fresh water from every part of it, which fell upon us as fast as the first droppings of a shower. The inhabitants and Neapolitans, who have heard of Tiberius's grottoes, will have this to be one of them; but there are several reasons that shew it to be natural. For besides the little use we can conceive of such a dark cavern of salt waters, there are no where any marks of the chisel; the sides are of a soft mouldering stone, and one sees many of the like hollow spaces worn in the bottoms of the rocks, as they are more or less able to resist the impressions of the water that beats against them.

Not far from this grotto lie the *Sirenum Scopuli*, which Virgil and Ovid mention in Æneas's voyage; they are two or three sharp rocks that stand about a stone's-throw from the south side of the island, and are generally beaten by waves and tempests, which are much more violent on the south than on the north of Caprea.

Jamque adeò Scopulos Sirenum advecta subibat;
Difficiles quondam, multorumque ossibus albos:
Tum rauca assiduo longè sale saxa sonabant.
Æn. 5. v. 864.

Glides by the Sirens cliffs, a shelfy coast,
Long infamous for ships and sailors lost,
And

And white with bones: Th'impetuous ocean roars,
And rocks rebellow from the sounding shores.

Dryden.

I have before said that they often find medals in this island. Many of those they call the Spintriæ, which Aretin has copied, have been dug up here. I know none of the antiquaries that have written on this subject, and find nothing satisfactory of it where I thought it most likely to be met with, in Patin's edition of Suetonius illustrated by medals. Those I have conversed with about it, are of opinion they were made to ridicule the brutality of Tiberius, though I cannot but believe they were stamped by his order. They are unquestionably antique, and no bigger than medals of the third magnitude. They bear on one side some lewd invention of that hellish society, which Suetonius calls *Monstrosi concubitûs repertores*, and on the other the number of the medal. I have seen of them as high as to twenty. I cannot think they were made as a jest on the Emperor, because raillery on coins is of a modern date. I know but two in the upper empire, besides the Spintriæ, that lie under any suspicion of it. The first is one of Marcus Aurelius, where, in compliment to the Emperor and Empress, they have stamped on the reverse the figure of Venus caressing Mars, and endeavouring to detain him from the wars.

——*Quoniam*

———*Quoniam belli fera munera Mavors*
Armipotens regit, in gremium qui sæpe tuum se
Rejicit, æterno devinctus vulnere amoris.
Lucr. Lib. i. v. 33.

Because the brutal bus'ness of the war
Is manag'd by thy dreadful servant's care,
Who oft retires from fighting fields, to prove
The pleasing pains of thy eternal love. Dryden.

The Venus has Faustina's face; her lover is a naked figure, with a helmet on his head, and a shield on his arm.

Tu scabie frueris mali, quod in Aggere rodit
' *Qui tegitur parmâ et galeâ*'— Juv. Sat. 5. v. 153.

Such scabbed fruit you eat, as, in his tent,
' With helmet arm'd and shield,' the soldier gnaws.

This unluckily brings to mind Fauſtina's fondneſs for the gladiator, and is therefore interpreted by many as a hidden piece of ſatire. But, beſides that ſuch a thought was inconſiſtent with the gravity of a ſenate, how can one imagine that the fathers would have dared to affront the wife of Aurelius, and the mother of Commodus, or that they could think of giving an offence to an Empreſs whom they afterwards deified, and to an Emperor that was the darling of the army and people?

The other medal is a golden one of Gallienus, preſerved in the French King's cabinet; it is inſcribed *Gallienæ Auguſtæ, Pax Ubique,* and was ſtamped at a time when the Emperor's father was in bondage, and the empire torn in pieces by ſeveral pretenders to it. Yet, if one conſiders the ſtrange ſtupidity of this Emperor, with the ſenſeleſs ſecurity which appears in ſeveral of his ſayings that are ſtill left on record, one may very well believe this coin was of his own invention. We may be ſure, if raillery had once entered the old Roman coins, we ſhould have been overſtock'd with medals of this nature; if we conſider there were often rival Emperors proclaimed at the ſame time, who endeavoured at the leſſening of each other's character, and that moſt of them were ſucceeded by ſuch as were enemies to their predeceſſor. Theſe medals of Tiberius were never current money, but rather of the nature of medalions, which ſeem to have been made on purpoſe to perpetuate the diſcoveries of that infamous ſociety. Suetonius tells us, that their monſtrous inventions were regiſtered ſeveral ways, and preſerv'd in the Emperor's private apartment. *Cubicula pluriſariam diſpoſita tabellis ac Sigillis laſciviſſimarum picturarum et figurarum adornavit, libriſque Elephantidis inſtruxit: ne cui in Operâ edenda exemplar*

plar impetratæ Schemæ deeſſet. i. e. He adorned his apartments, which were variouſly diſpoſed, with pictures and ſeals, repreſenting the lewdeſt images, and furniſhed them with the books of Elephantis, that no one might be at a loſs for examples to copy after. The Elephantis here mentioned is probably the ſame Martial takes notice of for her book of poſtures.

In Sabellum.

Facundes mihi de libidinoſis
Legiſti nimium, Sabella, verſus.
Quales nec Didymi ſciunt puellæ,
Nec molles Elephantidos libelli.
Sunt illic Veneris novæ figuræ:
Quales, &c.   Lib. xii. Epigr. 43.

'Too much, Sabellus, you delight
In poems, that to luſt excite,
Where Venus, varying ſtill her ſhape,
Provokes to inceſt or a rape:
Not ſuch the lewdeſt Harlots know,
Nor Elephantis' books can ſhew.

Ovid mentions the ſame kind of pictures that found a place even in Auguſtus's cabinet.

Scilicet in domibus veſtris, ut priſca virorum
 Artifici fulgent corpora picta manu;
Sic quæ concubitus varios Veneriſque figuras
 Exprimat, eſt aliquo parva tabella loco.
     De Triſt. Lib. ii. v. 523.

As ancient Heroes, by the painter's hand
Immortaliz'd, in thy rich gallery ſtand,

Immodest pictures in some corner lie,
With feats of lust to catch the wanton eye.

 There are several of the Sigilla, or seals, Suetonius speaks of, to be met with in collections of ancient Intaglios.
 But, I think, what puts it beyond all doubt that these coins were rather made by the Emperor's order, than as a satire on him is, because they are now found in the very place that was the scene of these his unnatural lusts.

—— *Quem rupes Caprearum tetra latebit*
Incesto possessa Seni ? —— Cl. de quarto Consf. Hon.

Who has not heard of Caprea's guilty shore,
Polluted by the rank old Emperor?

FROM

FROM NAPLES TO ROME, by SEA.

I Took a felucca at Naples to carry me to Rome, that I might not be forced to run over the same fights a second time, and might have an opportunity of seeing many things in a road, which our voyage-writers have not so particularly described. As, in my journey from Rome to Naples, I had Horace for my guide, so I had the pleasure of seeing my voyage from Naples to Rome described by Virgil. It is indeed much easier to trace out the way Æneas took, than that of Horace, because Virgil has marked it out by capes, islands, and other parts of nature, which, are not so subject to change or decay, as are towns, cities, and the works of art. Mount Pausilypo makes a beautiful prospect to those who pass by it: At a small distance from it lies the little island of Nisida, adorned with a great variety of plantations, rising one above another in so beautiful an order, that the whole island looks like a large terrace-garden. It has two little ports, and is not at present troubled with any of those noxious steams that Lucan mentions.

―――*Tali spiramine Nesis*
Emittit Stygium nebulosis Aëra saxis. Lib. vi. v. 90.
Nesis' high rocks such Stygian air produce,
And the blue breathing pestilence diffuse.

From Nisida we rowed to cape Miseno. The extremity of this cape has a long cleft in it, which was enlarged and cut into shape by Agrippa, who made this the great port for the Roman fleet that served in the Mediterranean; as that of Ravenna held the ships designed for the Adriatic and Archipelago. The highest end of this promontory rises in the fashion of a sepulchre or monument to those that survey it from the land, which perhaps might occasion Virgil's burying Misenus under it. I have seen a grave Italian author, who has written a very large book on the Campania Felice, that, from Virgil's description of this mountain, concludes it was called Aërius before Misenus had given it a new name.

At pius Æneas ingenti mole Sepulchrum
Imponit, suaque arma viro remumque tubamque
Monte sub Aerio, que nunc Misenus ab illo
Dicitur, æternumque tenet per sæcula nomen.
Æn. vi. v. 232.

But good Æneas order'd on the shore
A stately tomb; whose top a trumpet bore,
A soldier's faulchion, and a seaman's oar.

Thus

Thus was his friend interr'd; and deathless fame
Still to the lofty cape consigns his name. *Dry.*

There are still to be seen a few ruins of old Misenum; but the most considerable antiquity of the place is a set of galleries that are hewn into the rock, and are much more spacious than the Piscina Mirabilis. Some will have them to have been a reservoir of water; but others more probably suppose them to have been Nero's baths. I lay the first night on the isle of Procita, which is pretty well cultivated, and contains about four thousand inhabitants, who are all vassals to the Marquis de Vasto.

The next morning I went to see the isle of Ischia, that stands further out into the sea. The ancient Poets call it Inarime, and lay Typhœus under it, by reason of its eruptions of fire. There has been no eruption for near these three hundred years. The last was very terrible, and destroyed a whole city. At present there are scarce any marks left of a subterraneous fire; for the earth is cold, and over-run with grass and shrubs, where the rocks will suffer it. There are indeed several little cracks in it, through which there issues a constant smoke; but it is probable this arises from the warm springs that feed the many baths, with which this island is plentifully stocked. I observed, about one of these breathing passages, a spot of myrtles that flourish within the steam of these vapours, and have a continual moisture hanging upon them. On the south of Ischia lies a round lake of about three quarters of a mile diameter, separated from the sea by a narrow tract of land. It was formerly a Roman Port. On the north end of this island stands the town and castle, on an exceeding high rock, divided from the body of the island, inaccessible to an enemy on all sides. This island is larger, but much more rocky and barren than Procita. Virgil makes them both shake at the fall of part of the mole of Baiæ, that stood at a few miles distance from them.

Qualis in Euboico Baiarum littore quondam
Saxea pila cadit, magnis quam molibus ante
Constructam jaciunt pelago : Sic illa ruinam
Prona trahit, penitusque vadis illisa recumbit :
Miscent se Maria et nigræ attolluntur arenæ,
Tum sonitu Prochyta alta tremit, durumque cubile
Inarime, Jovis imperiis imposta Typhæo.
Æn. ix. v. 710.

Not with less ruin than the Baian mole
(Rais'd on the seas the surges to control)
At once comes tumbling down the rocky wall;
Prone to the deep the stones disjointed fall
Off the vast pile; the scatter'd ocean flies; [arise.
Black sands, discolour'd froth, and mingled mud
The frighted billows roll, and seek the shores:
Trembles high Prochyta, and Ischia roars:
Typhœus roars beneath by Jove's command,
Astonish'd at the flaw that shakes the land;
Soon shifts his weary side, and scarce awake,
With wonder feels the weight press lighter on
   his back. Dryden.

I do not see why Virgil, in this noble comparison, has given the epithet of Alta to Prochyta; for it is not only no high island in itself, but is much lower than Ischia, and all the points of land that lie within its neighbourhood. I should think
Alta

Alta was joined adverbially with Tremit, did Virgil make use of so equivocal a syntax. I cannot forbear inserting, in this place, the lame imitation Silius Italicus has made of the foregoing passage.

Haud aliter structo Tyrrhena ad littora Saxo,
Pugnatura fretis. subter cærisque procellis
Pila immane sonans, impingitur ardua ponto;
Immugit Nereus, divisaque cærula pulsu
Illisum accipiunt irata sub æquora montem. Lib. iv.

So vast a fragment of the Baian mole,
That, fix'd amid the Tyrrhene waters, braves
The beating tempests and insulting waves.
Thrown from its basis with a dreadful sound,
Dashes the broken billows all around,
And with resistless force the surface cleaves,
That in its angry waves the falling rock receives.

The next morning going to Cumæ through a very pleasant path, by the Mare Mortuum, and the Elysian fields, we saw in our way a great many ruins of sepulchres, and other ancient edifices. Cumæ is at present utterly destitute of inhabitants, so much is it changed since Lucan's time, if the poem to Pisa be his.

——*Acidaliâ quæ condidit Alite muros*
Euboicam referens fœcunda Neapolis urbem.

Where the fam'd walls of fruitful Naples lie,
That may for multitudes with Cumæ vie.

They show here the remains of Apollo's temple, which all the writers of the antiquities of this place suppose to have been the same Virgil describes in his sixth Æneid, as built by Dædalus, and that the very story, which Virgil there mentions, was actually engraven on the front of it.

Redditus his primûm terris tibi, Phœbe, sacravit
Remigium Alarum, posuitque immania Templa.
In foribus lethum Androgeo : tum pendere pœnas
Cecropidæ jussi, miserum ! Septena quotannis
Corpora Natorum : Stat ductis sortibus urna.
Contra elata mari respondet Gnossia tellus, &c.
Æn. vi. v. 19.

To the Cumæan coast at length he came,
And, here alighting, built his costly frame
Inscrib'd to Phœbus, here he hung on high
The steerage of his wings that cut the sky;
Then o'er the lofty gate his art embofs'd
Androgeos' death, and off 'rings to his ghost,
Sev'n youths from Athens yearly sent to meet
The fate appointed by revengeful Crete ;
And next to those the dreadful urn was plac'd,
In which the destin'd names by lots were cast.
Dryden.

Among other subterraneous works there is the beginning of a passage, which is stopp'd up, within less than an hundred yards of the entrance, by the earth that is fallen into it. They suppose it to have been the other mouth of the Sibyl's grotto. It lies indeed in the same line with the entrance near the Avernus, is fac'd alike with the Opus Reticulatum, and has still the marks of chambers that have been cut into the sides of it. Among the many fables and conjectures which have been made on this grotto, I think it is highly probable, that it was once inhabited by such as perhaps thought it a better shelter against the sun than

than any other kind of building, or at least that it
was made with smaller trouble and expence. As
for the mosaic and other works that may be found
in it, they may very well have been added in later
ages, according as they thought fit to put the place
to different uses. The story of the Cimmerians
is indeed clogged with improbabilities, as Strabo
relates it; but it is very likely there was in it some
foundation of truth. Homer's description of the
Cimmerians, whom he places in these parts, answers very well to the inhabitants of such a long
dark cavern.

The gloomy race, in subterraneous cells,
Among surrounding shades and darkness dwells;
Hid in th' unwholsome covert of the night,
They shun the approaches of the chearful light:
The sun ne'er visits their obscure retreats,
Nor when he runs his course, nor when he sets.
Unhappy mortals!——   Odyss. Lib. x.

*Tu quoque littoribus nostris, Æneïa nutrix,
Æternam moriens famam, Cajeta, dedisti:
Et nunc servat honos sedem tuus, ossaque nomen
Hesperia in magnâ, si qua est ea gloria, signat.*
                               Æn. vii. v. 1.

And thou, O matron of immortal fame,
Here dying, to the shore hast left thy name;
Cajeta still the place is call'd from thee,
The nurse of great Æneas' infancy.
Here rest thy bones in rich Hesperia's plains;
Thy name ('tis all a ghost can have) remains.
                               Dryden.

I saw at Cajeta the rock of marble, said to be
cleft by an earthquake at our Saviour's death.
There is written over the chapel door, that leads
into

into the crack, the words of the Evangelist *Ecce terræ motus factus est magnus:* Behold, there was a great earthquake! I believe every one who sees this vast rent in so high a rock, and observes how exactly the convex parts of one side tally with the concave of the other, must be satisfied that it was the effect of an earthquake, though I question not but it either happened long before the time of the Latin writers, or in the darker ages since; for otherwise I cannot but think they would have taken notice of its original. The port, town, castle, and antiquities of this place have been often described.

We touched next at Monte Circeio, which Homer calls Insula Æa, whether it be that it was formerly an island, or that the Greek sailors of his time thought it so. It is certain they might easily have been deceived by its appearance, as being a very high mountain joined to the main land by a narrow tract of earth, that is many miles in length, and almost of a level with the surface of the water. The end of this promontory is very rocky, and mightily exposed to the winds and waves, which perhaps gave the first rise to the howlings of wolves, and the roarings of lions, that used to be heard thence. This I had a very lively idea of, being forced to lie under it a whole night. Virgil's description of Æneas passing by this coast can never be enough admired. It is worth while to observe how, to heighten the horror of the description, he has prepared the reader's mind, by the solemnity of Cajeta's funeral, and the dead stilness of the night.

At pius exequiis Æneas rite solutis,
Aggere composito tumuli, postquam alta quierunt
Æquora,

Æquora, tendit iter velis, portumque relinquit.
Adspirant auræ in noctem, nec candida cursus
Luna negat: Splendet tremulo sub lumine pontus.
Proxima Circææ raduntur littora terræ:
Dives inaccessos ubi Solis filia lucos
Assiduo resonat cantu, tectisque superbis
Urit odoratam nocturna in lumina cedrum,
Arguto tenues percurrens pectine telas:
Hinc exaudiri gemitus, iræque Leonum
Vincla recusantum, et serâ sub nocte rudentum:
Setigerique sues atque in præsepibus ursi
Sævire, ac formæ magnorum ululare luporum:
Quos hominum ex facie Dea sæva potentibus herbis
Induerat Circe in vultus ac terga ferarum.
Quæ ne monstra pii paterentur talia Troës
Delati in portus, neu littora dira subirent,
Neptunus ventis implevit vela secundis,
Atque fugam dedit, et præter vada fervida vexit.
                                        Æn. vii. v. 5.

Now when the Prince her funeral rites had paid,
He plow'd the Tyrrhene seas with sails display'd;
From land a gentle breeze arose, by night
Serenely shone the stars, the moon was bright,
And the sea trembled with her silver light.
Now near the shelves of Circe's shores they run,
(Circe the rich, the daughter of the sun)
A dang'rous coast: The goddess wastes her days
In joyous songs, the rocks resound her lays.
In spinning or the loom, she spends her night,
And cedar brands supply her father's light.
From hence were heard, (rebellowing to the main)
The roars of lions that refuse the chain,
The grunts of bristled boars, and groans of bears,
And herds of howling wolves that stun the sailors
            ears.   These

These from their caverns, at the close of night,
Fill the sad isle with horror and affright. (pow'r,
Darkling they mourn their fate, whom Circe's
(That watch'd the moon, and planetary hour)
With words and wicked herbs, from human kind
H.d alter'd, and in brutal shapes confin'd.
Which monsters, left the Trojan's pious host
Should bear, or touch upon th' inchanted coast;
Propitious Neptune steer'd their course by night
With rising gales, that sped their happy flight.
Dryden.

Virgil calls this promontory *Ææa Infula Circes* in the third Æneid; but it is the hero, and not the Poet that speaks. It may however be looked upon as an intimation, that he himself thought it an island in Æneas's time. As for the thick woods, which not only Virgil but Homer mentions in the beautiful description that Plutarch and Longinus have taken notice of, they are most of them grubbed up since the promontory has been cultivated and inhabited; though there are still many spots of it which show the natural inclination of the soil leans that way.

The next place we touched upon was Nettuno, where we found nothing remarkable besides the extreme poverty and laziness of the inhabitants. At two miles distance from it lie the ruins of Antium, that are spread over a great circuit of land. There are still left the foundations of several buildings, and, what are always the last parts that perish in a ruin, many subterraneous grottos and passages of a great length. The foundations of Nero's port are still to be seen. It was altogether artificial, and composed of huge moles running round it, in a kind of circular figure, except where the ships were

were to enter, and had about three quarters of a mile in its shortest diameter. Though the making of this port must have cost prodigious sums of money, we find no model of it, and yet the same Emperor has a medal struck in his own name for the port of Ostia, which in reality was a work of his predecessor Claudius. The last Pope was at considerable charges to make a little kind of harbour in this place, and to convey fresh water to it, which was one of the artifices of the grand Duke, to divert his holiness from his project of making Civita-vecchia a free port. There lies, between Antium and Nettuno, a cardinal's Villa, which is one of the pleasantest for walks, fountains, shades, and prospects that I ever saw.

Antium was formerly famous for the temple of fortune that stood in it. All agree there were two fortunes worshipped here, which Suetonius calls *Fortunæ Antiates*, and Martial the *Sorores Antii*. Some are of opinion, that by these two goddesses were meant the Nemeses, one of which rewarded good men, and the other punished the wicked. Fabretti and others are apt to believe, that by the two fortunes were only meant in general the goddess who sent prosperity, or she who sent afflictions to mankind, and produce in their behalf an ancient monument found in this very place, and superscribed *Fortunæ Felici* ; which indeed may favour one opinion as well as the other, and shows at least they are not mistaken in the general sense of their division. I do not know whether any body has taken notice, that this double function of the goddess gives a considerable light and beauty to the ode which Horace has addressed to her. The whole poem is a prayer

to

to fortune, that she would prosper Caesar's arms, and confound his enemies, so that each of the goddesses has her task assigned in the Poet's prayer; and we may observe the invocation is divided between the two deities, the first line relating indifferently to either. That which I have marked speaks to the goddess of prosperity, or, if you please, to the Nemesis of the good, and the other to the goddess of adversity, or to the Nemesis of the wicked.

O Diva gratum quæ regis Antium,
' *Præsens vel imo tollere de gradu*
' *Mortale corpus,' vel superbos*
 Vertere funeribus triumphos! &c. Od. xxv. lib. i.

Great goddess, Antium's guardian power,
Whose force is strong, and quick to raise
The lowest to the highest place;
 ' Or with a wond'rous fall
 ' To bring the haughty lower,
' And turn proud triumphs to a funeral,' &c.
Creech.

If we take the first interpretation of the two fortunes for the double Nemesis, the compliment to Caesar is the greater, and the fifth stanza clearer than the commentators usually make it; for the *Clavi trabales, cunei, uncus, liquidumque plumbum,* were actually used in the punishment of criminals.

Our next stage brought us to the mouth of the Tiber, into which we entered with some danger, the sea being generally very rough in the parts, where the river rushes into it. The season of the year, the muddiness of the stream, with the many green trees hanging over it, put me in mind of the delightful image that Virgil has given us when Æneas took the first view of it. *Atque*

Atque hic Æneas ingentem ex æquore lucum
Prospicit; hunc inter fluvio Tiberinus amœno,
Vorticibus rapidis et multâ flavus arenâ,
In mare prorumpit: variæ circumque supraque
Assuetæ ripis volucres et fluminis alveo,
Æthera mulcebant cantu, lucoque volabant.
Flectere iter Sociis, terræque advertere proras
Imperat, et lætus fluvio succedit opaco. Æn. vii. v. 29.

The Trojan from the main beheld a wood,
Which thick with shades, and a brown horror stood:
Betwixt the trees the Tiber took his course,
With whirlpools dimpled, and with downward force
That drove the sand along, he took his way,
And roll'd his yellow billows to the sea.
About him, and above, and round the wood,
The birds that haunt the borders of his flood,
'That bath'd within, or bask'd upon his side,
To tuneful songs their narrow throats apply'd.
The captain gives command, the joyful train
Glide through the gloomy shade, and leave the main. Dryden.

It is impossible to learn from the ruins of the port of Ostia what its figure was when it stood whole and entire. I shall therefore set down the medal, that I have before-mentioned, which represents it as it was formerly.

It

It is worth while to compare Juvenal's description of this port with the figure it makes on the coin.

Tandem intrat pofitas inclufa per æquora moles,
Tyrrhenamque Pharon, porrectaque brachia, rurfus
Quæ pelago occurrunt medio, longéque relinquunt
Italiam : non fic igitur mirabere portus
Quos Natura dedit——   Juv. Sat. xii. v. 75.

At laſt within the mighty mole ſhe gets,
Our Tyrrhene Pharos, that the mid ſea meets
With its embrace, and leaves the land behind;
A work ſo wond'rous nature ne'er defign'd.
                                                    Dryden.

The ſeas may very properly be ſaid to be incloſed *(Inclufa)* between the two ſemicircular moles that almoſt ſurround them. The Coloſſus, with ſomething like a lighted torch in its hand, is probably the Pharos in the ſecond line. The two moles,

moles, that we must suppose are joined to the land behind the *Pharos*, are very poetically described by the

————*Porrectaque brachia, rursus*
Quæ pelago occurrunt medio, longeque relinquunt
Italiam————

as they retire from one another in the compass they make, till their two ends almost meet a second time in the midst of the waters, where the figure of *Neptune* sits. The poet's reflection on the haven is very just, since there are few natural ports better land-locked, and closed on all sides than this seems to have been. The figure of *Neptune* has a rudder by him, to mark the convenience of the harbour for navigation, as he is represented himself at the entrance of it, to shew it stood in the sea. The dolphin distinguishes him from a river-god, and figures out his dominion over the seas. He holds the same fish in his hand on other medals. What it means we may learn from the *Greek* epigram on the figure of a Cupid, that had a dolphin in one hand, and a flower in the other.

Οὐδὲ μάτην παλάμαις κατέχει δελφῖνα κὴ ἄνθος,
Τῇ μὲν γὰρ γαῖαν τῇδε θάλασσαν ἔχει.

A proper emblem graces either hand,
In one he holds the sea, in one the land.

Half a day more brought us to *Rome*, through a road that is commonly visited by travellers.

ROME.

ROME.

IT is generally obferved, that modern *Rome* ſtands higher than the ancient; ſome have computed it about fourteen or fifteen feet, taking one place with another. The reaſon given for it is, that the preſent city ſtands upon the ruins of the former; and indeed I have often obſerved, that where any conſiderable pile of building ſtood anciently, one ſtill finds a riſing ground, or a little kind of hill, which was doubtleſs made up out of the fragments and rubbiſh of the ruined edifice. But beſides this particular cauſe, we may aſſign another that has very much contributed to the raiſing the ſituation of ſeveral parts of *Rome*; it being certain the great quantities of earth that have been waſhed off the hills by the violence of ſhowers, had no ſmall ſhare in it. This any one may be ſenſible of, who obſerves how far ſeveral buildings, that ſtand near the roots of the mountains, are ſunk deeper in the earth than thoſe that have been on the tops of hills, or in open plains; for which reaſon the preſent face of *Rome* is much more even and level than it was formerly; the ſame cauſe, that has raiſed the low grounds, having contributed to ſink thoſe that were higher.

There are in *Rome* two ſets of antiquities, the *Chriſtian* and the *Heathen*. The former, though of a freſher date, are ſo embroiled with fable and legend,

gend, that one receives but little satisfaction from searching into them. The other give a great deal of pleasure to such as have met with them before in ancient authors; for a man who is in Rome can scarce see an object that does not call to mind a piece of a Latin Poet, or historian. Among the remains of old Rome, the grandeur of the commonwealth shews itself chiefly in works that were either necessary or convenient, such as temples, highways, aqueducts, walls, and bridges of the city. On the contrary, the magnificence of Rome, under the Emperors, was rather for ostentation or luxury, than any real usefulness or necessity, as in baths, amphitheatres, circus's, obelisks, triumphant pillars, arches, and Mausoleums; for what they added to the aqueducts was rather to supply their baths and Naumachias, and to embellish the city with fountains, than out of any real necessity there was for them. These several remains have been so copiously described by abundance of travellers, and other writers, particularly by those concerned in the learned collection of Grævius, that it is very difficult to make any new discoveries on so beaten a subject. There is however so much to be observed in so spacious a field of antiquities, that it is almost impossible to survey them without taking new hints, and raising different reflexions, according as a man's natural turn of thoughts, or the course of his studies direct him.

No part of the antiquities of Rome pleased me so much as the ancient statues, of which there is still an incredible variety. The workmanship is often the most exquisite of any thing in its kind. A man would wonder how it were possible for so much life to enter into marble, as may be discovered in some of the best of them; and even in

the

the meanest one has the satisfaction of seeing the faces, postures, airs and dress of those that have lived so many ages before us. There is a strange resemblance between the figures of the several heathen deities, and the descriptions that the Latin Poets have given us of them; but as the first may be looked upon as the ancienter of the two, I question not but the Roman Poets were the copiers of the Greek statuaries. Tho' on other occasions we often find the statuaries took their subjects from the Poets. The Laocoon is too known an instance, among many others that are to be met with at Rome. In the Villa Aldobrandina are the figures of an old and young man, engaged together at the Cæstus, who are probably the Dares and Entellus of Virgil; where by the way one may observe the make of the ancient Cæstus, that it only consisted of many large thongs about the hand, without any thing like a piece of lead at the end of them, as some writers of antiquities have falsly imagined.

I question not but many passages in the old Poets hint at several parts of sculpture, that were in vogue in the authors time, though they are now never thought of, and that therefore such passages lose much of their beauty in the eye of a modern reader, who does not look upon them in the same light with the author's Cotemporaries. I shall only mention two or three out of Juvenal, that his commentators have not taken notice of: The first runs thus;

Multa pudicitiæ veteris vestigia forsan,
Aut aliqua extiterint, et sub Jove, sed Jove nondum
Barbato.———   Sat. vi. v. 14.

Some

Some thin remains of chaftity appear'd
Ev'n under Jove, but Jove without a beard. *Dry.*

I appeal to any reader, if the humour here would not appear much more natural and unforced to a people that saw every day some or other statue of this god with a thick bushy beard, as there are still many of them extant at Rome, than it can to us who have no such idea of him, especially if we consider there was in the same city a temple dedicated to the young Jupiter, called Templum Vejovis, where, in all probability, there stood the particular statue of a * Jupiter Imberbis. Juvenal, in another place, makes his flatterer compare the neck of one that is feebly built to that of Hercules holding up Antæus from the earth.

Et longum invalidi collum cervicibus æquat
Herculis Antæum procul à tellure tenentis.
Sat. iii. v. 88.

His long crane neck and narrow shoulders praise ;
You'd think they were describing Hercules
Lifting Antæus—————   *Dryden.*

What a strained unnatural similitude must this seem to a modern reader, but how full of humour, if we suppose it alludes to any celebrated statues of these two champions, that stood perhaps in some public place or highway near Rome? and, what makes it more than probable there were such statues, we meet with the figures, which Juvenal here describes, on antique Intaglios and medals. Nay, Propertius has taken notice of the very statues.

————*Luctantum in pulvere signa*
Herculis Antæique————   Lib. iii. Eleg. 22. v. 9.

* Vid. Ovid. de Faftis, Lib. iii.
Antæus

Antæus here and stern Alcides strive,
And both the grappling statues seem to live.

I cannot forbear observing here, that the turn of the neck and arms is often commended in the Latin Poets among the beauties of a man, as in Horace we find both put together, in that beautiful description of jealousy:

> *Dum tu, Lydia, Telephi*
>   *Cervicem roseam, & cerea Telephi*
> *Laudas Brachia, væ meum*
>   *Fervens difficili bile tumet jecur.*
> *Tunc nec mens mihi, nec color*
>   *Certâ sede manent: humor in genas*
> *Furtim labitur, arguens*
>   *Quàm lentis penitus macerer ignibus.*
>   Od. 13. Lib. i. v. 1.

While Telephus's youthful charms,
His rosy neck, and winding arms,
With endless rapture you recite,
And in the tender name delight;
My heart, enrag'd by jealous heats,
With numberless resentment beats;
From my pale cheeks the colour flies,
And all the man within me dies;
By fits my swelling grief appears
In rising sighs, and falling tears,
That shew too well the warm desires,
The silent, slow, consuming fires,
Which on my inmost vitals prey,
And melt my very soul away.

This we should be at a loss to account for, did we not observe in the old Roman statues, that these two parts were always bare, and exposed to view, as much as our hands and face are at present. I cannot leave Juvenal without taking notice that his

Ventilat æstivum digitis sudantibus aurum,
Nec sufferre queat majoris pondera Gemmæ.
Sat. i.v. 28.
Charg'd with light summer rings his fingers sweat,
Unable to support a gem of weight; Dryden.

was not anciently so great an hyperbole as it is now; for I have seen old Roman rings so very thick about, and with such large stones in them, that it is no wonder a fop should reckon them a little cumbersome in the summer season of so hot a climate.

 It is certain that satire delights in such allusions and instances as are extremely natural and familiar: When therefore we see any thing in an old satirist that looks forced and pedantic, we ought to consider how it appeared in the time the Poet writ, and whether or no there might not be some particular circumstances to recommend it to the readers of his own age, which we are now deprived of. One of the finest ancient statues in Rome is a Meleager with a spear in his hand, and the head of a wild boar on one side of him. It is of Parian marble, and as yellow as ivory. One meets with many other figures of Meleager in the ancient Basso Relievos, and on the sides of the Sarcophagi, or funeral monuments. Perhaps it was the arms or device of the old Roman hunters;

which conjecture I have found confirmed in a passage of Manilius, that lets us know the pagan hunters had Meleager for their patron, as the christians have their St. Hubert. He speaks of the constellation which makes a good sportsman.

———— *Quibus aspirantibus orti*
Te, Meleagre, colunt ————   Manil. Lib. v.

They, on whose birth this constellation shone,
Thee, Meleager, for their patron own.

I question not but this sets a verse, in the fifth satire of Juvenal, in a much better light than if we suppose that the Poet aims only at the old story of Meleager, without considering it as so very common and familiar a one among the Romans.

————*Flavi dignus ferro Meleagri*
Spumat aper ————   Juv. Sat. 5. v. 115.

A boar intire, and worthy of the sword
Of Meleager, smokes upon the board.   Bowles.

In the beginning of the ninth satire, Juvenal asks his friend, why he looks like Marsya when he was overcome?

Scire velim quare toties mihi, Nævole, tristis
Occurris fronte obducta, seu Marsya victus? v. 1.

Tell me why sauntring thus from place to place,
I meet thee, Nævolus, with a clouded face?
                            Dryden's Juveral.

Some

Some of the commentators tell us, that Marsya was a lawyer who had lost his cause; others say that this passage alludes to the story of the satyr Marsyas, who contended with Apollo; which I think is more humorous than the other, if we consider there was a famous statue of Apollo fleaing Marsya in the midst of the Roman Forum, as there are still several ancient statues of Rome on the same subject.

There is a passage in the sixth satire of Juvenal, that I could never tell what to make of, until I had got the interpretation of it from one of Bellorio's ancient Basso Relievos.

Magnorum Artificum frangebat pocula miles,
Ut phaleris gauderet Equus: cælataque cassis
Romuleæ simulachra feræ mansuescere jussæ
Imperii fato, et geminos sub rupe Quirinos,
Ac nudam effigiem clypeo fulgentis et hasta,
Pendentisque Dei perituro ostenderat hosti.

Juv. Sat. xi. v. 102.

Or else a helmet for himself he made,
Where various warlike figures were inlaid:
The Roman wolf suckling the twins was there,
And Mars himself, arm'd with his shield and spear,
Hov'ring above his crest, did dreadful show,
As threatning death to each resisting foe.

Dryden's Juvenal.

Juvenal here describes the simplicity of the old Roman soldiers, and the figures that were generally engraven on their helmets. The first of them was the wolf giving suck to Romulus and Remus: The second, which is comprehended in the two last verses is not so intelligible. Some of the commentators tell us, that the god here mentioned is

Mars, that he comes to see his two sons sucking the wolf, and that the old sculptors generally drew their figures naked, that they might have the advantage of representing the different swelling of the muscles, and the turns of the body. But they are extremely at a loss to know what is meant by the word *Pendentis*; some fancy it expresses only the great embossment of the figure; others believe it hung off the helmet in Alto Relievo, as in the foregoing translation. Lubin supposes, that the god Mars was engraven on the shield, and that he is said to be hanging, because the shield which bore him hung on the left shoulder. One of the old interpreters is of opinion, that by hanging is only meant a posture of bending forward to strike the enemy. Another will have it, that whatever is placed on the head may be said to hang, as we call hanging-gardens such as are planted on the top of the house. Several learned men, who like none of these explications, believe there has been a fault in the transcriber, and that *Pendentis* ought to be *Perdentis*; but they quote no manuscript in favour of their conjecture. The true meaning of the words is certainly as follows. The Roman soldiers, who were not a little proud of their founder, and the military genius of their republic, used to bear on their helmets the first history of Romulus, who was begot by the god of war, and suckled by a wolf. The figure of the god was made as if descending on the priestess Ilia, or as others call her Rhea Silvia. The occasion required his body should be naked.

Tu quoque inermis eras cum te formosa Sacerdos
 Cepit, ut hinc urbi Semina magna dares.
Ovid. de Fast. Lib. iii. v. 10.

Then

'Then too, our mighty fire, thou stood'ft difarm'd,
When thy rapt foul the lovely prieftefs charm'd,
That Rome's high founder bore——

though on other occafions he is drawn, as Horace has defcribed him, *Tunica cinctum adamantina* — girt with a veft of adamant. The fculptor however, to diftinguifh him from the reft of the gods, gave him, what the medallifts call his proper attributes, a fpear in one hand, and a fhield in the other. As he was reprefented defcending, his figure appeared fufpended in the air over the veftal virgin, in which fenfe the word Pendentis is extremely proper and poetical. Befides the antique Baffo Relievo, that made me firft think of this interpretation, I have fince met with the fame figures on the reverfes of a couple of ancient coins, which were ftamped in the reign of Antoninus Pius, as a compliment to that Emperor, whom, for his excellent government and conduct of the city of Rome, the fenate regarded as a fecond kind of founder.

Ilia Vestalis (quid enim vetat inde moveri)
  Sacra lavaturas mane petebat aquas:
Fessa resedit humi, ventosque accepit aperto
  Pectore, turbatas restituitque comas.
Dum sedet, umbrosæ salices volucresque canoræ
  Fecerunt Somnos & leve murmur aquæ.
Blanda quies victis furtim subrepit ocellis,
  Et cadit a mento languida facta manus.

Mar

Mars videt hanc, visamque cupit, potiturque cupita:
  Et sua divina furta fefellit ope.
Somnus abit: jacet illa gravis; jam scilicet intra
  Viscera Romanæ conditor urbis erat.
                    Ovid. de Fastis. Lib. iii. v. 11.

As the fair vestal to the fountain came,
(Let none be startled at a vestal's name)
Tir'd with the walk, she laid her down to rest,
And to the winds expos'd her glowing breast
To take the freshness of the morning air,
And gather'd in a knot her flowing hair:
While thus she rested on her arm reclined,
The hoary willows waving with the wind,
And feather'd quires that warbled in the shade,
And purling streams that through the meadow
    stray'd,
In drowsy murmurs lull'd the gentle maid.
The god of war beheld the virgin lie,
The god beheld her with a lover's eye,
And by so tempting an occasion press'd,
The beauteous maid, whom he beheld, possess'd:
Conceiving, as she slept, her fruitful womb
Swell'd with the founder of immortal Rome.

I cannot quit this head without taking notice of a line in Seneca the tragedian.

———*Primus emergit solo*
Dextra ferocem cornibus premens taurum
Zetus————   Sen. OEdip. Act 3.

—First Zetus rises through the ground,
Bending the bull's tough neck with pain,
That tosses back his horns in vain.

I cannot doubt but the Poet had here in view the posture of Zetus in the famous groupe of figures, which represents the two brothers binding Dirce to the horns of a mad bull.

I could not forbear taking particular notice of the several musical instruments that are to be seen in the hands of the Apollos, muses, fauns, satyrs, bacchanals, and shepherds, which might certainly give a great light to the dispute for preference between the antient and modern music. It would perhaps be no impertinent design to take off all their models in wood, which might not only give us some notion of the ancient music, but help us to pleasanter instruments than are now in use. By the appearance they make in marble, there is not one string instrument that seems comparable to our violins; for they are all play'd on, either by the bare fingers, or the Plectrum; so that they were incapable of adding any length to their notes, or of varying them by those insensible swellings and wearings-away of sound upon the same string, which give so wonderful a sweetness to our modern music. Besides, that the string instruments must have had very low and feeble voices, as may be guessed from the small proportion of wood about them, which could not contain air enough to render the strokes, in any considerable measure, full and sonorous. There is a great deal of difference in the make, not only of the several kinds of instruments, but even among those of the same name. The Syringa, for example, has sometimes four, and sometimes more pipes, as high as to twelve. The same variety of strings may be observed on their harps, and of stops on their Tibiæ; which shows the little foundation that such writers have gone upon, who from a verse perhaps in Virgil's ec'ogues, or a short passage in a Classic author, have

been

been so very nice in determining the precise shape of the ancient musical instruments, with the exact number of their pipes, strings, and stops. It is indeed the usual fault of the writers of antiquities, to straiten and confine themselves to particular models. They are for making a kind of stamp on every thing of the same name, and, if they find any thing like an old description of the subject they treat on, they take care to regulate it, on all occasions according to the figure it makes in such a passage: As the learned German author, quoted by Monsieur Baudelot, who had probably never seen any thing of a houshold-god, more than a Canopus, affirms roundly, that all the ancient Lares were made in the fashion of a jug-bottle. In short, the antiquaries have been guilty of the same fault as the system-writers, who are for cramping their subjects into as narrow a space as they can, and for reducing the whole extent of a science into a few general maxims. This a man has occasion of observing more than once in the several fragments of antiquity that are still to be seen in Rome. How many dresses are there for each particular deity? what a variety of shapes in the ancient urns, lamps, lachrymary vessels, Priapus's, houshold-gods, which have some of them been represented under such a particular form, as any one of them has been described with in an ancient author, and would probably be all so, were they not still to be seen in their own vindication? Madam Dacier, from some old cuts of Terence, fancies that the Larva or Persona of the Roman actors, was not only a vizard for the face, but had false hair to it, and came over the whole head like a helmet. Among all the statues at Rome, I remember to have seen but two that are the figures of actors, which are both in the Villa Matthei.

One sees on them the fashion of the old sock and Larva, the latter of which answers the description that is given of it by this learned lady, though I question not but several others were in use; for I have seen the figure of Thalia, the comic muse, sometimes with an entire head-piece in her hand, sometimes with about half the head and a little friz, like a tower running round the edges of the face, and sometimes with a mask for the face only, like those of a modern make. Some of the Italian actors wear at present these masks for the whole head. I remember formerly I could have no notion of that fable in Phædrus, before I had seen the figures of these intire head-pieces.

Personam Tragicam forte Vulpes viderat :
O quanta Species, inquit, cerebrum non habet !
Lib. i. Fab. 7.

As wily Reynard walk'd the streets at night,
On a tragedian's mask he chanc'd to light ;
Turning it o'er he mutter'd with disdain,
How vast a head is here without a brain !

I find Madam Dacier has taken notice of this passage in Phædrus, upon the same occasion ; but not so the following one in Martial, which alludes to the same kind of masks ;

Non omnes fallis, scit te Proserpina canum ;
  Personam capiti detrahet illa tuo.
Lib. iii. Epigr. 43.

Why should'st thou try to hide thyself in youth ?
Impartial Proserpine beholds the truth,
And, laughing at so fond and vain a task,
Will strip thy hoary noddle of its mask.

In

In the Villa Borghese is the bust of a young Nero, which shows us the form of an ancient Bulla on the breast, which is neither like a heart, as Macrobius describes it, nor altogether resembles that in Cardinal Chigi's cabinet; so that, without establishing a particular instance into a general rule, we ought, in subjects of this nature, to leave room for the humour of the artist or wearer. There are many figures of gladiators at Rome, though I do not remember to have seen any of the Retiarius, the Samnite, or the antagonist to the Pinnirapus. But what I could not find among the statues, I met with in two antique pieces of mosaic, which are in the possession of a Cardinal. The Retiarius is engaged with the Samnite, and has had so lucky a throw, that his net covers the whole body of his adversary from head to foot; yet his antagonist recovered himself out of the toils, and was conqueror, according to the inscription. In another piece is represented the combat of the Pinnirapus, who is armed like the Samnite, and not like the Retiarius, as some learned men have supposed: On the helmet of his antagonist are seen the two Pinnæ, that stand up on either side like the wings in the Petasius of a Mercury, but rise much higher and are more pointed.

There is no part of the Roman antiquities that we are better acquainted with, than what relates to their sacrifices. For as the Old Romans were very much devoted to their religion, we see several parts of it entering their ancient Basso Relievos, statues, and medals; not to mention their altars, tombs, monuments, and those particular ornaments of architecture, which were borrowed from it. An heathen ritual could not instruct a man better than these several pieces of antiquity, in the particular ceremonies and punctilios that attended the different kinds of sacrifices. Yet there is a much greater variety in the make of the sacrificing instruments, than one finds in those who have treated of them, or have given us their pictures. For not to insist too long on such a subject, I saw in Signior Antonio Politi's collection a Patera without any rising in the middle, as it is generally engraven, and another with a handle to it, as Macrobius describes it, though it is quite contrary to any that I have ever seen cut in marble; and I have observed perhaps several hundreds. I might here inlarge on the shape of the triumphal chariot, which is different in some pieces of sculpture from what it appears in others; and on the figure of the Discus, that is to be seen in the hand of the celebrated Castor at Don Livio's, which is perfectly round, and not oblong, as some antiquaries have represented it, nor has it any thing like a sling fastened to it, to add force to the toss

Protinus imprudens, actusque cupidine lusus
Tollere Tænarides orbem properabat——
——De Hyacinthi disco.
Ovid. Metam. Lib. x. v. 182.

Th' unwary youth, impatient for the cast,
Went to snatch up the rolling orb in haste.

Notwithstanding there are so great a multitude of clothed statues at Rome, I could never discover the several different Roman garments; for it is very difficult to trace out the figure of a vest, through all the plaits and foldings of the drapery; besides that the Roman garments did not differ from each other so much by the shape, as by the embroidery and colour,

lour, the one of which was too nice for the statuary's observation, as the other does not lie within the expression of the chissel. I observed, in abundance of Bas Reliefs, that the Cinctus Gabinus is nothing else but a long garment, not unlike a surplice, which would have trailed on the ground had it hung loose, and was therefore gathered about the middle with a girdle. After this it is worth while to read the laborious description that Ferrarius has made of it. *Cinctus Gabinus non aliud fuit quam cum togæ lacinia lævo brachio subducta in tergum ita rejiciebatur, ut contracta retraberetur ad pectus, atque ita in nodum necteretur; qui nodus sive cinctus togam contrahebat, brevioremque et strictiorem reddidit. De re Vestiar.* Lib. i. Cap. 14. The Cinctus Gabinus was nothing more, than, when the bottom of the garment, being thrown over the left shoulder behind the back, was brought round to the breast in such a manner, as to be gathered into a knot; which knot or cincture, straitened the garment, and made it both less and tighter. Lipsius's description of the Samnite armour, seems drawn out of the very words of Livy; yet not long ago a statue, which was dug up at Rome, dressed in this kind of armour, gives a much different explication of Livy from what Lipsius has done. This figure was superscribed *BA. TO. NI.* from whence Fabretti concludes, that it was a monument erected to the gladiator Bato, who, after having succeeded in two combats, was killed in the third, and honourably interred, by order of the Emperor Caracalla. The manner of punctuation after each syllable is to be met with in other antique inscriptions. I confess I could never learn where this figure is now to be seen; but I think it may serve as an instance

stance of the great uncertainty of this science of antiquities*.

In a palace of Prince Cesarini I saw busts of all the Antonine family, which were dug up about two years since, not far from Albano, in a place where is supposed to have stood a Villa of Marcus Aurelius. There are the heads of Antoninus Pius, the Faustina's, Marcus Aurelius, Lucius Verus, a young Commodus, and Annius Verus, all incomparably well cut.

Though the statues that have been found among the ruins of old Rome are already very numerous, there is no question but posterity will have the pleasure of seeing many noble pieces of sculpture which are still undiscovered; for doubtless there are greater treasures of this nature under ground, than what are yet brought to light. They have often dug into lands that are described in old authors, as the places where such particular statues and obelisks stood, and have seldom failed of success, in their pursuits. There are still many such promising spots of ground that have never been searched into. A great part of the Palatine mountain, for example, lies untouched, which was formerly the seat of the imperial palace, and may be presumed to abound with more treasures of this nature than any other part of Rome..

Ecce Palatino crevit reverentia monti,
Exultatque habitante Deo, potioraque Delphis
Supplicibus late populis oracula pandit.
Non alium certe decuit rectoribus orbis
Esse Larem, nulloque magis se colle potestas.

* Vid. Fabr. de Columnâ Trajani.

Æstimat

Æstimat et summi sentit fastigia juris,
Attollens apicem subjectis regia rostris
Tot circum delubra videt, tantisque Deorum
Cingitur excubiis———
              Claud. de sexto Consulat. Honorii.

The Palatine, proud Rome's imperial seat,
(An awful pile!) stands venerably great :
Thither the kingdoms and the nations come,
In supplicating crowds to learn their doom :
To Delphi less th' enquiring worlds repair,
Nor does a greater god inhabit there :
This sure the pompous mansion was design'd
To please the mighty rulers of mankind ;
Inferior temples rise on either hand,
And on the borders of the palace stand,
While o'er the rest her head she proudly rears,
And lodg'd amidst her guardian gods appears.

  But whether it be that the richest of these discoveries fall into the Pope's hands, or for some other reason, it is said that the Prince Farnese, who is the present owner of this seat, will keep it from being turned up, until he sees one of his own family in the chair. There are undertakers in Rome who often purchase the digging of fields, gardens, or vineyards, where they find any likelihood of succeeding, and some have been known to arrive at great estates by it. They pay according to the dimensions of the surface they are to break up, and after having made essays into it, as they do for coal in England, they rake into the most promising parts of it, though they often find to their disappointment, that others have been beforehand with them. However they generally gain enough by the
                                          rubbish

rubbish and bricks, which the present architects value much beyond those of a modern make, to defray the charges of their search. I was shown two spaces of ground, where part of Nero's golden house stood, for which the owner has been offered an extraordinary sum of money. What encouraged the undertakers are several very ancient trees, which grow upon the spot, from whence they conclude that these particular tracts of ground must have lain untouched for some ages. It is pity there is not something like a public register, to preserve the memory of such statues as have been found from time to time, and mark the particular places where they have been taken up, which would not only prevent many fruitless searches for the future, but might often give a considerable light into the quality of the place, or the design of the statue.

But the great magazine for all kinds of treasure, is supposed to be the bed of the Tiber. We may be sure when the Romans lay under the apprehensions of seeing their city sacked by a barbarous enemy, as they have done more than once, that they would take care to bestow such of their riches this way as could best bear the water: besides what the insolence of a brutish conqueror may be supposed to have contributed, who had an ambition to waste and destroy all the beauties of so celebrated a city. I need not mention the old common-shore of Rome, which ran from all parts of the town with the current and violence of an ordinary river, nor the frequent inundations of the Tiber, which may have swept away many of the ornaments of its banks, nor the several statues that the Romans themselves flung into it, when they would revenge themselves on the

the memory of an ill citizen, a dead tyrant, or a discarded favourite. At Rome they have so general an opinion of the riches of this river, that the Jews have formerly proffered the Pope to cleanse it so they might have for their pains, what they found in the bosom of it. I have seen the valley near Ponte molle, which they proposed to fashion into a new channel for it, until they had cleared the old for its reception. The Pope however would not comply with the proposal, as fearing the heats might advance too far before they had finished their work, and produce a pestilence among his people; though I do not see why such a design might not be executed now with as little danger as in Augustus's time, were there as many hands employed upon it. The city of Rome would receive a great advantage from the undertaking, as it would raise the banks and deepen the bed of the Tiber, and by consequence free them from those frequent inundations to which they are so subject at present; for the channel of the river is observed to be narrower within the walls, than either below or above them.

Before I quit this subject of the statues, I think it is very observable, that, among those which are already found, there should be so many not only of the same persons, but made after the same design. One would not indeed wonder to see several figures of particular deities and emperors, who had a multitude of temples erected to them, and had their several sets of worshippers and admirers. Thus Ceres, the most beneficent and useful of the heathen divinities, has more statues than any other of the gods or goddesses, as several of the Roman Empresses took a pleasure to be represented in her dress. And I believe one finds as many figures of that excellent Emperor Marcus Aurelius, as of all the rest together;

together; because the Romans had so great a veneration for his memory, that it grew into a part of their religion to preserve a statue of him in almost every private family. But how comes it to pass, that so many of these statues are cut after the very same model, and not only of these, but of such as had no relation, either to the interest or devotion of the owner, as the dying Cleopatra, the Narcissus, the fawn leaning against the trunk of a tree, the boy with a bird in his hand, the Leda and her swan, with many others of the same nature? I must confess I always looked on figures of this kind as the copies of some celebrated master-piece, and question not but they were famous originals, that gave rise to the several statues which we see with the same air, posture, and attitudes. What confirms me in this conjecture, there are many ancient statues of the Venus de Medicis, the Silenus with the young Bacchus in his arms, the Hercules Farnese, the Antinous, and other beautiful originals of the ancients, that are already drawn out of the rubbish, where they lay concealed for so many ages. Among the rest I have observed more that are formed after the design of the Venus of Medicis, than of any other; from whence I believe one may conclude, that it was the most celebrated statue among the ancients, as well as among the moderns. It has always been usual for sculptors to work upon the best models, as it is for those that are curious to have copies of them.

I am apt to think something of the same account may be given of the resemblance that we meet with in many of the antique Basso Relievos. I remember I was very well pleased with the device of one that I met with on the tomb of a young Roman lady, which had been made for her by her mother.

mother. The sculptor had chosen the rape of Proserpine for his device, where in one end you might see the god of the dead (Pluto) hurrying away a beautiful young virgin (Proserpine) and at the other the grief and distraction of the mother (Ceres) on that occasion. I have since observed the same device upon several Sarcophagi, that have inclosed the ashes of men or boys, maids or matrons; for when the thought took, though at first it received its rise from such a particular occasion as I have mentioned, the ignorance of the sculptors applied it promiscuously. I know there are authors who discover a mystery in this device.

A man is sometimes surprised to find so many extravagant fancies as are cut on the old pagan tombs. Masks, hunting-matches, and bacchanals, are very common; sometimes one meets with a lewd figure of a Priapus, and in the Villa Pamphilia is seen a satyr coupling with a goat. There are however many of a more serious nature, that shadow out the existence of the soul after death, and the hopes of a happy immortality. I cannot leave the Basso Relievos, without mentioning one of them, where the thought is extremely noble. It is called Homer's Apotheosis, and consists of a groupe of figures cut in the same block of marble, and rising one above another by four or five different ascents. Jupiter sits at the top of it with a thunderbolt in his hand, and, in such a majesty as Homer himself represents him, presides over the ceremony.

There,

There, far apart, and high above the rest,
The thund'rer sat; where old Olympus shrouds
His hundred heads in heav'n, and props the clods.
                                                Pope.

Immediately beneath him are the figures of the nine muses, supposed to be celebrating the praises of the Poet. Homer himself is placed at one end of the lowest row, sitting in a chair of state, which is supported on each side by the figure of a kneeling woman. The one holds a sword in her hand to represent the Iliad or actions of Achilles, as the other has an Aplustre to represent the Odyssey, or voyage of Ulysses. About the Poet's feet are creeping a couple of mice, as an emblem of the Batrachomyomachia. Behind the chair stands time, and the genius of the earth, distinguished by their proper attributes, and putting a garland on the Poet's head, to intimate the mighty reputation he has gained in all ages, and in all nations of the world. Before him stands an altar with a bull ready to be sacrificed to the new god, and behind the victim a train of the several virtues that are represented in Homer's Works, or to be learned out of them, lifting up their hands in admiration of the Poet, and in applause of the solemnity. This antique piece of sculpture is in the possession of the constable Colonna, but never shown to those who see the palace unless they particularly desire it.

Among the great variety of ancient coins which I saw at Rome, I could not but take particular notice of such as relate to any of the buildings or statues that are still extant. Those of the first kind have been already published by the writers of the Roman antiquities, and may be most of them met with in the last edition of Donatus, as the pillars of
                                                Trajan

Trajan and Antonine, the arches of Drusus Germanicus and Septimius Severus, the temples of Janus, Concord, Vesta, Jupitertonans, Apollo and Faustina, the Circus Maximus, Agonalis, and that of Caracalla, or, according to Fabretti, of Galienus, of Vespasian's amphitheatre, and Alexander Severus's baths; though, I must confess, the subject of the last may be very well doubted of. As for the Metasudans and Pons Ælius, which have gained a place among the buildings that are now standing, and to be met with on old reverses of medals; the coin that shows the first is generally rejected as spurious, nor is the other, tho' cited in the last edition of Monsieur Vaillant, esteemed more authentic by the present Roman medalists, who are certainly the most skilful in the world, as to the mechanical part of this science. I shall close up this set of medals with a very curious one, as large as a medalion, that is singular in its kind. On one side is the head of the Emperor Trajan, the reverse has on it the Circus Maximus, and a view of the side of the Palatine mountain that faces it, on which are seen several edifices, and among the rest the famous temple of Apollo, that has still a considerable ruin standing. This medal I saw in the hands of Monseigneur Strozzi, brother to the Duke of that name, who has many curiosities in his possession, and is very obliging to a stranger who desires the sight of them. It is a surprising thing, that among the great pieces of architecture represented on the old coins, one can never meet with the Pantheon, the Mausoleum of Augustus, Nero's golden house, the Moles Adriani, the Septizonium of Severus, the baths of Dioclesian, &c. But since it was the custom of the Roman Emperors thus to register their most remarkable buildings as well as actions, and since there are several in either

of

of these kinds not to be found on medals, more extraordinary than those that are, we may, I think, with great reason suspect our collections of the old coins to be extremely deficient, and that those which are already found out scarce bear a proportion to what are yet undiscovered. A man takes a great deal more pleasure in surveying the ancient statues, who compares them with medals, than it is possible for him to do without some little knowledge this way; for these two arts illustrate each other; and as there are several particulars in history and antiquities which receive a great light from ancient coins, so would it be impossible to decipher the faces of the many statues that are to be seen at Rome, without so universal a key to them. It is this that teaches to distinguish the Kings and Consuls, Emperors and Empresses, the deities and virtues, with a thousand other particulars relating to a statuary, and not to be learnt by any other means. In the Villa Pamphilia stands the statue of a man in woman's clothes, which the antiquaries do not know what to make of, and therefore pass it off for an Hermaphrodite: But a learned medalist in Rome has lately fixed it to Clodius, who is so famous for having intruded into the solemnities of the Bona Dea in a woman's habit; for one sees the same features and make of face in a medal of the Clodian family.

I have seen on coins the four finest figures perhaps that are now extant: The Hercules Farnese, the Venus of Medicis, the Apollo in the Belvidere, and the famous Marcus Aurelius on horseback. The oldest medal that the first appears upon is on one of Lucius Verus. We may conclude, I think, from hence, that these statues were extremely celebrated
among

among the old Romans, or they would never have been honoured with a place among the Emperor's coins. We may further obferve, that all four of them make their firft appearance in the Antonine family; for which reafon I am apt to think they are all of them the product of that age. They would probably have been mentioned by Pliny the naturalift, who lived in the next reign, fave one, before Antoninus Pius, had they been made in his time. As for the brazen figure of Marcus Aurelius on horfeback, there is no doubt of its being of this age, though I muft confefs it may be doubted, whether the medal I have cited reprefents it. All I can fay for it is, that the horfe and man on the medal are in the fame pofture as they are on the ftatue, and that there is a refemblance of Marcus Aurelius's face; for I have feen this reverfe on a medalion of Don Livio's cabinet, and much more diftinctly in another very beautiful one, that is in the hands of Signior Marcus Antonio. It is generally objected, that Lucius Verus would rather have placed the figure of himfelf on horfeback upon the reverfe of his own coin, than the figure of Marcus Aurelius. But it is very well known that an Emperor often ftamped on his coins the face or ornaments of his Collegue, as an inftance of his refpect or friendfhip for him; and we may fuppofe Lucius Verus would omit no opportunity of doing honour to Marcus Aurelius, whom he rather revered as his father, than treated as his partner in the empire. The famous Antinous in the Belvidere muft have been made too about this age; for he died towards the middle of Adrian's reign, the immediate predeceffor of Antoninus Pius. This intire figure, though not to be found in medals, may be feen in feveral precious ftones. Monfieur La Chauffe, the author of the Mufæum Romanum,

fhewed

shewed me an Antinous that he has published in his last volume, cut in a Cornelian, which he values at fifty pistoles. It represents him in the habit of a Mercury, and is the finest Intaglia that I ever saw.

Next to the statues, there is nothing in Rome more surprizing than that amazing variety of ancient pillars of so many kinds of marble. As most of the old statues may be well supposed to have been cheaper to their first owners, than they are to a modern purchaser, several of the pillars are certainly rated at a much lower price at present than they were of old. For, not to mention what a huge column of Granite, Serpentine, or Porphyry must have cost in the quarry, or in its carriage from Ægypt to Rome, we may only consider the great difficulty of hewing it into any form, and of giving it the due turn, proportion and polish. It is well known how these sorts of marble resist the impressions of such instruments as are now in use. There is indeed a Milanese at Rome who works in them; but his advances are so very slow, that he scarce lives upon what he gains by it. He showed me a piece of Porphyry worked into an ordinary salver, which had cost him four months continual application, before he could bring it into that form. The ancients had probably some secret to harden the edges of their tools, without recurring to those extravagant opinions of their having an art to mollify the stone, or that it was naturally softer at its first cutting from the rock or, what is still more absurd, that it was an artificial composition, and not the natural product of mines and quarries. The most valuable pillars about Rome, for the marble of which they are made, are the four columns of oriental jasper in St. Paulina's chapel at St. Mary Maggiore; two of oriental granite in St. Pudenziana; one of transparent oriental

ental jasper in the Vatican library; four of Nero-Bianco in St. Cecilia Transtevere; two of Brocatello, and two of oriental agate in Don Livio's palace; two of Giallo Antico in St. John Lateran, and two of Verdi Antique in the Villa Pamphilia. These are all intire and solid pillars, and made of such kinds of marble as are no where to be found but among antiquities, whether it be that the veins of it are undiscovered, or that they were quite exhausted upon the ancient buildings. Among these old pillars I cannot forbear reckoning a great part of an alabaster column, which was found in the ruins of Livia's Portico. It is of the colour of fire, and may be seen over the high Altar of St. Maria in Campitello; for they have cut it into two pieces, and fixed it in the shape of a cross in a hole of the wall that was made on purpose to receive it; so that the light, passing through it from without, makes it look, to those who are in the church, like a huge transparent cross of amber. As for the workmanship of the old Roman pillars, Monsieur Desgodetz, in his accurate measures of these ruins, has observed, that the ancients have not kept to the nicety of proportion, and the rules of art, so much as the moderns in this particular. Some, to excuse this defect, lay the blame of it on the workmen of Ægypt, and of other nations, who sent most of the ancient pillars ready shaped to Rome: Others say, that the ancients knowing architecture was chiefly designed to please the eye, only took care to avoid such disproportions as were gross enough to be observed by the sight, without minding whether or no they approached to a mathematical exactness: Others will have it rather to be an effect of art, and of what the Italians call the Gusto grande, than of any negligence in the architect; for they say, the ancients

always

always confidered the fituation of a building, whether it was high or low, in an open fquare or in a narrow ftreet, and more or lefs deviated from their rules of art, to comply with the feveral diftances and elevations from which their works were to be regarded. It is faid there is an Ionic pillar in the Santa Maria Tranftevere, where the marks of the compafs are ftill to be feen on the volute, and that Palladio learnt from hence the working of that difficult problem; but I never could find time to examine all the old columns of that church. Among the pillars I muft not pafs over the two nobleft in the world, thofe of Trajan and Antonine. There could not have been a more magnificent defign than that of Trajan's pillar. Where could an Emperor's afhes have been fo nobly lodged, as in the midft of his metropolis, and on the top of fo exalted a monument, with the greateft of his actions underneath him? Or, as fome will have it, his ftatue was on the top, his urn at the foundation, and his battles in the midft. The fculpture of it is too well known to be here mentioned. The moft remarkable piece in Antonine's pillar is the figure of Jupiter Pluvius, fending down rain on the fainting army of Marcus Aurelius, and thunderbolts on his enemies, which is the greateft confirmation poffible of the ftory of the chriftian legion, and will be a ftanding evidence for it, when any paffage in an old author may be fuppofed to be forged. The figure, that Jupiter here makes among the clouds, puts me in mind of a paffage in the Æneid, which gives juft fuch another image of him. Virgil's Interpreters are certainly to blame, that fuppofe it is nothing but the air which is here meant by Jupiter.

Quantus ab occafu veniens pluvialibus hædis
Verberat imber humum, quam multa grandine nimbi

*In vada præcipitant, quum Jupiter horridus austris
Torquet aquosam hyemem, et cælo cava nubila rumpit.*
Æn. ix. v. 668.

The combat thickens, like the storm that flies
From westward, when the show'ry kids arise:
Or patt'ring hail comes pouring on the main,
When Jupiter descends in harden'd rain,
Or bellowing clouds burst with a stormy sound,
And with an armed winter strew the ground.
Dryden.

I have seen a medal, that, according to the opinion of many learned men, relates to the same story. The Emperor is intitled on it Germanicus, (as it was in the wars of Germany that this circumstance happened) and carries on the reverse a thunderbolt in his hand; for the heathens attributed the same miracle to the piety of the Emperor, that the christians ascribed to the prayers of their legion. *Fulmen de cælo precibus suis contra hostium Machinamentum Marcus extorsit, suis pluvia impetrata cum sui laborarent.*
Jul. Capit.

The Emperor Marcus Aurelius, by his prayers, extorted thunder from heaven against the enemy's battering engine, having obtained rain for his army, when it was oppressed with thirst.

Claudian takes notice of this miracle, and has given the same reason for it.

―――――*Ad templa vocatus,
Clemens Marce, redis, cum gentibus undique cinctam
Exuit Hesperiam paribus fortuna periclis.
Laus ibi nulla ducum, nam flammeus imber in hostem
Decidit, hunc dorso trepidum fumante ferebat*
Ambustus

Ambuſtus ſonipes ; hic tabeſcente ſolutus
Subſedit galea, liquefaƐtaque fulgure cuſpis
Canduit, et ſubitis fluxere vaporibus enſes.
Tunc, contenta polo, mortalis neſcia teli
Pugna fuit. Chaldæa mago ſeu carmine ritu
Armavere Deos : ſeu quod reor, omne tonantis
Obſequium Marci mores potuere mereri.

De ſexto Conſ. Hon.

So mild Aurelius to the gods repaid
The grateful vows that in his fears he made,
When Latium from unnumber'd foes was freed:
Nor did he then by his own force ſucceed;
But with deſcending ſhow'rs of brimſtone fir'd,
The wild barbarian in the ſtorm expir'd.
Wrapt in devouring flames the horſeman rag'd,
And ſpurr'd his ſteed in equal flames engag'd:
Another pent in his ſcorch'd armour glow'd,
While from his head the melting helmet flow'd;
Swords by the lightning's ſubtle force diſtill'd,
And the cold ſheath with running metal fill'd:
No human arm its weak aſſiſtance brought,
But heav'n, offended heav'n the battle fought;
Whether dark magic and Chaldean charms
Had fill'd the ſkies, and ſet the god in arms;
Or good Aurelius (as I more believe)
Deſerv'd whatever aid the thunderer could give.

 I do not remember that M. Dacier, among ſeveral quotations on this ſubject, in the life of Marcus Aurelius, has taken notice, either of the forementioned figure on the pillar of Marcus Antoninus, or of the beautiful paſſage I have quoted ou of Claudian.

 It is pity the obeliſks in Rome had not been charged with ſeveral parts of the Ægyptian hiſtories inſtead of hieroglyphics; which might have given no ſmall
light

light to the antiquities of that nation, which are now quite funk out of fight in thofe remoter ages of the world. Among the triumphal arches, that of Conftantine is not only the nobleft of any in Rome, but in the world. I fearched narrowly into it, efpecially among thofe additions of fculpture made in the Emperor's own age, to fee if I could find any mark of the apparition, that is faid to have preceded the very victory which gave occafion to the triumphal arch. But there are not the leaft traces of it to be met with, which is not very ftrange, if we confider that the greateft part of the ornaments were taken from Trajan's arch, and fet up to the new conqueror, in no fmall hafte, by the fenate and people of Rome, who were then moft of them heathens. There is however fomething in the infcription, which is as old as the arch itfelf, which feems to hint at the Emperor's vifion. *Imp. Cæf. Fl. Conftantino maximo P. F. Augufto S. P. Q. R. quod* inftinctu Divinitatis *mentis magnitudine cum exercitu fuo tam de Tyranno quam de omni ejus Factione uno tempore juftis Rempublicam ultus eft armis arcum triumphis infignem dicavit.* To the Emperor Conftantine, &c. the fenate and people of Rome have dedicated this triumphal arch, becaufe, through a Divine Impulfe, with a greatnefs of mind, and by force of arms he delivered the commonwealth at once from the tyrant and all his faction. There is no ftatue of this Emperor at Rome with a crofs to it, though the ecclefiaftical hiftorians fay there were many fuch erected to him. I have feen his medals that were ftamped with it, and a very remarkable one of his fon Conftantius, where he is crowned by a victory on the reverfe, with this infcription, *In hoc Signo Victor*

Victor eris. **R** This triumphal arch, and some other buildings of the same age, show us that architecture held up its head after all the other arts of designing were in a very weak and languishing condition, as it was probably the first among them that revived. If I was surprised not to find the cross in Constantine's arch, I was as much disappointed not to see the figure of the temple of Jerusalem on that of Titus, where are represented the golden candlestick, the table of shew-bread, and the river Jordan. Some are of opinion, that the composite pillars of this arch were made in imitation of the pillars of Solomon's temple, and observe that these are the most antient of any that are found of that order.

It is almost impossible for a man to form, in his imagination, such beautiful and glorious scenes as are to be met with in several of the Roman churches and chapels; for having such a prodigious stock of ancient marble within the very city, and at the same time so many different quarries in the bowels of their country, most of their chapels are laid over with such a rich variety of incrustations, as cannot possibly be found in any other part of the world. And notwithstanding the incredible sums of money, which have been already laid out this way, there is still the same work going forward in other parts of Rome, the last still endeavouring to outshine those that went before them. Painting, sculpture and architecture, are at present far from being in a flourishing condition; but it is thought they may
all

all recover themselves under the present pontificate, if the wars and confusions of Italy will give them leave. For as the pope is himself a master of polite learning, and a great encourager of arts, so at Rome any of these arts immediately thrives under the encouragement of the Prince, and may be fetched up to its perfection in ten or a dozen years, which is the work of an age or two in other countries, where they have not such excellent models to form themselves upon.

I shall conclude my observations on Rome with a letter of King Henry the eighth to Anne of Bullein, transcribed out of the famous manuscript in the Vatican, which the Bishop of Salisbury assures us is written with the King's own hand.

' The cause of my writing at this time is to
' hear of your health and prosperity, of which
' I would be as glad as in a manner of my own,
' praying God that it be his pleasure to send us
' shortly together, for, I promise, I long for it;
' howbeit I trust it shall not be long too, and
' seeing my darling is absent, I can no less do
' than send her some flesh, prognosticating that
' hereafter thou must have some of mine, which
' if he please, I would have now. As touching
' your sister's mother, I have consigned Walter
' Welsh to write to my Lord Manwring my mind
' therein; whereby I trust he shall not have power
' to dissuade her; for surely, whatever is said, it
' cannot so stand with his honour, but that he
' must needs take his natural daughter in her
' extreme necessity. No more to you at this
' time

'time, my own darling, but that with a whistle
'I wish we were together one evening; by the
'hand of yours,

HENRY.

These letters are always shown to an Englishman that visits the Vatican library.

TOWNS

Within the Neighbourhood of

ROME.

I Spent three or four days on Tivoli, Frescati, Palistrina and Albano. In our way to Tivoli I saw the rivulet of Salforata, formerly called Albula, and smelt the stench that arises from its waters some time before I saw them. Martial mentions this offensive smell in an epigram of the fourth book, as he does the rivulet itself in the first.

Quod siccæ redolet locus lacunæ,
Crudarum nebulæ quod Albularum. Lib. vi. Epigr. 4.

The dying marshes such a stench convey,
Such the rank steams of reeking Albula.

Itur ad Herculeæ gelidas qua Tiburis arces,
  Canaque sulphureis Albula fumat aquis.
                                    Lib. i. Epigr. 5.

As from high Rome to Tivoli you go
Where Albula's sulphureous waters flow.

The little lake that gives rise to this river, with its floating islands, is one of the most extraordinary natural curiosities about Rome. It lies in the very flat of Campania; and as it is the drain of these parts, it is no wonder that it is so impregnated with sulphur. It has at bottom so thick a sediment of it, that, upon throwing in a stone, the water boils for a considerable time over the place which has been stirred up. At the same time are seen little flakes of scurf rising up, that are probably the parts which compose the islands; for they often mount of themselves, though the water is not troubled.

I question not but this lake was formerly much larger than it is at present, and that the banks have grown over it by degrees, in the same manner as the islands have been formed on it. Nor is it improbable but that, in process of time, the whole surface of it may be crusted over, as the islands inlarge themselves, and the banks close in upon them. All about the lake, where the ground is dry, we found it to be hollow by the trampling of our horses feet. I could not discover the least traces of the Sibyls temple and grove, which stood on the borders of this lake. Tivoli is seen at a distance lying along the brow of a hill. Its situation has given Horace occasion to call it Tibur Supinum, as Virgil perhaps for the same reason intitles it Superbum. The Villa de Medicis with its water-works, the cascade of the Teverone, and the ruins of the Sibyls temple (of which Vignola has made a little copy at St. Peter's de Montorio) are described in every itinerary. I must confess I was most pleased with a beautiful prospect that none of them have mentioned, which lies at about a mile distance from the town. It opens on one side into the Roman

Cam-

Campania, where the eye loses itself on a smooth spacious plain. On the other side is a more broken and interrupted scene, made up of an infinite variety of inequalities and shadowings that naturally arise from an agreeable mixture of hills, groves and valleys. But the most enlivening part of all is the river Teverone, which you see at about a quarter of a mile's distance throwing itself down a precipice, and falling by several cascades from one rock to another, until it gains the bottom of the valley, where the sight of it would be quite lost, did not it sometimes discover itself through the breaks and openings of the woods that grow about it. The Roman painters often work upon this landskip, and I am apt to believe that Horace had his eye upon it in those two or three beautiful touches which he has given us of these seats. The Teverone was formerly called the Anio.

Me nec tam patiens Lacedæmon,
Nec tam Larissæ percussit campus opimæ,
  Quam domus Albunææ resonantis,
Et præceps Anio, et Tiburni lucus, et udæ,
  Mobilibus pomaria rivis.   Lib. i. Od. vii. v. 10.

Not fair Larissa's fruitful shore,
Nor Lacedæmon, charms me more
Than high Albunea's airy walls,
Resounding with her water-falls,
And Tivoli's delightful shades,
And Anio rolling in cascades,
That through the flow'ry meadows glides,
And all the beauteous scene divides.

I remember Monsieur Dacier explains Milibus by Ductilibus, and believes that the word elates to

the

the conduits, pipes, and canals, that were made to diſtribute the waters up and down, according to the pleaſure of the owner. But any one who ſees the Teverone muſt be of another opinion, and conclude it to be one of the moſt moveable rivers in the world, that has its ſtream broken by ſuch a multitude of caſcades, and is ſo often ſhifted out of one channel into another. After a very turbulent and noiſy courſe of ſeveral miles among the rocks and mountains, the Teverone falls into the valley before mentioned, where it recovers its temper, as it were by little and little, and after many turns and windings glides peaceably into the Tiber. In which ſenſe we are to underſtand Silius Italicus's deſcription, to give it its proper beauty.

Sulphureis gelidus qua ſerpit lenitur undis,
Ad genitorem Anio labens ſine murmure Tibrim.

Here the loud Anio's boiſt'rous clamours ceaſe,
That with ſubmiſſive murmurs glides in peace
To his old ſire the Tiber———

At Freſcati I had the ſatisfaction of ſeeing the firſt ſketch of Verſailles in the walks and water-works. The proſpect from it was doubtleſs much more delightful formerly, when the Campania was ſet thick with towns, villas, and plantations. Cicero's Tuſculum was at a place called Grotto Ferrate, about two miles off this town, though moſt of the modern writers have fixed it at Freſcati. Nardini ſays, there was found among the ruins at Grotto Ferrate a piece of ſculpture, which Cicero himſelf mentions in one of his familiar epiſtles. In going to Freſcati we had a fair view of mount Algido.

On our way to Palæstrina we saw the lake Regillus, famous for the apparition of Castor and Pollux, who were here seen to give their horses drink after the battle between the Romans and the son-in-law of Tarquin. At some distance from it we had a view of the Lacus Gabinus, that is much larger than the former. We left the road for about half a mile to see the sources of a modern aqueduct. It is entertaining to observe how the little springs and rills, that break out of the sides of the mountain, are gleaned up, and conveyed through little covered channels into the main hollow of the aqueduct. It was certainly very lucky for Rome, seeing it had occasion for so many aqueducts, that there chanced to be such a range of mountains within its neighbourhood. For by this means they could take up their water from what height they pleased, without the expence of such an engine as that of Marli. Thus the Claudian aqueduct ran thirty-eight miles, and sunk after the proportion of five foot and a half every mile, by the advantage only of a high source and the low situation of Rome. Palæstrina stands very high, like most other towns in Italy, for the advantage of the cool breezes; for which reason Virgil calls it Altum, and Horace Frigidum Præneste. Statius calls it Præneste Sacrum, because of the famous temple of Fortune that stood in it. There are still great pillars of granite, and other fragments of this antient temple. But the most considerable remnant of it is a very beautiful Mosaic pavement, the finest I have ever seen in marble. The parts are so well joined together, that the whole piece looks like a continued picture. There are in it the figures of a rhinoceros, of elephants, and of several other animals, with little landskips, which look very lively and well painted, though they are made

out

out of the natural colours and shadows of the marble. I do not remember ever to have met with an old Roman Mosaic, composed of little pieces of clay half vitrified, and prepared at the glass-houses, which the Italians call Smalte. These are much in use at present, and may be made of what colour and figure the workman pleases; which is a modern improvement of the art, and enables those who are employed in it to make much finer pieces of Mosaic than they did formerly.

In our excursion to Albano we went as far as Nemi, that takes its name from the Nemus Dianæ. The whole country thereabouts is still over-run with woods and thickets. The lake of Nemi lies in a very deep bottom, so surrounded on all sides with mountains and groves, that the surface of it is never ruffled with the least breath of wind, which, perhaps, together with the clearness of its waters, gave it formerly the name of Diana's Looking-glass.

—— *Speculumque Dianæ.*   Virg.

Prince Cæsarini has a palace at Jensano, very near Nemi in a pleasant situation, and set off with many beautiful walks. In our return from Jensano to Albano, we passed through la Ricca, the Aricia of the ancients, Horace's first stage from Rome to Brundisi. There is nothing at Albano so remarkable as the prospect from the Capuchins garden, which for the extent and variety of pleasing incidents is, I think, the most delightful one that I ever saw. It takes in the whole Campania, and terminates in a full view of the Mediterranean. You have a sight at the same time of the Alban lake, which lies just by in an oval figure of about seven miles

miles round, and, by reason of the continued circuit of high mountains that incompass it, looks like the Area of some vast amphitheatre. This, together with the several green hills and naked rocks, within the neighbourhood, makes the most agreeable confusion imaginable. Albano keeps up its credit still for wine, which perhaps would be as good as it was anciently, did they preserve it to as great an age; but as for olives, there are now very few here, though they are in great plenty at Tivoli;

―――*Albani pretiosa senectus.* Juv. Sat. xiii. v. 214.

Cras bibet Albanis aliquid de montibus aut de
Setinis, cujus patriam titulumque Senectus
Delevit multa veteris fuligine testa. Id. Sat. 5. v. 33.

Perhaps to-morrow he may change his wine,
And drink old sparkling Alban, or Setine;
Whose title and whose age with mould o'ergrown,
The good old cask for ever keeps unknown.
Bowles.

―――*Palladiæ seu collibus uteris Albæ.*
Mart. Lib. v. Epigr. 1.

Whether the hills of Alba you prefer,
Whose rising tops the fruitful olive bear.

Albanæ―――*Olivæ.* Id. Lib. . Epigr. 16.

Th' Albanian olives.

The places mentioned in this chapter were all of them formerly the cool retirements of the Romans, where they used to hide themselves among the
woods

woods and mountains, during the excessive heats of their summer; as Baiæ was the general winter rendezvous.

Jam terras volucremque polum fuga veris Aquosi
Laxat, et Icariis cœlum latratibus urit.
Ardua jam densæ rarescunt mænia Romæ:
Hos Præneste sacrum, nemus hos glaciale Dianæ,
Algidus aut horrens, aut Tuscula protegit Umbra,
Tiburis hi lucos, Anienaque frigora captant. Sil. iv. 1.

Albanos quoque Tusculosque colles
Et quodcunque jacet sub urbe frigus:
Fidenas veteres, brevesque Rubras,
Et quod Virgineo cruore gaudet
Annæ pomiferum nemus Perennæ.
Mart. Lib. 1. Epigr. 123.

All shun the raging dog-star's sultry heat,
And from the half-unpeopled town retreat:
Some hid in Nemi's gloomy forests lie,
To Palestrina some for shelter fly;
Others to catch the breeze or breathing air,
To Tusculum or Algido repair;
Or in moist Tivoli's retirements find
A cooling shade, and a refreshing wind.

On the contrary, at present, Rome is never fuller of nobility than in summer-time: for the country towns are so infested with unwholsome vapours, that they dare not trust themselves in them while the heats last. There is no question but the air of the Campania would be now as healthful as it was formerly, were there as many fires burning in it, and as many inhabitants to manure the soil. Leaving Rome about the latter end of October, in my way to Sienna,

Sienna, I lay the first night at a little village in the territories of the ancient Veii.

Hæc tum nomina erant, nunc sunt sine nomine Campiæ
Virg. Æn. vi. v. 776.

These then were names, now fields without a name.

The ruins of their capital city are at present so far lost, that the geographers are not able to determine exactly the place where they once stood; So literally is that noble prophecy of Lucan fulfilled, of this and other places of Latium.

―――*Gentes Mars iste futuras*
Obruet, et populos venientis in orbem
Erepto natale feret ; tunc omne Latinum
Fabula nomen erit : Gabios, Veiosque, Coramque
Pulvere vix tectæ poterunt monstrare ruinæ,
Albanosque lares Laurentinosque penates,
Rus vacuum, quod non habitet nisi nocte coacta
Invitus―――――
Lib. vii. v. 389

Succeeding nations by the sword shall die,
And swallow'd up in dark oblivion lie;
Almighty Latium, with her cities crown'd,
Shall like an antiquated fable found;
The Veian and the Gabian tow'rs shall fall,
And one promiscuous ruin cover all;
Nor, after length of years, a stone betray
The place where once the very ruins lay :
High Alba's walls and the Lavinian Strand,
(A lonely desert, and an empty land)
Shall scarce afford, for needful hours of rest,
A single house to their benighted guest.

We here saw the lake Bacca, that gives rise to the Cremera, on whose banks the Fabii were slain.

Tercentum numerabat avos, quos turbine Martis
Abstulit una Dies, cum fors non æqua labori
Patricio Cremeræ maculavit sanguine ripas.

Sil. Ital. Lib. i.

Fabius a num'rous ancestry could tell,
Three hundred heroes that in battle fell,
Near the fam'd Cremera's disast'rous flood,
That ran polluted with Patrician blood

We saw afterwards, in the progress of our voyage, the lakes of Vico and Bolsena. The last is reckoned one and twenty miles in circuit, and is plentifully stocked with fish and fowl. There are in it a couple of Islands, that are perhaps the two floating isles mentioned by Pliny, with that improbable circumstance of their appearing sometimes like a circle, and sometimes like a triangle, but never like a Quadrangle. It is easy enough to conceive how they might become fixed, though they once floated; and it is not very credible, that the naturalist could be deceived in his account of a place that lay, as it were, in the neighbourhood of Rome. At the end of this lake stands Montefiascone, the habitation of Virgil's Æqui Falisci, Æn. 7. and on the side of it, the town of the Volsinians, now called Bolsena.

Aut positis nemorosa inter juga Volsiniis.

Juv. Sat. iii. v 191.

————Volsinium stood
Cover'd with mountains, and inclos'd with wood.
I saw

I saw in the churchyard of Bolsena an antique funeral monument (of that kind which they called a Sarcophagus) very intire, and what is particular, engraven on all sides with a curious representation of a Bacchanal. Had the inhabitants observed a couple of lewd figures at one end of it, they would not have thought it a proper ornament for the place where it now stands. After having travelled hence to Aquapendente, that stands in a wonderful pleasant situation, we came to the little brook which separates the Pope's dominions from the great Duke's. The frontier castle of Radicofani is seated on the highest mountain in the country, and is as well fortified as the situation of the place will permit. We here found the natural face of the country quite changed from what we had been entertained with in the Pope's dominions. For instead of the many beautiful scenes of green mountains and fruitful valleys, that we had been presented with for some days before, we saw now nothing but a wild naked prospect of rocks and hills, worn out on all sides with gutters and channels, and not a tree or shrub to be met with in a vast circuit of several miles. This savage prospect put me in mind of the Italian proverb, that, ' The Pope has the flesh, and the ' great Duke the bones of Italy.' Among a large extent of these barren mountains I saw but a single spot that was cultivated, on which there stood a convent.

SIENNA,

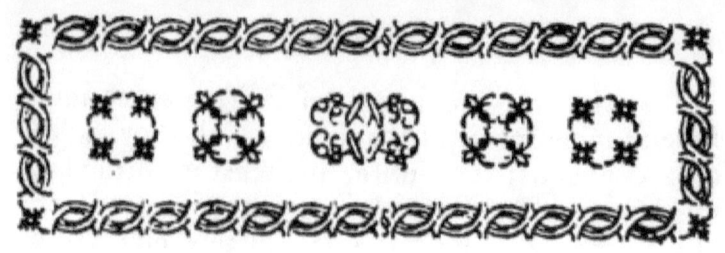

SIENNA, LEGHORNE, PISA.

SIENNA stands high, and is adorned with a great many towers of brick, which in the time of the commonwealth were erected to such of the members as had done any considerable service to their country. These towers gave us a sight of the town a great while before we entered it. There is nothing in this city so extraordinary as the cathedral, which a man may view with pleasure after he has seen St. Peter's, though it is quite of another make, and can only be looked upon as one of the master-pieces of Gothic architecture. When a man sees the prodigious pains and expence that our forefathers have been at in these barbarous buildings, one cannot but fancy to himself what miracles of architecture they would have left us had they only been instructed in the right way; for when the devotion of those ages was much warmer than it is at present, and the riches of the people much more at the disposal of the priests here was so much money consumed on these Gothic cathedrals,

cathedrals, as would have finished a greater variety of noble buildings, than have been raised either before or since that time.

One would wonder to see the vast labour that has been laid out on this single cathedral. The very spouts are loaden with ornaments; the windows are formed like so many scenes of perspective, with a multitude of little pillars retiring one behind another: the great columns are finely engraven with fruits and foliage that run twisting about them from the very top to the bottom; the whole body of the church is chequered with different lays of white and black marble, the pavement curiously cut out in designs and scripture-stories, and the front covered with such a variety of figures, and over-run with so many little mazes and labyrinths of sculpture, that nothing in the world can make a prettier shew to those, who prefer false beauties and affected ornaments, to a noble and majestic simplicity. Over-against this church stands a large hospital, erected by a shoe-maker, who has been beatified, though never sainted. There stands a figure of him superscribed, *Sutor ultra Crepidam.*—A shoemaker beyond his last. I shall speak nothing of the extent of this city, the cleanliness of its streets, nor the beauty of its piazza, which so many travellers have described. As this is the last republic that fell under the subjection of the Duke of Florence, so it is still supposed to retain many hankerings after its ancient liberty. For this reason when the keys and pageants of the Duke's towns and governments pass in procession before him, on St. John Baptist's day, I was told that Sienna comes in the rear of his dominions and is pushed forward by those that follow, to shew the reluctancy it has to appear in such a solemnity. I

shall

shall say nothing of the many gross and absurd traditions of St. Catharine of Sienna, who is the great saint of this place. I think there is as much pleasure in hearing a man tell his dreams, as in reading accounts of this nature. A traveller, that thinks them worth his observation, may fill a book with them at every great town in Italy.

From Sienna we went forward to Leghorne, where the two ports, the bagnio, and Donatelli's statue of the great Duke, amidst the four slaves chained to this pedestal, are very noble sights. The square is one of the largest, and will be one of the most beautiful in Italy, when this statue is erected in it, and a town-house built at one end of it to front the church that stands at the other. They are at a continual expence to cleanse the ports, and keep them from being choaked up, which they do by the help of several engines that are always at work, and employ many of the great Duke's slaves. Whatever part of the harbour they scoop in, it has an influence on all the rest; for the sea immediately works the whole bottom to a level. They draw a double advantage from the dirt that is taken up, as it clears the port, and at the same time dries up several marshes about the town, where they lay it from time to time. One can scarce imagine how great profits the Duke of Tuscany receives from this single place, which are not generally thought so considerable, because it passes for a free port. But it is very well known how the great Duke, on a late occasion, notwithstanding the privileges of the merchants, drew no small sums of money out of them; though still in respect of the exorbitant dues that are paid at most other ports, it deservedly retains the name of free. It brings into his dominions a great increase of people from all other nations.

hey

They reckon in it near ten thousand Jews, many of them very rich, and so great traffickers, that our English factors complain they have most of our country trade in their hands. It is true the strangers pay little or no taxes directly; but out of every thing they buy there goes a large gabel to the government. The very ice-merchant at Leghorne pays above a thousand pounds sterling annually for his privilege, and the tobacco-merchant ten thousand. The ground is sold by the great Duke at a very high price, and houses are every day rising on it. All the commodities that go up into the country, of which there are great quantities, are clogged with impositions as soon as they leave Leghorne. All the wines, oils, and silks, that come down from the fruitful valleys of Pisa, Florence, and other parts of Tuscany, must make their way through several duties and taxes before they can reach the port. The canal that runs from the sea into the Arno gives a convenient carriage to all goods that are to be shipped off, which does not a little enrich the owners: and in proportion as private men grow wealthy, their legacies, law-suits, daughters portions, &c. increase, in all which the great Duke comes in for a considerable share. The Lucquese, who traffic at this port, are said to bring in a great deal into the Duke's coffers. Another advantage, which may be of great use to him, is, that at five or six days warning he might find credit in this town for very large sums of money, which no other Prince in Italy can pretend to. I need not take notice of the reputation that this port gives him among foreign princes; but there is one benefit arising from it, which, though never thrown into the account, is doubtless very considerable. It is well known how the Pisans and Florentines long regretted

the

the loss of their ancient liberty, and their subjection to a family that some of them thought themselves equal to, in the flourishing times of their commonwealths. The town of Leghorne has accidentally done what the greatest fetch of politics would have found difficult to have brought about; for it has almost unpeopled Pisa, if we compare it with what it was formerly; and every day lessens the number of the inhabitants of Florence. This does not only weaken those places, but at the same time turns many of their busiest spirits, from their old notions of honour and liberty, to the thoughts of traffic and merchandise: And as men engaged in the road of thriving are no friends to changes and revolutions, they are at present worn into a habit of subjection, and push all their pursuits another way. It is no wonder therefore that the great duke has such apprehensions of the Pope's making Civita Vecchia a free port, which may in time prove so very prejudicial to Leghorne. It would be thought an improbable story, should I set down the several methods that are commonly reported to have been made use of, during the last pontificate, to put a stop to this design. The great Duke's money was so well bestowed in the conclave, that several of the cardinals dissuaded the Pope from the undertaking, and at last turned all his thoughts upon the little port which he made at Antium, near Nettuno. The chief workmen, that were to have conveyed the water to Civita Vecchia, were bought off; and when a poor Capuchin, that was thought proof against all bribes, had undertaken to carry on the work, he died a little after he had entered upon it. The present Pope however, who is very well acquainted with the secret history, and the weakness of his predecessor, seems resolved

resolved to bring the project to its perfection. He has already been at vast charges in finishing the aqueduct, and had some hopes that, if the war should drive our English merchants from Sicily and Naples they would settle here. His holiness has told some English gentlemen, that those of our nation should have the greatest privileges of any but the subjects of the church. One of our countrymen, who makes a good figure at Rome, told me the Pope has this design extremely at his heart, but that he fears the English will suffer nothing like a resident or counsel in his dominions, though at the same time he hoped the business might as well be transacted by one that had no public character. This gentleman has so busied himself in the affair, that he has offended the French and Spanish Cardinals, in so much that Cardinal Janson refused to see him, when he would have made his apology for what he had said to the Pope on this subject. There is one great objection to Civita Vechia, that the air of the place is not wholesome; but this, they say, proceeds from want of inhabitants, the air of Leghorne having been worse than this before the town was well peopled.

The great profits, which have accrued to the Duke of Florence from his free port, have set several of the states of Italy on the same project. The most likely to succeed in it would be the Genoese, who lie more convenient than the Venetians, and have a more inviting form of government, than that of the church, or that of Florence. But as the port of Genoa is so very ill guarded against storms, that no privileges can tempt the merchants from Leghorne into it, so dare not the Genoese make any other of their ports free, lest it should draw to it most of their commerce and inhabitants, and by consequence ruin their chief city.

From Leghorne I went to Pisa, where there is still the shell of a great city, though not half furnished with inhabitants. The great church, baptistery, and leaning tower, are very well worth seeing, and are built after the same fancy with the cathedral of Sienna. Half a day's journey more brought me into the republic of Lucca.

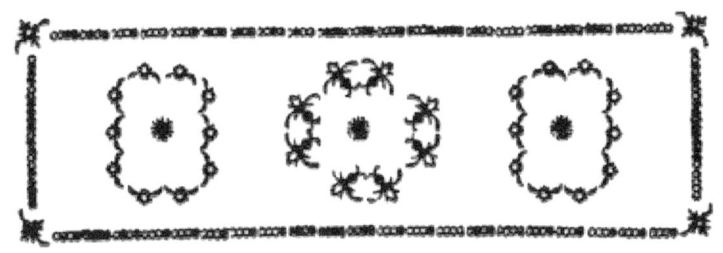

THE REPUBLIC OF LUCCA.

IT is very pleasant to see how the small territories of this little republic are cultivated to the best advantage, so that one cannot find the least spot of ground, that is not made to contribute its utmost to the owner. In all the inhabitants there appears an air of chearfulness and plenty, not often to be met with in those of the countries which lie about 'em. There is but one gate for strangers to enter at, that it may be known what numbers of them are in the town. Over it is written in letters of gold, *Libertas*.

This republic is shut up in the great Duke's dominions, who at present is very much incensed against it, and seems to threaten it with the fate of Florence, Pisa, and Sienna. The occasion as follows.

The Lucquese plead prescription for hunting in one of the Duke's forests, that lies upon their frontiers, which about two years since was strictly forbidden them, the Prince intending to preserve the game for his own pleasure. Two or three sportsmen of the republic, who had the hardiness to offend against the prohibition, were seized, and kept in a neighbouring prison. Their countrymen, to the number of threescore, attacked the place where they were kept in custody, and rescued them. The great Duke redemands his prisoners, and, as a further satisfaction, would have the governor of the town, where the threescore assailants had combined together, delivered into his hands; but receiving only excuses, he resolved to do himself justice. Accordingly he ordered all the Lucquese to be seized that were found on a market-day, in one of his frontier towns. These amounted to fourscore, among whom were persons of some consequence in the republic. They are now in prison at Florence, and, as it is said, treated hardly enough; for there are fifteen of the number dead within less than two years. The King of Spain, who is protector of the commonwealth, received information from the great Duke of what had passed, who approved of his proceedings, and ordered the Lucquese by his governor of Milan, to give a proper satisfaction. The republic, thinking themselves ill used by their protector, as they say at Florence, have sent to Prince Eugene to desire the Emperor's protection, with an offer of winter-quarters, as it is said, for four thousand Germans. The great Duke rises on them in his demands, and will not be satisfied with less than a hundred thousand crowns, and a solemn embassy to beg pardon for the past, and promise amendment for the future. Thus
stands

stands the affair at present, that may end in the ruin of the commonwealth, if the French succeed in Italy. It is pleasent however to hear the discourse of the common people of Lucca, who are firmly persuaded that one Lucquese can beat five Florentines, who are grown low-spirited, as they pretend, by the great Duke's oppressions and have nothing worth fighting for. They say, they can bring into the field twenty or thirty thousand fighting men, all ready to sacrifice their lives for their liberty They have a good quantity of arms and ammunition, but few horse. It must be owned these people are more happy, at least in imagination, than the rest of their neighbours, because they think themselves so; though such a chimerical happiness is not peculiar to republicans, for we find the subjects of the most absolute Prince in Europe are as proud of their monarch as the Lucquese of being subject to none. Should the French affairs prosper in Italy, it is possible the great Duke may bargain for the republic of Lucca, by the help of his great treasures. as his predecessors did formerly with the Emperor for that of Sienna. The great Dukes have never yet attempted any thing on Lucca, as not only fearing the arms of their protector, but because they are well assured, that, should the Lucquese be reduced to the last extremity, they would rather throw themselves under the government of the Genoese, or some stronger neighbour, than submit to a state for which they have so great an aversion. And the Florentines are very sensible, that it is much better having a weak state within their dominions, than the branch of one as strong as themselves. But should so formidable a power, as that of the French King, support them in their attempts, there is no government in Italy that would dare to interpose.

This republic, for the extent of its dominions, is esteemed the richest and best peopled state of Italy. The whole administration of the government passes into different hands at the end of every two months, which is the greatest security imaginable to their liberty, and wonderfully contributes to the quick dispatch of all public affairs: But in any exigence of state, like that they are now pressed with, it certainly asks much longer time to conduct any design, for the good of the commonwealth to its maturity and perfection.

FLORENCE.

I Had the good luck to be at Florence when there was an opera acted, which was the eighth that I had seen in Italy. I could not but smile to read the solemn protestation of the Poet in the first page, where he declares that he believes neither in the fates, deities, or destinies; and that, if he has made use of the words, it is purely out of a poetical liberty, and not from his real sentiments, for that in all these particulars he believes as the holy mother church believes and commands.

PROTESTA.

Le voci Fato, Deita, Destino, e simili, che per entro questo Drama trovarai, son messe per ischerzo poetico, e non per Sentimento vero, credendo sempre in tutto quello, che crede, e comanda Santa Madre chiesa.

There are some beautiful palaces in Florence; and as Tuscan pillars and Rustic work owe their original to this country, the architects always take care to give them a place in the great edifices that are raised in Tuscany. The Duke's new palace is a very noble pile, built after this manner, which makes it look extremely solid and majestic. It is not unlike that of Luxemburg at Paris, which was built by Mary of Medicis, and for that reason perhaps the workmen fell into the Tuscan humour. I found in the court of this palace what I could not meet with any where in Rome: I mean an antique statue of Hercules lifting up Antæus from the earth, which I have already had occasion to speak of. It was found in Rome, and brought hither under the reign of Leo the tenth. There are abundance of pictures in the several apartments, by the hands of the greatest masters.

But it is the famous gallery of the old palace, where are perhaps the noblest collections of curiosities to be met with in any part of the whole world. The gallery itself is made in the shape of an L, according to Mr. Lassel; but, if it must needs be like a letter, it resembles the Greek Π most. It is adorned with admirable pieces of sculpture, as well modern as ancient. Of the last sort I shall mention those that are rarest either for the persons they represent, or the beauty of the sculpture. Among the busts of the Emperors and Empresses, there are these that follow, which are all very scarce, and some of them almost singular in their kind: Agrippa, Caligula, Otho, Nerva, Ælius Verus, Pertinax, Geta, Didius Julianus, Albinus extremely well wrought, and, what is seldom seen, in allabaster, Gordianus Africanus the elder, Eliogabalus, Galien the elder, and the younger Pupienus. I have put Agrippa among the Emperors, because he is generally ranged so in sets of medals, as some that follow among the empresses have no other right to the company they are joined with: Domitia, Agrippina wife of Germanicus, Antonia, Matidia, Plotina, Mallia Scantilla, falsly inscribed under her bust Julia Severi, Aquilia Severa, Julia Mæse.

I hava

I have generally obferved at Rome, which is the great magazine of thefe antiquities, that the fame heads which are rare in medals, are alfo rare in marble, and indeed one may commonly affign the fame reafon for both, which was the fhortnefs of the Emperors reigns, that did not give the workmen time to make many of their figures; and as the fhortnefs of their reigns was generally occafioned by the advancement of a rival, it is no wonder that nobody worked on the figure of a deceafed Emperor, when his enemy was on the throne. This obfervation however does not always hold. An Agrippa or Caligula, for example, is a common coin, but a very extraordinary buft; and a Tiberius a rare coin, but a common buft; which one would the more wonder at, if we confider the indignities that were offered to this Emperor's ftatues after his death. The Tiberius in Tiberim is a known inftance.

Among the bufts of fuch Emperors as are common enough, there are feveral in the gallery that deferve to be taken notice of for the excellence of the fculpture; as thofe of Auguftus, Vefpafian, Adrian, Marcus Aurelius, Lucius Verus, Septimius Severus, Caracalla, Geta. There is in the fame gallery a beautiful buft of Alexander the great, cafting up his face to heaven, with a noble air of grief or difcontentednefs in his looks. I have feen two or three antique bufts of Alexander in the fame air and pofture, and am apt to think the fculptor had in his thoughts the conqueror's weeping for new worlds, or fome other the like circumftance of his hiftory. There is alfo in porphyry the head of a fawn, and of the god Pan. Among the intire figures I took particular notice of a veftal virgin, with the holy fire burning before her,

L 5 This

This statue, I think, may decide that notable controversy among the antiquaries, whether the vestals, after having received the tonsure, ever suffered their hair to come again; for it is here full grown, and gathered under the Veil. The brazen figure of the consul, with the ring on his finger, reminded me of Juvenal's *majoris pondera Gemmæ*. There is another statue in brass, supposed to be of Apollo, with this modern inscription on the pedestal, which I must confess I do not know what to make of, *Ut potui huc veni musis et fratre relicto*. I saw in the same gallery the famous figure of the wild boar, the gladiator, the Narcissus, the Cupid and Psyche, the Flora, with some modern statues that several others have described. Among the antique figures there is a fine one of Morpheus in touchstone. I have always observed, that this god is represented by the ancient statuaries under the figure of a boy asleep, with a bundle of poppy in his hand. I at first took it for a Cupid, until I had taken notice that it had neither bow nor quiver. I suppose Dr. Lister has been guilty of the same mistake, in the reflexions he makes on what he calls the sleeping Cupid with poppy in his hands.

—————————*Qualia namque
Corpora nudorum Tabula pinguntur Amorum,
Talis erat ; sed ne faciat discrimina cultus,
Aut huic adde leves aut illis deme pharetras.*
Ovid. Metam. Lib. 10. v. 515.

Such are the Cupids that in paint we view;
But that the likeness may be nicely true,
A loaden quiver to his shoulders tie,
Or bid the Cupids lay their quivers by.

It

It is probable they chose to represent the god of sleep under the figure of a boy, contrary to all our modern designers, because it is that age, which has its repose the least broken by cares and anxieties. Statius, in his celebrated invocation of sleep, addresses himself to him under the same figure.

Crimine quo merui, juvenis placidissime Divum,
Quove errore miser, donis ut solus egerem,
Somne, tuis? tacet omne pecus, volucresque feræque, &c.
Sylv. 4. Lib. 5. v. 1.

Tell me, thou best of gods, thou gentle youth,
Tell me my sad offence; that only I,
While hush'd at ease thy drousy subjects lie,
In the dead silence of the night complain,
Nor taste the blessings of thy peaceful reign.

I never saw any figure of sleep that was not of black marble, which has probably some relation to the night, that is the proper season for rest. I should not have made this remark, but that I remember to have read in one of the ancient authors, that the Nile is generally represented in stone of this colour, because it flows from the country of the Æthiopians; which shows us that statuaries had sometimes an eye to the person they were to represent, in the choice they made of their marble. There are still at Rome some of these black statues of the Nile which are cut in a kind of touchstone.

Usque coloratis amnis devexus ab Indis.
Virg. Georg. 4. v. 293.

Rolling its tide from Ethiopian lands.

At one end of the gallery stand two antique marble pillars, curiously wrought with the figures of the old Roman arms and instruments of war. After a full survey of the gallery, we were led into four or five chambers of curiosities that stand on the side of it. The first was a cabinet of antiquities, made up chiefly of idols, talismans, lamps, and hieroglyphics. I saw nothing in it that I was not before acquainted with, except the four following figures in brass.

I. A little image of Juno Sispita, or Sospita, which perhaps is not to be met with any where else but on medals. She is clothed in a goat's skin, the horns sticking out above her head. The right arm is broken that probably supported a shield, and the left a little defaced, though one may see it held something in its grasp formerly. The feet are bare. I remember Tully's description of this goddess in the following words. *Illam nostram Sospitam, quam tu nunquam ne in Somniis, vides nisi cum pelle Caprina, cum hasta, cum scutulo, cum calceolis repandis.*— Our goddess Sospita, whom you never see, even in a dream, without a goat-skin, a spear, a little shield, and broad sandals.

FLORENCE. 241

A Medal of Juno Sispita, Vid. Ful Ursin. in Familia Thoria & Porcilio.

This is a Reverse of Anton. Pius

II. An antique model of the famous Laocoon and his two sons, that stands in the Belvidera at Rome. This is the more remarkable, as it is intire in those parts where the statue is maimed. It was by the help of this model that Bandinelli finished his admirable copy of the Laocoon, which stands at one end of this gallery.

III. An Apollo or Amphion. I took notice of this little figure for the singularity of the instrument, which I never before saw in ancient sculpture. It is not unlike a violin, and played on after the same manner. I doubt however, whether this figure be not of a later date than the rest, by the meanness of the workmanship.

IV. A Corona Radialis with only eight spikes to it. Every one knows the usual number was twelve, some say in allusion to the signs of the Zodiac, and others to the labours of Hercules.

— *In-*

——Ingenti mole Latinus
Quadrijugo vehitur curru; cui tempora circum
Aurati bis Sex Radii fulgentia cingunt,
Solis avi Specimen——   Virg. Æn. 12. v. 161.

Four steeds the chariot of Latinus bear:
Twelve golden beams around his temples play,
To mark his lineage from the god of day.
                                        Dryden.

The two next chambers are made up of several artificial curiosities in ivory, amber, crystal, marble, and precious stones, which all voyage-writers are full of. In the chamber that is shewn last, stands the celebrated Venus of Medicis. The statue seems much less than the life, as being perfectly naked, and in company with others of a larger make: It is notwithstanding as big as the ordinary size of a woman, as I concluded from the measure of her wrist; for from the bigness of any one part it is easy to guess at all the rest, in a figure of such nice proportions. The softness of the flesh, the delicacy of the shape, air, and posture, and the correctness of design in this statue are inexpressible. I have several reasons to believe that the name of the sculptor on the pedestal is not so old as the statue. This figure of Venus put me in mind of a speech she makes in one of the Greek epigrams.

Γυμνὴν οἶδε Πάρις με καὶ Ἀγχίσης καὶ Ἄδωνις,
   Τὰς τρεῖς οἶδα μόνας· Πραξιτέλης δὲ πόθι;

Anchises, Paris, and Adonis too,
Have seen me naked and expos'd to view?
All these I frankly own without denying;
But where has this Praxiteles been prying?
                                        There

There is another Venus in the same circle, that would make a good figure any where else. There are among the old Roman statues several of Venus in different postures and habits, as there are many particular figures of her made after the same design. I fancy it is not hard to find among them some that were made after the three statues of this goddess, which Pliny mentions. In the same chamber is the Roman slave whetting his knife and listening, which from the shoulders upward is incomparable. The two wrestlers are in the same room. I observed here likewise a very curious bust of Annius Verus, the young son of Marcus Aurelius, who died at nine years of age. I have seen several other busts of him at Rome, though his medals are exceeding rare.

The great Duke has ordered a large chamber to be fitted up for old inscriptions, urns, monuments, and the like sets of antiquities. I was shown several of them which are not yet put up. There are the two famous inscriptions that give so great a light to the histories of Appius, who made the highway, and of Fabius the dictator; they contain a short account of the honours they passed through, and the actions they performed. I saw too the busts of Tranquillina, mother to Gordianus Pius, and of Quintus Herrenius, son to Trajan Decius, which are extremely valuable for their rarity; and a beautiful old figure made after the celebrated hermaphrodite in the Villa Borghese. I saw nothing that has not been observed by several others in the Argentaria, the tabernacle of St. Lawrence's chapel, and the chamber of painters. The chapel of St. Lawrence will be perhaps the most costly piece of work on the face of the earth, when compleated; but it advances so very slowly, that it is not impossible

ble but the family of Medicis may be extinct before their burial place is finished.

The great Duke has lived many years separate from the Dutchess, who is at present in the court of France, and intends there to end her days. The Cardinal his brother is old and infirm, and could never be induced to resign his purple for the uncertain prospect of giving an heir to the dukedom of Tuscany. The great Prince has been married several years without any children ; and notwithstanding all the precautions in the world were taken for the marriage of the Prince his younger brother (as the finding out a lady for him who was in the vigour and flower of her age, and had given marks of her fruitfulness by a former husband) they have all hitherto proved unsuccessful. There is a branch of the family of Medicis in Naples. The head of it has been owned as a kinsman by the great Duke, and it is thought will succeed to his dominions, in case the Princes his sons die childless; though it is not impossible but, in such a conjuncture, the commonwealths, that are thrown under the great dutchy, may make some efforts towards the recovery of their ancient liberty.

I was in the library of manuscripts belonging to St. Lawrence, of which there is a printed catalogue. I looked into the Virgil, which disputes its antiquity with that of the Vatican. It wants the *Ille ego qui quondam*, &c. and the twenty-two lines in the second Æneid, beginning at *Jamque adeo super unus eram.*—I must confess I always thought this passage left out with a great deal of judgment by Tucca and Varius, as it seems to contradict a part in the sixth Æneid, and represents the hero in a passion, that is, at least, not at all becoming the greatness of his character. Besides, I think the apparition

of

of Venus comes in very properly to draw him away from the fight of Priam's murder; for without such a machine to take him off, I cannot see how the hero could, with honour, leave Neoptolemus triumphant, and Priam unrevenged. But since Virgil's friends thought fit to let drop this incident of Helen, I wonder they would not blot out, or alter a line in Venus's speech, that has a relation to the Rencounter, and comes in improperly without it;

Non tibi Tyndoridæ facies invisa Lacænæ,
Culpatusve Paris——   Æn. 2. v. 601

Not Helen's face, nor Paris was in fault.
                                Dryden.

Florence for modern statues I think excels even Rome; but these I shall pass over in silence, that I may not transcribe out of others.

The way from Florence to Bolonia runs over several ranges of mountains, and is the worst road, I believe, of any over the Apennines; for this was my third time of crossing them. It gave me a lively idea of Silius Italicus's description of Hannibal's march.

Quoque magis subiere jugo atque evadere nisi
Erexere gradum, crescit labor, ardua supra
Sese aperit fessis, et nascitur altera moles. Lib. 3.

From steep to steep the troops advanc'd with pain,
In hopes at last the topmost cliff to gain;
But still by new ascents the mountain grew,
And a fresh toil presented to their view.

I shall conclude this chapter with the descriptions
                                which

which the Latin Poets have given us of the Apennines. We may observe in them all, the remarkable qualities of this prodigious length of mountains that run from one extremity of Italy to the other, and give rise to an incredible variety of rivers that water this delightful country.

———*Nubifer Apenninus.*
Ovid. Metam. Lib. 2. v. 226.

Cloud-bearing Apennines.

———*Qui Siculum porrectus ad usque Pelorum,*
Finibus ab Ligurum, populos amplectitur omnes
Italiæ, geminumque latus stringentia longe
Utraque perpetuo discriminat æquora tractu.
Claud. de sexto Cons. Hon.

Which, stretching from Liguria's distant bounds
To where the strait of Sicily resounds,
Extends itself thro' all Italia's sons,
Embracing various nations as it runs:
And from the summit of its rocky chain
Beholds, on either hand, the hoarse-resounding main.

——————*Mole nivali*
Alpibus æquatum attollens caput Apenninus.
Sil. Ital. Lib. 2.

The Apennine, crown'd with perpetual snow,
High as the tow'ring Alps erects its lofty brow.

Horrebat glacie Saxa inter lubrica Summo
Piniferum cælo miscens caput Apenninus:
Condiderat Nix alta trabes, et vertice celso
Canus apex stricta surgebat ad astra pruina. Id. Lib. 4.
Deform'd

Deform'd with ice, the shady Apennine
Mix'd with the skies; and, cover'd deep with snows,
High as the stars his hoary summit rose.

Umbrosis mediam qua collibus Apenninus
Erigit Italiam, nullo qua vertice tellus
Altius intumuit, propiusque accessit Olympo :
Mons inter geminas medius se porrigit undas
Inferni, superique maris : collesque coercent,
Hinc Tyrrhena vado frangentes æquora Pisæ,
Illinc Dalmaticis obnoxia fluctibus Ancon.
Fontibus hic vastis immensos concipit amnes,
Fluminaque in geminas spargit divortia ponti.
Lucan. Lib. 2. v. 396.

In pomp the shady Apennines arise,
And lift th' aspiring nation to the skies ;
No land like Italy erects the sight
By such a vast ascent, or swells to such a height :
Her num'rous states the tow'ring hills divide,
And see the billows rise on either side ;
At Pisa here the range of mountains ends,
And there to high Ancona's shores extends :
In their dark womb a thousand rivers lie,
That with continu'd streams the double sea supply.

BOLONIA,

BOLONIA, MODENA,

PARMA, TURIN, &c.

AFTER a very tedious journey over the Apennines, we at laſt came to the river that runs at the foot of them, and was formerly called the little Rhine. Following the courſe of this river, we arrived in a ſhort time at Bolonia.

———*Parvique Bolonia Rheni.*   Sil. Ital. Lib. 8.

Bolonia water'd by the petty Rhine.

We here quickly felt the difference of the northern from the ſouthern ſide of the mountains, as well in the coldneſs of the air, as in the badneſs of the wine. This town is famous for the richneſs of the ſoil that lies about it, and the magnificence of its convents, It is likewiſe eſteemed the third in Italy for pictures, as having been the ſchool of the Lombard painters. I ſaw in it three rarities of different kinds, which pleaſed me more than any other ſhows of the place. The firſt was an authentic ſilver medal of the younger Brutus, in the hands of an eminent antiquary. One may ſee the character of the

the person in the features of the face, which is exquisitely well cut. On the reverse is the cap of liberty, with a dagger on each side of it, subscribed *Id. Mar.* for the ides of March, the famous date of Cæsar's murder. The second was a picture of Raphael's in St. Giouanni in Monte. It is extremely well preserved, and represents St. Cecilia with an instrument of music in her hands. On one side of her are the figures of St. Paul, and St. John; and on the other, of Mary Magdalene, and St. Austin. There is something wonderfully divine in the airs of this picture. I cannot forbear mentioning, for my third curiosity, a new stair-case that strangers are generally carried to see, where the easiness of the ascent within so small a compass, the disposition of the lights, and the convenient landing, are admirably well contrived. The wars of Italy, and the season of the year, made me pass through the dutchies of Modena, Parma, and Savoy, with more haste than I would have done at another time. The soil of Modena and Parma is very rich and well cultivated. The palaces of the Princes are magnificent, but neither of them is yet finished. We procured a licence of the Duke of Parma to enter the theatre and gallery, which deserve to be seen as well as any thing of that nature in Italy. The theatre is, I think, the most spacious of any I ever saw, and at the same time so admirably well contrived, that from the very depth of the stage the lowest sound may be heard distinctly to the farthest part of the audience, as in a whispering-place; and yet if you raise your voice as high as you please, there is nothing like an echo to cause in it the least confusion. The gallery is hung with a numerous collection of pictures, all done by celebrated hands. On one side of the

gallery

gallery is a large room adorned with inlaid tables, cabinets, works in amber, and other pieces of great art and value. Out of this we were led into another great room, furnished with old inscriptions, idols, busts, medals, and the like antiquities. I could have spent a day with great satisfaction in this apartment, but had only time to pass my eye over the medals, which are in great number, and many of them very rare. The scarcest of all is a Pescennius Niger on a medalion well preserved. It was coined at Antioch, where this Emperor trifled away his time until he lost his life and empire. The reverse is a Dea Salus. There are two of Otho, the reverse a Serapis; and two of Messalina and Poppæa in middle brass, the reverses of the Emperor Claudius. I saw two medalions of Plotina and Matildia, the reverse to each a Pietas: with two medals of Pertinax, the reverse of one Vota Decennalia, and of the other Diis Custodibus; and another of Gordianus Africanus, the reverse I have forgot.

The principalities of Modena and Parma are much about the same extent, and have each of them two large towns, besides a great number of little villages. The Duke of Parma however is much richer than the Duke of Modena. Their subjects would live in great plenty amidst so rich and well cultivated a soil, were not the taxes and impositions so very exorbitant; for the courts are much too splendid and magnificent for the territories that lie about them, and one cannot but be amazed to see such a profusion of wealth laid out in coaches, trappings, tables, cabinets, and the like precious toys, in which there are few Princes of Europe who equal them, when at the same time they

they have not had the generosity to make bridges over the rivers of their countries, for the convenience of their subjects, as well as strangers, who are forced to pay an unreasonable exaction at every ferry upon the least rising of the waters. A man might well expect in these small governments, a much greater regulation of affairs, for the ease and benefit of the people, than in large over-grown states, where the rules of justice, beneficence, and mercy, may be easily put out of their course in passing through the hands of deputies, and a long subordination of officers. And it would certainly be for the good of mankind to have all the mighty empires and monarchies of the world cantoned out into petty states and principalities, that, like so many large families, might lie under the eye and observation of their proper governors; so that the care of the Prince might extend itself to every individual person under his protection. But since such a general scheme can never be brought about, and, if it were, it would quickly be destroyed by the ambition of some particular state aspiring above the rest, it happens very ill at present to be borne under one of these petty sovereigns, that will be still endeavouring, at his subjects cost, to equal the pomp and grandeur of greater Princes, as well as to outvy those of his own rank.

For this reason there are no people in the world, who live with more ease and prosperity, than the subjects of little commonwealths, as on the contrary there are none who suffer more under the grievances of a hard government, than the subjects of little principalities. I left the road of Milan on my right, having before seen that city, and after having passed through

Asti,

Asti, the frontier town of Savoy, I at last came within sight of the Po, which is a fine river even at Turin, though within six miles of its source. This river has been made the scene of two or three poetical stories. Ovid has chosen it out to throw his Phaeton into it, after all the smaller rivers had been dried up in the conflagration.

I have read some botanical critics, who tell us the Poets have not rightly followed the traditions of antiquity, in metamorphosing the sisters of Phaeton into poplars, who ought to have been turn'd into larch-trees; for that it is this kind of tree which sheds a gum, and is commonly found on the banks of the Po. The change of Cycnus into a swan, which closes up the disasters of Phaeton's family, was wrought on the same place where the sisters were turned into trees. The descriptions that Virgil and Ovid have made of it cannot be sufficiently admired.

Claudian has set off his description of the Eridanus with all the poetical stories that have been made of it.

―――Ille caput placidis sublime fluentis
Extulit, & totis lucem spargentia ripis
Aurea roranti micuerunt cornua vultu
Non illi madidum vulgaris arundine crinem
Velat honos; rami caput umbravere virentes
Heliadum, totisque fluunt electra capillis.
Palla tegit latos humeros, curruque paterno
Intextus Phaeton glaucos incendit amictus:
Fultaque sub gremio cælatis nobilis astris
Æthereum probat urna decus. Namque omnia luctus
Argumenta sui Titan signavit Olympo,
Mutatumque senem plumis, et fronde sorores,

Et

Et fluvium, nati qui vulnera lavit anheli,
Stat gelidis Auriga plagis ; vestigia fratris
Germanæ servant Hyades, Cycnique sodalis
Lacteus extentas aspergit circulus alas.
Stellifer Eridanus sinuatis fluctibus errans,
Clara noti convexa rigat⸺
     Claudian. de sexto Conf. Honorii.

His head above the floods he gently rear'd,
And as he rose his golden horns appear'd,
That on the forehead shone divinely bright,
And o'er the banks diffus'd a yellow light :
No interwoven reeds a garland made,
To hide his brows within the vulgar shade :
But poplar wreaths around his temple spread,
And tears of amber trickled down his head :
A spacious veil from his broad shoulders flew,
That set th' unhappy Phaeton to view :
The flaming chariot and the steeds it show'd,
And the whole fable in the mantle glow'd :
Beneath his arm an urn supported lies,
With stars embellish'd and fictitious skies.
For Titan, by the mighty loss dismay'd,
Among the heav'ns th' immortal fact display'd,
Lest the remembrance of his grief should fail,
And in the constellations wrote his tale.
A swan in memory of Cycnus shines ;
The mourning sisters weep in watry signs ;
The burning chariot, and the charioteer,
In bright Bootes and his wane appear ;
Whilst in a track of light the waters run,
That wash'd the body of his blasted son.

 The river Po gives a name to the chief street of Turin, which fronts the Duke's palace, and when

when finish'd will be one of the noblest in Italy for its length. There is one convenience in this city that I never observed in any other, and which makes some amends for the badness of the pavement. By the help of a river, that runs on the upper side of the town, they can convey a little stream of water through all the most considerable streets, which serves to cleanse the gutters, and carries away all the filth that is swept into it. The manager opens his sluice every night, and distributes the water into what quarters of the town he pleases. Besides the ordinary convenience that arises from it, it is of great use when a fire chances to break out; for at a few minutes warning they have a little river running by the very walls of the house that is burning. The court of Turin is reckoned the most splendid and polite of any in Italy; but by reason of its being in mourning, I could not see it in its magnificence. The common people of this state are more exasperated against the French than even the rest of the Italians. For the great mischiefs they have suffered from them are still fresh upon their memories, and, notwithstanding this interval of peace, one may easily trace out the several marches, which the French armies have made through their country, by the ruin and desolation they have left behind them. I passed through Piedmont and Savoy, at a time when the Duke was forced, by the necessity of his affairs, to be in alliance with the French.

I came directly from Turin to Geneva, and had a very easy journey over mount Cennis, though about the beginning of December, the snows having not yet fallen. On the top of this high mountain is a large plain, and in the midst of the plain

a beau-

a beautiful lake which would be very extraordinary, were there not several mountains in the neighbourhood rising over it. The inhabitants thereabout pretend that it is unfathomable, and I question not but the waters of it fill up a deep valley, before they come to a level with the surface of a plain. It is well-stocked with trouts, though they say it is covered with ice three quarters of the year.

There is nothing in the natural face of Italy that is more delightful to a traveller, than the several lakes which are dispersed up and down among the many breaks and hollows of the Alps and Appennines. For as these vast heaps of mountains are thrown together with so much irregularity and confusion, they form a great variety of hollow bottoms, that often lie in the figure of so many artificial basons; where, if any fountains chance to rise, they naturally spread themselves into lakes, before they can find any issue for their waters. The ancient Romans took a great deal of pains to hew out a passage for these lakes to discharge themselves into some neighbouring river, for the bettering of the air, or the recovering of the soil that lay underneath them. The draining of the Fucinus by the Emperor Claudius, with the prodigious multitude of spectators who attended it, and the famous Naumachia and splendid entertainment, which were made upon it before the sluices were opened, is a well known piece of history. In all our journey through the Alps, as well when we climbed as when we descended them, we had still a river running along with the road, that probably at first occasioned the discovery of this passage. I shall end this chapter with a description

scription of the Alps, as I did the last with those of the Appennines. The Poet perhaps would not have taken notice, that there is no spring nor summer on these mountains, but because in this respect the Alps are quite different from the Appennines, which have as delightful green spots among them as any in Italy.

Cuncta gelu canâque æternùm grandine tecta,
Atque ævi glaciem cohibent: riget ardua montis
Ætherei facies, surgentique obvia Phœbo
Duratas nescit flammis mollire pruinas:
Quantùm Tartareus regni pallentis hiatus
Ad manes imos atque atræ stagna paludis
A superâ tellure patet, tam longa per auras
Erigitur tellus, & cælum intercipit Umbrâ.
Nullum ver usquam, nullique Æstatis honores;
Sola jugis habitat diris, sedesque tuetur
Perpetuas deformis Hyems: illa undique nubes.
Huc atras agit, et mixtos cum grandine nimbos,
Nam cuncti flatus ventique furentia regna
Alpinâ posuere domo, caligat in altis
Obtutus saxis, abeuntque in nubila montes.

Sil. Ital. Lib. 3.

Stiff with eternal ice, and hid in snow
That fell a thousand centuries ago,
The mountain stands; nor can the rising sun
Unfix her frosts, and teach 'em how to run:
Deep as the dark infernal waters lie
From the bright regions of the chearful sky,
So far the proud ascending rocks invade
Heav'n's upper realms, and cast a dreadful shade:
No spring nor summer on the mountain seen
Smiles with gay fruits, or with delightful green;
But

But hoary winter, unadorn'd and bare,
Dwells in the dire retreat, and freezes there;
There she assembles all her blackest storms,
And the rude hail in rattling tempests forms;
Thither the loud tumultuous winds resort,
And on the mountain keep their boist'rous court,
That in thick show'rs her rocky summit shrowds,
And darkens all the broken view with clouds.

GENEVA

GENEVA

AND THE

LAKE.

NEAR St. Julian in Savoy the Alps begin to enlarge themselves on all sides, and open into a vast circuit of ground, which, in respect of the other parts of the Alps, may pass for a plain champain country. This extent of lands, with the Leman lake, would make one of the prettiest and most defensible dominions in Europe, was it all thrown into a single state, and had Geneva for its metropolis. But there are three powerful neighbours, who divide among them the greatest part of this fruitful country. The Duke of Savoy has the Chablais, and all the fields that lie beyond the Arve, as far as to the Ecluse. The King of France is master of the whole country of Gex; and the canton of Bern comes in for that of Vaud. Geneva and its little territories lie in the heart of these three states. The greatest part of the town stands upon a hill, and has its view bounded on all sides by several ranges of mountains, which are however at so great a distance, that they leave open a wonderful variety of beautiful prospects. The situation of these mountains has some particular effects on the country, which they inclose. As first, they cover it from all winds, except the south and north. It is to the last of these winds that the inhabitants of Geneva ascribe the healthfulness of their air; for as the Alps surround them on all sides, they form a vast kind of bason, where there would be a constant stagnation of vapours, the country being so well watered, did not the north wind put them in motion, and scatter them from time to time. Another effect the Alps have on Geneva is, that the sun here rises later and sets sooner than it does to other places of the same latitude. I have often observed that the tops of the neighbouring mountains have been covered with light above half an hour after the sun is down, in respect of those who live at Geneva. These mountains likewise very much increase their summer heats, and make up an horizon that has something in it very singular and agreeable. On one side you have the long tract of hills, that goes under the name of mount Jura, covered with vineyards and pasturage, and on the other huge precipices of naked rocks rising up in a thousand odd figures, and cleft in some places, so as to discover high mountains of snow that lie several leagues behind them. Towards the south the hills rise more insensibly, and leave the eye a vast uninterrupted prospect for many miles. But the most beautiful view of all is the lake, and the borders of it that lie N. of the town.

This lake resembles a sea in the colour of its waters, the storms that are raised on it, and the ravage it makes on its banks. It receives too a different name from the coasts it washes, and in summer has something like an ebb and flow, which arises from the melting of the snows that fall into it more copiously at noon than at other times of the day. It has five different states bordering on it, the kingdom of France, the dutchy of Savoy, the canton of Bern, the bishopric of Sion, and the republic of Geneva. I have seen papers fixed up in the canton of Bern, with this magnificent preface; 'Whereas we have been informed of several abuses 'committed in our ports and harbours on the lake, '&c.'

I made a little voyage round the lake, and touched on the several towns that lie on its coasts, which took up near five days, though the wind was pretty fair for us all the while.

The right side of the lake from Geneva belongs to the Duke of Savoy, and is extremely well cultivated. The greatest entertainment we found in coasting it were the several prospects of woods, vineyards, meadows, and corn-fields which lie on the borders of it, and run up all the sides of the Alps, where the barrenness of the rocks, or the steepness of the ascent will suffer them. The wine however on this side of the lake is by no means so good as that on the other, as it has not so open a soil, and is less exposed to the sun. We here passed by Yvoire, where the Duke keeps his gallies, and lodged at Tonon, which is the greatest town on the lake belonging to the Savoyard. It has four convents, and they say about six or seven thousand inhabitants. The lake is here about twelve miles in breadth. At a little distance from Tonon stands Ripaille, where is a convent of Carthusians. They have a large forest cut out into walks, that are extremely thick and gloomy, and very suitable to the genius of the inhabitants. There are Vistas in it of a great length, that terminate upon the lake. At one side of the walks you have a near
prospect

prospect of the Alps, which are broken into so many steeps and precipices, that they fill the mind with an agreeable kind of horror, and form one of the most irregular mis-shapen scenes in the world. The house, that is now in the hands of the Carthusians, belonged formerly to the hermits of St. Maurice, and is famous in history for the retreat of an Anti-Pope, who called himself Felix the fifth. He had been Duke of Savoy, and after a very glorious reign took on him the habit of a hermit, and retired into this solitary spot of his dominions. His enemies will have it, that he lived here in great ease and luxury; from whence the Italians to this day make use of the proverb, *Andare a Ripaglia*, and the French, *Faire Ripaille*, to express a delightful kind of life. They say too, that he had great managements with several ecclesiastics before he turned hermit, and that he did it in the view of being advanced to the pontificate. However it was, he had not been here half a year, before he was chosen Pope by the council of Basil, who took upon them to depose Eugenio the fourth. This promised fair at first; but by the death of the Emperor, who favoured Amadeo, and the resolution of Eugenio, the greatest part of the church threw itself again under the government of their deposed head. Our Anti-pope however was still supported by the council of Basil, and owned by Savoy, Switzerland, and a few other little states. This schism lasted in the church nine years, after which Felix voluntarily resigned his title into the hands of Pope Nicholas the fifth; but on the following conditions, that Amadeo should be the first Cardinal in the conclave; that the Pope should always receive him standing, and offer him his mouth to kiss; that he should be perpetual Cardinal legate in the states of Savoy, and Switzerland, and in the archbishoprics of Geneva, Sion, Bress, &c. And lastly, that all the Cardinals of his creation should be recognized by the Pope. After he had made a peace so acceptable to the church, and so honourable to himself, he spent the remainder of his life with great devotion at Ripaille, and died with an extraordinary reputation of sanctity.

At Tonon they shewed us a fountain of water that is in great esteem for its wholsomness. They say it weighs two ounces in a pound less than the same measure of the lake-water, notwithstanding this last is very good to drink, and as clear as can be imagined. A little above Tonon is a castle and small garrison. The next day we saw other small towns on the coast of Savoy, where there is nothing but misery and poverty. The nearer you come to the end of the lake, the mountains on each side grow thicker and higher, until at last they almost meet. One often sees on the tops of the mountains several sharp rocks that stand above the rest; for as these mountains have been doubtless much higher than they are at present, the rains have washed away abundance of the soil, that has left the veins of stones shooting out of them; as in a decayed body the flesh is still shrinking from the bones. The natural histories of Switzerland talk very much of the fall of these rocks, and the great damage they have sometimes done, when their foundations have been mouldered with age, or rent by an earthquake. We saw in several parts of the Alps, that bordered upon us, vast pits of snow, as several mountains that lie at a greater distance are wholly covered with it. I fancied the confusion of mountains and hollows, I here observed, furnished me with a more probable reason than any

any I have met with for those periodical fountains in Switzerland, which flow only at such particular hours of the day. For as the tops of these mountains cast their shadows upon one another, they hinder the sun's shining on several parts at such certain times, so that there are several heaps of snow which have the sun lying upon them for two or three hours together, and are in the shade all the day afterwards. If therefore it happens that any particular fountain takes its rise from any of these reservoirs of snow, it will naturally begin to flow on such hours of the day as the snow begins to melt: but as soon as the sun leaves it again to freeze and harden, the fountain dries up, and receives no more supplies until about the same time the next day, when the heat of the sun again sets the snows running that fall into the same little conduits, traces, and canals, and by consequence break out and discover themselves always in the same place. At the very extremity of the lake the Rhone enters, and, when I saw it, brought along with it a prodigious quantity of water, the rivers and lakes of this country being much higher in summer than in winter, by reason of the melting of the snows. One would wonder how so many learned men could fall into so great an absurdity, as to believe this river could preserve itself unmixed with the lake, till its going out again at Geneva, which is a course of many miles. It was extremely muddy at its entrance, when I saw it, though as clear as rock water at its going out. Besides, that it brought in much more water than it carried off. The river indeed preserves itself for about a quarter of a mile in the lake, but is afterwards so wholly mixed and lost with the waters of the lake, that one discovers nothing like a stream
until

until within about a quarter of a mile of Geneva. From the end of the lake to the source of the Rhone is a valley of about four days journey in length, which gives the name of Vallesins to its inhabitants, and is the dominion of the Bishop of Sion. We lodged the second night at Villa Neuve, a little town in the canton of Bern, where we found good accommodations, and a much greater appearance of plenty than on the other side of the lake. The next day, having passed by the castle of Chillon, we came to Versoy, another town in the canton of Bern, where Ludlow retired after having left Geneva and Lausanne. The magistrates of the town warned him out of the first by the solicitation of the Dutchess of Orleans, as the death of his friend Lisle made him quit the other. He probably chose this retreat as a place of the greatest safety, it being an easy matter to know what strangers are in the town, by reason of its situation. The house he lived in has this inscription over the door;

Omne solum forti patria
quia Patris.

The first part is a piece of verse in Ovid, as the last is a cant of his own. He is buried in the best of the churches with the following epitaph.

Sisle gradum et respice.

Hic jacet Edmond Ludlow, Anglus Natione, Provinciæ Wiltoniensis, filius Henrici Equestris ordinis, Senatorisque Parliamenti, cujus quoque fuit ipse membrum, Patrum stemmate clarus et nobilis, virtute propriâ nobilior, Religione protestans et insigni pietate coruscus, Ætatis Anno 23 Tribunus

bunus Militum, paulo post exercitûs prætor primarius. Tunc Hibernorum domitor, in pugnâ intrepidus et vitæ prodigus, in victoriâ clemens et mansuetus, patriæ Libertatis Defensor, et potestatis Arbitrariæ propugnator acerrimus; cujus causâ ab eâdem patria 32 annis extorris, meliorique fortuna dignus apud Helvetios se recepit, ibique ætatis Anno 73 Moriens sui desiderium relinquens sedes æternas lætus advolavit.

Hocce Monumentum, in perpetuam veræ et sinceræ pietatis erga maritum defunctum memoriam, dicat et vovet Domina Elizabeth de Thomas, ejus strenua et mæstissima, tam in infortuniis quam in matrimonio consors dilectissima, quæ animi magnitudine et vi amoris conjugalis mota eum in exilium ad obitum usque constanter secuta est. Anno Dom. 1693.

Here lies Edmund Ludlow, by birth an Englishman, of the county of Wilts; son of Sir Henry Ludlow, Knight; a member of parliament, as his father had likewise been; more distinguished by his virtue than his family, though an ancient and good one; by religion a protestant, and remarkable for his eminent piety: In the 23d year of his age he had the command of a regiment, and, soon after, the post of lieutenant-general: In which quality he subdued the Irish, being intrepid in fight, and exposing himself to the greatest dangers; but in victory merciful and humane: A defender of the liberty of his country, and a strenuous opposer of arbitrary power: upon which account being banished 32 years from his native country, and worthy of a better fortune, he retired into Switzerland, where he died, universally regretted, in the 73d year of his age.

This

This monument was erected, in perpetual memory of her true and sincere affection towards her deceased husband, by Dame Elizabeth Thomas, his beloved wife, and afflicted, but constant, partner, as well in misfortunes, as in wedlock; who, excited by her own greatness of mind, and the force of conjugal love, followed him into banishment, and constantly bore him company to his death, *A. D.* 1693.

Ludlow was a constant frequenter of sermons and prayers, but would never communicate with them either of Geneva or Vevy. Just by his monument is a tomb stone with the following inscription.

Depositorium.

Andreæ Broughton Armigeri Anglicani Maydstonensis in Comitatu Cantii ubi bis prætor Urbanus. Dignatusque etiam fuit sententiam Regis Regum profari. Quam ob causam expulsus patriâ suâ, peregrinatione ejus finitâ, solo senectutis morbo affectus, requiescens a laboribus suis in Domino obdormivit, 23 *die Feb. Anno D.* 1687, *ætatis suæ* 84. The remains of Andrew Broughton, Esq; an Englishman, of Maidstone in the county of Kent, of which place he was twice mayor. He had the honour likewise to pronounce the sentence of the King of Kings. Upon which account being banished from his country, after his travels were at an end, affected with no other disease than that of old age, he rested from his labours, and fell asleep in the Lord, the 23d of February, *A. D.* 1687, in the 84th year of his age. The inhabitants of the place could give no account of this Broughton; but I suppose, by his epitaph, it is

the

the same person that was clerk to the pretended high court of justice, which passed sentence on the royal martyr.

The next day we spent at Lausanne, the greatest town on the lake, after Geneva. We saw the wall of the cathedral church that was opened by an earthquake, and shut again some years after by a second. The crack can but be just discerned at present, though there are several in the town still living who have formerly passed through it. The Duke of Schomberg, who was killed in Savoy, lies in this church, but without any monument or inscription over him. Lausanne was once a republic, but is now under the canton of Bern, and governed, like the rest of their dominions, by a bailiff, who is sent them every three years from the Senate of Bern. There is one street of this town that has the privilege of acquitting or condemning any person of their own body, in matters of life and death. Every inhabitant of it has his vote, which makes a house here sell better than in any other part of the town. They tell you that not many years ago it happened, that a cobler had the casting vote for the life of the criminal, which he very graciously gave on the merciful side. From Lausanne to Geneva we coasted along the country of the Vaud, which is the fruitfullest and best cultivated part of any among the Alps. It belonged formerly to the Duke of Savoy, but was won from him by the canton of Bern, and made over to it by the treaty of St. Julian, which is still very much regretted by the Savoyard. We called in at Morge, where there is an artificial port, and a show of more trade than in any other town on the lake. From Morge we came to Nyon. The Colonia Equestris, that Julius Cæsar settled in this country, is generally supposed to have been planted in this place. They have often dug up old Roman inscriptions and statues, and as I walked in the town I observed in the walls of several houses the fragments of vast Corinthian pillars, with several other pieces of architecture, which must have formerly belonged to some very noble pile of building. There is no author that mentions this colony, yet it is certain by several old Roman inscriptions that there was such an one. Lucan indeed speaks of a part of Cæsar's army, that came to him from the Leman lake in the beginning of the civil war.

Deseruere cavo tentoria fixa Lemanno.
Lib. 1. v. 396.

They left their tents pitch'd on the Leman lake.

At about five miles distance from Nyon they show still the ruins of Cæsar's wall, that reached eighteen miles in length from mount Jura to the borders of the lake, as he has described it in the first book of his commentaries. The next town upon the lake is Versoy, which we could not have an opportunity of seeing, as belonging to the King of France. It has the reputation of being extremely poor and beggarly. We sailed from hence directly for Geneva, which makes a very noble show from the lake. There are near Geneva several quarries of freestone that run under the lake. When the water is at the lowest they make within the borders of it a little square inclosed with four walls. In this square they sink a pit, and dig for freestone; the walls hindering the waters from coming in upon them, when the lake rises and runs on all sides of them. The great convenience of carriage makes these stones much cheaper than any that can be found upon firm land. One sees several deep pits that have been made at several times as one sails over them. As the lake approaches Geneva it grows still narrower and narrower, until at last it changes its name into the Rhone, that turns all the mills of the town, and is extremely rapid, notwithstanding its waters are very deep. As I have seen great part of the course of this river, I cannot but think it has been guided by the particular hand of Providence. It rises in the very heart of the Alps, and has a long valley that seems hewn out on purpose to give its waters passage amidst so many rocks and mountains which are on all sides of it. This brings it almost in a direct line to Geneva. It would there overflow all the country, were there not one particular cleft that divides a vast circuit of mountains, and conveys it off to Lyons. From Lyons there is another great rent, which runs across the whole country in almost another straight line, and notwithstanding the vast height of the mountains that rise about it, gives it the shortest course it can take to fall into the sea. Had such a river as this been left to itself to have found its way out from among the Alps, whatever windings it had made it must have formed several little seas, and have laid many countries under water before it had come to the end of its course. I shall not make any remarks upon Geneva, that is a republick so well known to the English. It lies at present under some difficulties by reason of the Emperor's displeasure, who has forbidden the importation of their manufactures into any part of the empire, which will certainly raise a sedition among the people, unless the magistrates find some way to remedy it: and they say it is already done by the interposition of the states of Holland. The occasion of the Emperor's prohibition was their furnishing great sums to the King of France for the payment of his army in Italy. They obliged themselves to remit, after the rate of twelve hundred thousand pounds sterling *per Annum*, divided into so many monthly payments. As the interest was very great, several of the merchants of Lyons, who would not trust their King in their own name, are said to have contributed a great deal under the names of Geneva merchants. The republic fancies itself hardly treated by the Emperor, since it is not any action of the state, but a compact among private persons that have furnished out these several remittances. They pretend however to have put a stop to them, and by that means are in hopes again to open their commerce into the empire.

Fribourg, Bern, Soleurre, Zurich, St. Gaul, Lindaw, &c.

FROM Geneva I travelled to Lausanne, and thence to Fribourg, which is but a mean town for the capital of so large a canton: Its situation is so irregular, that they are forced to climb up to several parts of it by stair cases of a prodigious ascent. This inconvenience however gives them a very great commodity in case a fire breaks out in any part of the town; for by reason of several reservoirs on the tops of these mountains, by the opening of a sluice they convey a river into what part of the town they please. They have four churches, four convents of women, and as many for men. The little chapel called the Salutation, is very neat, and built with a pretty fancy. The college of the jesuits is, they say, the finest in Switzerland. There is a great deal of room in it, and several beautiful views from the different parts of it. They have a collection of pictures representing most of the fathers of their order, who have been eminent for their piety or learning. Among the rest, many Englishmen, whom we name rebels, and they martyrs. Henry

Henry Garnet's inscription says, that when the heretics could not prevail with him, either by force or promises, to change his religion, they hanged and quartered him. At the Capuchins I saw the escargatoire, which I took the more notice of, because I do not remember to have met with any thing of the same nature in other countries. It is a square place boarded in, and filled with a vast quantity of large snails, that are esteemed excellent food when they are well dressed. The floor is strowed about half a foot deep with several kinds of plants, among which the snails nestle all the winter season. When Lent arrives, they open their magazines, and take out of them the best meagre food in the world; for there is no dish of fish that they reckon comparable to a ragoût of snails.

About two leagues from Fribourg we went to see a hermitage, that is reckoned the greatest curiosity of these parts. It lies in the prettiest solitude imaginable, among woods and rocks, which at first sight dispose a man to be serious. There has lived in it a hermit these five and twenty years, who with his own hand has worked in the rock a pretty chapel, a sacristy, a chamber, kitchen, cellar, and other conveniencies. His chimney is carried up through the whole rock, so that you see the sky through it, notwithstanding the rooms lie very deep. He has cut the side of the rock into a flat for a garden, and by laying on it the waste earth that he has found in several of the neighbouring parts, has made such a spot of ground of it as furnishes out a kind of luxury for an hermit. As he saw drops of water distilling from several parts of the rock, by following the veins of them, he has made himself two or three fountains in the
bowels

bowels of the mountain, that serve his table, and water his little garden.

We had very bad ways from hence to Bern, a great part of them through woods of fir-trees. The great quantity of timber they have in this country makes them mend their highways with wood instead of stone. I could not but take notice of the make of several of their barns I here saw. After having laid a frame of wood for the foundation, they place at the four corners of it four huge blocks, cut in such a shape as neither mice nor any other sort of vermin can creep up the sides of them, at the same time that they raise the corn above the moisture that might come into it from the ground. The whole weight of the barn is supported by these four blocks.

What pleased me most at Bern was their public walks by the great church. They are raised extremely high, and, that their weight might not break down their walls and pilasters which surround them, they are built upon arches and vaults. Though they are, I believe, as high as most steeples in England from the streets and gardens that lie at the foot of them, yet, about forty years ago, a person in his drink fell down from the very top to the bottom, without doing himself any other hurt than the breaking of an arm. He died about four years ago. There is the noblest summer-prospect in the world from this walk ; for you have a full view of a huge range of mountains that lie in the country of the Grisons, and are buried in snow. They are about twenty five leagues distance from the town, though by reason of their height and their colour they seem much nearer. The cathedral church stands on one side of these walks, and is perhaps the most magnificent of any protestant church

church in Europe, out of England. It is a very bold work, and a master-piece in Gothic architecture.

I saw the arsenal of Bern, where they say there are arms for twenty thousand men. There is indeed no great pleasure in visiting these magazines of war after one has seen two or three of them; yet it is very well worth a traveller's while to look into all that lie in his way; for besides the idea it gives him of the forces of a state, it serves to fix in his mind the most considerable parts of its history. Thus in that of Geneva one meets with the ladders, petards, and other utensils which were made use of in their famous escalade, besides the weapons they took of the Savoyards, Florentines, and French in the several battles mentioned in their history. In this of Bern you have the figure and armour of the count who founded the town, and the famous Tell, who is represented as shooting at the apple on his son's head. The story is too well known to be repeated in this place. I here likewise saw the figure and armour of him that headed the peasants in the war upon Bern, with the several weapons which were found in the hands of his followers. They show too abundance of arms that they took from the Burgundians in the three great battles which established them in their liberty, and destroyed the great Duke of Burgundy himself, with the bravest of his subjects. I saw nothing remarkable in the chambers where the council meet, nor in the fortifications of the town. These last were made on occasion of the peasants insurrection, to defend the place for the future against the like sudden assaults. In their library I observed a couple of antique figures in metal, of a priest pouring wine between the horns of a bull.

The

The prieſt is veiled after the manner of the old Roman ſacrificers, and is repreſented in the ſame action that Virgil deſcribes in the fourth Æneid.

Ipſa tenens dextrâ pateram pulcherrima Dido,
Candentis vaccæ media inter cornua fundit. v. 60.

The beauteous Queen before her altar ſtands,
And holds the golden goblet in her hands:
A milk-white heifer ſhe with flow'rs adorns,
And pours the ruddy wine betwixt her horns.
Dryden.

This antiquity was found at Lauſanne.

The town of Bern is plentifully furniſhed with water, there being a great multitude of handſome fountains planted at ſet diſtances from one end of the ſtreets to the other. There is indeed no country in the world better ſupplied with water, than the ſeveral parts of Switzerland that I travelled through. One meets every where in the roads with fountains continually running into huge troughs that ſtand underneath them, which is wonderfully commodious in a country that ſo much abounds with horſes and cattle. It has ſo many ſprings breaking out of the ſides of the hills, and ſuch vaſt quantities of wood to make pipes of, that it is no wonder they are ſo well ſtocked with fountains.

On the road between Bern and Soleurre there is a monument erected by the republic of Bern, which tells us the ſtory of an Engliſhman, who is not to be met with in any of our own writers. The inſcription is in Latin verſe on one ſide of the ſtone, and in German on the other. I had not time to copy it; but the substance of it is this: "One Cussinus, an Englishman, to whom the Duke of Austria had given his sister in marriage, came to take her from among the Swiss by force of arms; but after having ravaged the country for some time, he was here overthrown by the canton of Bern."

Soleurre is our next considerable town, that seemed to me to have a greater air of politeness than any I saw in Switzerland. The French Ambassador has his residence in this place. His Master contributed a great sum of money to the jesuits church, which is not yet quite finished. It is the finest modern building in Switzerland. The old cathedral church stood not far from it. At the ascent that leads to it are a couple of antique pillars, which belonged to an old heathen temple, dedicated to Hermes: They seem Tuscan by their proportion. The whole fortification of Soleurre is faced with marble. But its best fortifications are the high mountains that lie within its neighbourhood, and separate it from the Franche Compté.

The next day's journey carried us through other parts of the canton of Bern, to the little town of Meldingen. I was surprized to find, in all my road through Switzerland, the wine that grows in the county of Vaud on the border of the lake of Geneva, which is very cheap, notwithstanding the great distance between the vineyards and the towns that sell the wine. But the navigable rivers of Switzerland are as commodious to them in this respect, as the sea is to the English. As soon as the vintage is over, they ship off their wine upon the lake, which furnishes all the towns that lie upon its borders. What they design for other parts of the country

country they unload at Vevy, and after about half a day's land carriage convey it into the river Aar, which brings it down the stream to Bern, Soleurre, and, in a word, distributes it through all the richest part of Switzerland; as it is easy to guess from the first sight of the map, which shews us the natural communication Providence has formed between the many rivers and lakes of a country that is at so great a distance from the sea. The canton of Bern is reckoned as powerful as all the rest together. They can send a hundred thousand men into the field; though the soldiers of the catholic cantons, who are much poorer, and therefore forced to enter oftner into foreign armies, are more esteemed than the protestants.

We lay one night at Meldingen, which is a little Roman catholic town with one church, and no convent. It is a republic of itself, under the protection of the eight ancient cantons. There are in it a hundred bourgeois, and about a thousand souls. Their government is modelled after the same manner with that of the cantons, as much as so small a community can imitate those of so large an extent. For this reason, though they have very little business to do, they have all the variety of councils and officers that are to be met with in the greater states. They have a town house to meet in, adorned with the arms of the eight cantons their protectors. They have three councils, the great council of fourteen, the little council of ten, and the privy council of three. The chief of the state are the two Avoyers: When I was there the reigning Avoyer, or Doge of the commonwealth, was son to the inn-keeper where I was lodged; his father having enjoyed the same honours before him. His revenue amounts to about

N   thirty

thirty pounds a year. The several councils meet every Thursday upon affairs of state, such as the reparation of a trough, the mending of a pavement, or any the like matters of importance. The river that runs through their dominions puts them to the charge of a very large bridge, that is all made of wood, and coped over head, like the rest in Switzerland. Those that travel over it pay a certain due towards the maintenance of this bridge. And as the French Ambassador has often occasion to pass this way, his master gives the town a pension of twenty pounds sterling which makes them extremely industrious to raise all the men they can for his service, and keeps this powerful republic firm to the French interest. You may be sure the preserving of the bridge, with the regulation of the dues arising from it, is the grand affair that cuts out employment for the several councils of state. They have a small village belonging to them, whither they punctually send a bailiff for the distribution of justice; in imitation still of the great cantons. There are three other towns that have the same privileges and protectors.

We dined the next day at Zurich, that is prettily situated on the out-let of the lake, and is reckoned the handsomest town in Switzerland. The chief places shewn to strangers are the arsenal, the library, and the town-house. This last is but lately finished, and is a very fine pile of building. The frontispiece has pillars of a beautiful black marble streaked with white, which is found in the neighbouring mountains. The chambers for the several councils, with the other apartments, are very neat. The whole building is indeed so well designed, that it would make a good figure even in Italy. It is pity they have spoiled the beauty of the

walls

walls with abundance of childish Latin sentences, that consist often in a jingle of words. I have indeed observed in several inscriptions of this country, that your men of learning here are extremely delighted in playing little tricks with words and figures; for your Swiss wits are not yet got out of the anagram and acrostic. The library is a very large room. pretty well filled. Over it is another room furnished with several artificial and natural curiosities. I saw in it a huge map of the whole country of Zurich drawn with a pencil, where they see every particular fountain or hillock in their dominions. I ran over their cabinet of medals, but do not remember to have met with any in it that are extraordinary rare. The arsenal is better than that of Bern, and they say has arms for thirty thousand men. At about a day's journey from Zurich we entered on the territories of the Abbot of St. Gaul. They are four hours riding in breadth, and twelve in length. The Abbot can raise in it an army of twelve thousand men well armed and exercised. He is sovereign of the whole country, and under the protection of the cantons of Zurich, Lucerne, Glaris and Switz. He is always chosen out of the abbey of Benedictines at St. Gaul. Every father and brother of the convent has a voice in the election, which must afterwards be confirmed by the Pope. The last Abbot was Cardinal Sfondrati, who was advanced to the purple about two years before his death. The Abbot takes the advice and consent of his chapter before he enters on any matter of importance, as the levying of a tax, or declaring of a war. His chief lay-officer is the grand *Maitre d'Hotel*, or high steward of the houshold, who is named by the Abbot, and has the management of all affairs under him. There are several other judges and diftributers of juftice appointed for the feveral parts of his dominions, from whom there always lies an appeal to the Prince. His refidence is generally at the Beredictine convent at St. Gaul, notwithftanding the town of St. Gaul is a little proteftant republic, wholly independent of the Abbot, and under the protection of the cantons.

One would wonder to fee fo many rich bourgeois in the town of St. Gaul, and fo very few poor people in a place that has fcarce any lands belonging to it, and little or no income but what arifes from its trade. But the great fupport and riches of this little ftate is in its linen manufacture, which employs almoft all ages and conditions of its inhabitants. The whole country about them furnifhes them with vaft quantities of flax, out of which they are faid to make yearly forty thoufand pieces of linen cloth, reckoning two hundred ells to the piece. Some of their manufacture is as finely wrought as any that can be met with in Holland; for they have excellent artifans, and great commodities for whitening. All the fields about the town were covered with their manufacture, that coming in the dufk of the evening we miftook them for a lake. They fend off their works upon mules into Italy, Spain, Germany, and all the adjacent countries. They reckon in the town of St. Gaul, and in the houfes that lie fcattered about it, near ten thoufand fouls, of which there are fixteen hundred bourgeois. They choofe their councils and burgomafters out of the body of bourgeois, as in the other governments of Switzerland, which are every where of the fame nature, the difference lying only in the numbers of fuch as are employed in ftate-affairs, which are proportioned to the grandeur of the ftates that employ them. The Abbey and the town

town bear a great averſion to one another; but in the general diet of the cantons their repreſentatives ſit together, and act by concert. The Abbot deputes his grand *Maitre d' Hotel*, and the town one of its burgo-maſters.

About four years ago, the town and abbey would have come to an open rupture, had it not been timely prevented by the interpoſition of their common protectors. The occaſion was this. A Benedictine monk, in one of their annual proceſſions, carried his croſs erected through the town, with a train of three or four thouſand peaſants following him. They had no ſooner entered the convent, but the whole town was in a tumult, occaſioned by the inſolence of the prieſt, who, contrary to all precedents, had preſumed to carry his croſs in that manner. The bourgeois immediately put themſelves in arms, and drew down four pieces of their cannon to the gates of the convent. The proceſſion, to eſcape the fury of the citizens, durſt not return by the way it came, but, after the devotions of the monks were finiſhed, paſſed out at a back-door of the convent, that immediately led into the Abbot's territories. The Abbot on his part raiſes an army blocks up the town on the ſide that faces his dominions, and forbids his ſubjects to furniſh it with any of their commodities. While things were juſt ripe for a war, the cantons, their protector, interpoſed as umpires in the quarrel, condemning the town that had appeared too forward in the diſpute to a fine of two thouſand crowns; and enacting at the ſame time, that as ſoon as any proceſſion entered their walls, the prieſt ſhould let the croſs hang about his neck without touching it with either hand until he came within the precincts of the abbey. The citizens could bring into the field near two thouſand

thousand men well exercised, and armed to the best advantage, with which they fancy they could make head against twelve or fifteen thousand peasants; for so many the Abbot could easily raise in his territories. But the protestant subjects of the abbey, who they say make up a good third of its people, would probably, in case of a war, abandon the cause of their Prince for that of their religion. The town of St. Gaul has an arsenal, library, town-houses, and churches proportionable to the bigness of the state. It is well enough fortified to resist any sudden attack, and to give the cantons time to come to their assistance. The abbey is by no means so magnificent as one would expect from its endowments. Their church has one huge nef with a double aisle to it. At each end is a large quire. The one of them is supported by vast pillars of stone, cased over with a composition that looks the most like marble of any thing one can imagine. On the cieling and walls of the church are lists of Saints, Martyrs, Popes, Cardinals, Archbishops, Kings, and Queens that have been of the Benedictine order. There are several pictures of such as have been distinguished by their birth, sanctity, or miracles, with inscriptions that let you into the name and history of the persons represented. I have often wished that some traveller would take the pains to gather together all the modern inscriptions which are to be met with in Roman catholic countries, as Gruter and others have copied out the ancient heathen monuments. Had we two or three volumes of this nature, without any of the collector's own reflections, I am sure there is nothing in the world could give a truer idea of the Roman catholic religion, nor expose more the pride, vanity, and self-interest of convents, the abuse of indulgences, the

folly

folly and impertinence of votaries, and in short, the superstition, credulity, and childishness of the Roman catholic religion. One might fill several sheets at St. Gaul, as there are few considerable convents or churches that would not afford large contributions.

As the King of France distributes his pensions through all parts of Switzerland, the town and abbey of St. Gaul come in too for their share. To the first he gives five hundred crowns *per Annum*, and to the other a thousand. This pension has not been paid these three years, which they attribute to their not acknowledging the duke of Anjou for King of Spain. The town and abbey of St. Gaul carry a bear in their arms. The Roman catholics have this bear's memory in very great veneration, and represent him as the first convert their saint made in the country. One of the most learned of the Benedictine monks gave me the following history of him, which he delivered to me with tears of affection in his eyes. St. Gaul, it seems, whom they call the great apostle of Germany, found all this country little better than a vast desart. As he was walking in it on a very cold day, he chanced to meet a bear in his way. The saint, instead of being startled at the rencounter ordered the bear to bring him a bundle of wood, and make him a fire. The bear served him to the best of his ability, and at his departure was commanded by the saint to retire into the very depth of the woods, and there to pass the rest of his life without ever hurting man or beast. From this time, says the monk, the bear lived irreproachably, and observed to his dying day the orders that the saint had given him.

I have often considered, with a great deal of pleasure, the profound peace and tranquility that reigns in Switzerland and its alliances. It is very wonderful to see such a knot of governments, which are so divided among themselves in matters of religion, maintain so uninterrupted a union and correspondence, that no one of them is for invading the rights of another, but remains content within the bounds of its first establishment. This, I think, must be chiefly ascribed to the nature of the people, and the constitution of their governments. Were the Swiss animated by zeal or ambition, some or other of their states would immediately break in upon the rest; or were the states so many principalities, they might often have an ambitious sovereign at the head of them, that would embroil his neighbours, and sacrifice the repose of his subjects to his own glory. But as the inhabitants of these countries are naturally of a heavy phlegmatic temper, if any of their leading members have more fire and spirit than comes to their share, it is quickly tempered by the coldness and moderation of the rest who sit at the helm with them. To this we may add, that the Alps is the worst spot of ground in the world to make conquests in, a great part of its governments being so naturally intrenched among woods and mountains. However it be, we find no such disorders among them as one would expect in such a multitude of states; for as soon as any public rupture happens, it is immediately closed up by the moderation and good offices of the rest that interpose.

As all the considerable governments among the Alps are commonwealths, so indeed it is a constitution the most adapted of any other to the poverty and barrenness of these countries. We may see only in a neighbouring government the ill consequence of having a despotic Prince, in a state that is moſt of it compoſed of rocks and mountains; for notwithſtanding there is a vaſt extent of lands, and many of them better than thoſe of the Swiſs and Griſons, the common people among the latter are much more at their eaſe, and in a greater affluence of all the conveniencies of life. A Prince's court eats too much into the income of a poor ſtate, and generally introduces a kind of luxury and magnificence, that ſets every particular perſon upon making a higher figure in his ſtation than is generally conſiſtent with his revenue.

It is the great endeavour of the ſeveral cantons of Switzerland, to baniſh from among them every thing that looks like pomp or ſuperfluity. To this end the miniſters are always preaching, and the governors putting out edicts, againſt dancing, gaming, entertainments, and fine cloaths. This is become more neceſſary in ſome of the governments, ſince there are ſo many refugees ſettled among them; for though the proteſtants in France affect ordinarily a greater plainneſs and ſimplicity of manners, than thoſe of the ſame quality who are of the Roman catholic communion, they have however too much of their country-gallantry for the genius and conſtitution of Switzerland. Should dreſſing, feaſting, and balls once get among the cantons, their military roughneſs would be quickly loſt, their tempers would grow too ſoft for their climate, and their expences out-run their incomes; beſides that the materials for their luxury muſt be brought from other nations, which would immediately ruin a country that has few commodities of its own to export, and is not overſtocked with money. Luxury indeed wounds a republic in its very vitals, as its natural conſequences are rapine, avarice, and injuſtice; for the more money a man ſpends, the more must he endeavour to augment his stock; which at last sets the liberty and votes of a commonwealth to sale, if they find any foreign power that is able to pay the price of them. We see no where the pernicious effects of luxury on a republic more than in that of the ancient Romans, who immediately found itself poor as soon as this vice got footing among them, though they were possessed of all the riches in the world. We find in the beginnings and increases of their commonwealth strange instances of the contempt of money, because indeed they were utter strangers to the pleasure that might be procured by it; or in other words, because they were wholly ignorant of the arts of luxury. But as soon as they once entered into a taste of pleasure, politeness, and magnificence, they fell into a thousand violencies, conspiracies, and divisions, that threw them into all the disorders imaginable, and terminated in the utter subversion of their commonwealth. It is no wonder therefore the poor commonwealths of Switzerland are ever labouring at the suppression and prohibition of every thing that may introduce vanity and luxury. Besides, the several fines that are set upon plays, games, balls, and feastings, they have many customs among them which very much contribute to the keeping up of their ancient simplicity. The bourgeois, who are at the head of the governments, are obliged to appear at all their public assemblies in a black cloke and a band. The womens dress is very plain, those of the best quality wearing nothing on their heads generally but furs, which are to be met with in their own country. The persons of different qualities in both sexes are indeed allowed their different ornaments; but these are generally such as are by no means costly, being rather designed as

marks

marks of diſtinction than to make a figure. The chief officers of Bern, for example, are known by the crowns of their hats, which are much deeper than thoſe of an inferior character. The peaſants are generally cloathed in a coarſe kind of canvas, that is the manufacture of the country. Their holiday cloaths go from father to ſon, and are ſeldom worn out, 'till the ſecond or third generation: So that it is common enough to ſee a countryman in the doublet and breeches of his great-grandfather.

Geneva is much politer than Switzerland, or any of its allies, and is therefore looked upon as the court of the Alps, whither the proteſtant cantons often ſend their children to improve themſelves in language and education. The Genevois have been very much refined, or, as others will have it, corrupted, by the converſation of the French proteſtants, who make up almoſt a third of their people. It is certain they have very much forgotten the advice that Calvin gave them in a great council a little before his death, when he recommended to them, above all things, an exemplary modeſty and humility, and as great a ſimplicity in their manners, as in their religion. Whether or no they have done well, to ſet up for making another kind of figure, time will witneſs. There are ſeveral that fancy the great ſums they have remitted into Italy, though by this means they make their court to the King of France at preſent, may ſome time or other give him an inclination to become the maſter of ſo wealthy a city.

As this collection of little ſtates abounds more in paſturage than in corn, they are all provided with their public granaries, and have the humanity to furniſh one another in public exigencies,

when

when the scarcity is not universal. As the administration of affairs, relating to these public granaries, is not very different in any of the particular governments, I shall content myself to set down the rules observed in it by the little commonwealth of Geneva, in which I had more time to inform myself of the particulars than in any other. There are three of the little council deputed for this office. They are obliged to keep together a provision sufficient to feed the people at least two years, in case of war or famine. They must take care to fill their magazines in times of the greatest plenty, that so they may afford cheaper, and increase the public revenue at a small expence of its members. None of the three managers must, upon any pretence, furnish the granaries from his own fields, that so they may have no temptation to pay too great a price, or put any bad corn upon the public. They must buy up no corn growing within twelve miles of Geneva, that so the filling of their magazines, may not prejudice their market, and raise the price of their provisions at home. That such a collection of corn may not spoil in keeping, all the inns and public houses are obliged to furnish themselves out of it, by which means is raised the most considerable branch of the public revenues; the corn being sold out at a much dearer rate than it is bought up at. So that the greatest income of the commonwealth, which pays the pensions of most of its officers and ministers, is raised on strangers and travellers, or such of their own body as have money enough to spend at taverns and public-houses.

It

It is the custom in Geneva and Switzerland, to divide their estates equally among all their children, by which means every one lives at his ease without growing dangerous to the republic; for as soon as an overgrown estate falls into the hands of one that has many children, it is broken into so many portions as render the sharers of it rich enough, without raising them too much above the level of the rest. This is absolutely necessary in these little republicks, where the rich merchants live very much within their estates, and by heaping up vast sums from year to year might become formidable to the rest of their fellow citizens, and break the equality, which is so necessary in these kinds of governments, were there not means found out to distribute their wealth among several members of their republick. At Geneva, for instance, are merchants reckoned worth twenty hundred thousand crowns, though, perhaps, there is not one of them who spends to the value of five hundred pounds a year.

Though the protestants and papists know very well, that it is their common interest to keep a steady neutrality in all the wars between the states of Europe, they cannot forbear siding with a party in their discourse. The catholics are zealous for the French King, as the protestants do not a little glory in the riches, power, and good success of the English and Dutch, whom they look upon as the bulwarks of the reformation. The ministers in particular have often preached against such of their fellow-subjects as enter into the troops of the French King; but so long as the Swifs see their interest in it, their poverty will always hold them fast to his service. They have indeed the exercise of their religion,

ligion, and their ministers with them; which is the more remarkable, because the very same Prince refused even those of the church of England, who followed their master to St. Germains, the public exercise of their religion.

Before I leave Switzerland, I cannot but observe, that the notion of witchcraft reigns very much in this country. I have often been tired with accounts of this nature from very sensible men that are most of them furnished with matters of fact which have happened, as they pretend, within the compass of their own knowledge. It is certain there have been many executions on this account, as in the canton of Bern there were some put to death during my stay at Geneva. The people are so universally infatuated with the notion, that, if a cow falls sick, it is ten to one but an old woman is clapped up in prison for it; and if the poor creature chance to think herself a witch, the whole country is for hanging her up without mercy. One finds indeed the same humour prevail in most of the rocky barren parts of Europe. Whether it be that poverty and ignorance, which are generally the products of these countries, may really engage a wretch in such dark practices, or whether or no the same principles may not render the people too credulous, and perhaps too easy to get rid of some of their unprofitable members.

A great affair that employs the Swiss politics at present is the Prince of Conti's succession to the Dutchy of Nemours in the government of Neuf-Chatel. The inhabitants of NeufrChatel can by no means think of submitting themselves to a Prince, who is a Roman catholic, and a subject of France. They were very attentive to his conduct in the
prin-

principality of Orange, which they did not question but he would rule with all the mildness and moderation imaginable, as it would be the best means in the world to recommend him to Neuf-Chatel. But notwithstanding it was so much his interest to manage his protestant subjects in that country, and the strong assurances he had given them in protecting them in all their privileges, and particularly in the free exercise of their religion, he made over his principality in a very little time, for a sum of money, to the King of France. It is indeed generally believed the Prince of Conti would rather still have kept his title to Orange; but the same respect, which induced him to quit this government, might at another time tempt him to give up that of Neuf-Chatel on the like conditions. The King of Prussia lays in his claim for Neuf-Chatel, as he did for the principality of Orange, and it is probable would be more acceptable to the inhabitants than the other; but they are generally disposed to declare themselves a free commonwealth, after the death of the Dutchess of Nemours, if the Swifs will support them. The protestant cantons seem much inclined to assist them, which they may very well do, in case the Dutchess dies, whilst the King of France has his hands so full of business on all sides of him. It certainly very much concerns them not to suffer the French King to establish his authority on this side mount Jura, and on the very borders of their country; but it is not easy to foresee what a round sum of money, or the fear of a rupture with France, may do among a people, who have tamely suffered the *Franche-Compte* to be seized on, and a fort to be built within cannon shot of one of their cantons.

There

There is a new sect sprung up in Switzerland, which spreads very much in the protestant cantons. The professors of it call themselves Pietists: And as enthusiasm carries men generally to the like extravagancies, they differ but little from several sectaries in other countries. They pretend in general to great refinements, as to what regards the practice of christianity, and to observe the following rules. To retire much from the conversation of the world: To sink themselves into an intire repose and tranquillity of mind: In this state of silence, to attend the secret illapse and flowings in of the holy spirit, that may fill their minds with peace and consolation, joys or raptures: To favour all his secret intimations, and give themselves up entirely to his conduct and direction, so as neither to speak, move or act, but as they find his impulse on their souls; to retrench themselves within the conveniencies and necessities of life: To make a covenant with all their senses, so far as to shun the smell of a rose or violet, and to turn away their eyes from a beautiful prospect: To avoid, as much as is possible, what the world calls innocent pleasures, lest they should have their affections tainted by any sensuality, and diverted from the love of him, who is to be the only comfort, repose, hope, and delight of their whole beings. This sect prevails very much among the protestants of Germany, as well as those of Switzerland, and has occasioned several edicts against it in the dutchy of Saxony. The professors of it are accused of all the ill practices, which may seem to be the consequence of their principles; as that they ascribe the worst of actions, which their own vicious tempers

throw

throw them upon, to the dictates of the holy
spirit; that both sexes, under pretext of devout
conversation, visit one another at all hours, and in
all places, without any regard to common decency,
often making their religion a cover for their immo-
ralities; and that the very best of them are possessed
with spiritual pride, and a contempt for all such as
are not of their own sect. The Roman catholics,
who reproach the protestants for their breaking into
such a multitude of religions, have certainly taken
the most effectual way in the world for the keeping
their flocks together; I do not mean the punishments
they inflict on mens persons, which are commonly
looked upon as the chief methods by which they
deter them from breaking through the pale of the
church, though certainly these lay a very great re-
straint on those of the Roman catholic persuasion.
But I take one great cause, why there are so few
sects in the church of Rome, to be the multitude of
convents, with which they every where abound,
that serve as receptacles for all those fiery zealots
who would set the church in a flame, were not
they got together in these houses of devotion. All
men of dark tempers, according to their degree
of melancholy or enthusiasm, may find convents
fitted to their humours, and meet with companions
as gloomy as themselves. So that what the protestants would call a fanatic, is, in the Roman
church, a religious of such or such an order; as
I have been told of an English merchant at Lisbon,
who, after some great disappointments in the world,
was resolved to turn quaker or capuchin; for, in
the change of religion, men of ordinary under-
standings do not so much consider the principles,
as the practice of those to whom they go over.

From

From St. Gaul I took horse to the lake of Constance, which lies at two leagues distance from it, and is formed by the entry of the Rhine. This is the only lake in Europe that disputes for greatness with that of Geneva; it appears more beautiful to the eye, but wants the fruitful fields and vineyards that border upon the other. It receives its name from Constance, the chief town on its banks. When the cantons of Bern and Zurich proposed, at a general diet, the incorporating Geneva in the number of the cantons, the Roman catholic party, fearing the protestant interest might receive by it too great a strengthening, proposed at the same time the incantoning of Constance, as a counterpoise; to which the protestants not consenting, the whole project fell to the ground. We crossed the lake to Lindaw, and in several parts of it observed abundance of little bubbles of air, that came working upward from the very bottom of the lake. The waterman told us, that they are observed always to rise in the same places, from whence they conclude them to be so many springs that break out of the bottom of the lake. Lindaw is an imperial town on a little island that lies at about three hundred paces from the firm land, to which it is joined by a huge bridge of wood. The inhabitants were all in arms when we passed through it, being under great apprehensions of the Duke of Bavaria, after his having fallen upon Ulm and Memminghen. They flatter themselves, that by cutting their bridge, they could hold out against his army: But, in all probability, a shower of bombs would quickly reduce the bourgeois to surrender. They were formerly bombarded by Gustavus Adolphus. We were

were advised by our merchants by no means to venture ourselves in the Duke of Bavaria's country, so that we had the mortification to lose the sight of Munich, Ausburg, and Ratisbon, and were forced to take our way to Vienna, through the Tirol, where we had very little to entertain us beside the natural face of the country.

TIROL,

TIROL,

INSPRUCK,

HALL, &c.

AFTER having coasted the Alps for some time, we at last entered them by a passage which leads into the long valley of the Tirol; and following the course of the river Inn, we came to Inspruck, that receives its name from this river, and is the capital city of the Tirol.

Inspruck is a handsome town, though not a great one, and was formerly the residence of the arch-Dukes who were Counts of Tirol: The palace where they used to keep their court is rather convenient than magnificent. The great hall is indeed a very noble room: the walls of it are painted in Fresco, and represent the labours of Hercules. Many of them look very finely, though a great part of the work has been cracked by earthquakes, which are very frequent in this country. There is a little wooden palace that borders on the other, whither the court used to retire at the first shake of an earthquake. I saw here the largest manage that I have met with any where else. At one end of it is a great partition designed for an opera. They

shewed

shewed us also a very pretty theatre. The last comedy that was acted on it was designed by the jesuits for the entertainment of the Queen of the Romans, who passed this way from Hanover to Vienna. The compliment, which the fathers made her majesty on this occasion, was very particular, and did not a little expose them to the raillery of the court. For the arms of Hanover being a horse, the fathers thought it a very pretty allusion to represent the Queen by Bucephalus, that would let no body get upon him but Alexander the great. The wooden horse that acted this notable part is still to be seen behind the scenes. In one of the rooms of the palace, which is hung with the pictures of several illustrious persons, they shewed us the portrait of Mary Queen of Scots, who was beheaded in the reign of Queen Elizabeth. The gardens about the house are very large, but ill kept. There is in the middle of them a beatiful statue in brass of an Arch-Duke Leopold on horseback. There are near it twelve other figures of water-nymphs and river-gods, well cast, and as big as the life. They were designed for the ornaments of a waterwork, as one might easily make a great variety of jetteaus, at a small expence, in a garden that has the river Inn running by its walls. The late Duke of Lorrain had this palace, and the government of the Tirol, assigned him by the Emperor, and his lady the Queen Dowager of Poland lived here several years after the death of the Duke her husband. There are covered gallies that lead from the palace to five different churches. I passed through a very long one, which reaches to the church of the Capuchin convent, where the Duke of Lorrain used often to assist at their midnight devotions. They shewed us in this convent the apart-

apartments of Maximilian, who was Arch-Duke and Count of Tirol about fourscore years ago. This Prince, at the same time that he kept the government in his hands, lived in this convent with all the rigour and austerity of a Capuchin. His antichamber and room of audience are little square chambers wainscotted. His private lodgings are three or four small rooms faced with a kind of fretwork, that makes them look like little hollow caverns in a rock. They preserve this apartment of the convent uninhabited, and shew in it the altar, bed and stove, as likewise a picture and a stamp of this devout Prince. The church of the Franciscan convent is famous for the monument of the Emperor Maximilian the first, which stands in the midst of it. It was erected to him by his grandson Ferdinand the first, who probably looked upon this Emperor as the founder of the Austrian greatness. For as by his own marriage he annexed the low-countries to the house of Austria, so, by matching his son to Joan of Arragon, he settled on his posterity the kingdom of Spain, and, by the marriage of his grand-son Ferdinand, got into his family the kingdoms of Bohemia and Hungary. This monument is only honorary; for the ashes of the Emperor lie elsewhere. On the top of it is a brazen figure of Maximilian on his knees, and on the sides of it a beautiful Bas-Relief representing the actions of this Prince. His whole history is digested into twenty-four square pannels of sculpture in Bas-Relief. The subject of two of them is his confederacy with Henry the eighth, and the wars they made together upon France. On each side of this monument is a row of very noble brazen statues much bigger than the life, most of them representing such as were some way or other related

related to Maximilian. Among the rest is one that the fathers of the convent tell us represents King Arthur the old British King. But what relation had that Arthur to Maximilian? I do not question therefore but it was designed for Prince Arthur, elder brother of Henry the eighth, who had espoused Catharine, sister of Maximilian, whose divorce afterwards gave occasion to such signal revolutions in England. This church was built by Ferdinand the first. One sees in it a kind of offer at modern architecture; but at the same time that the architect has shewn his dislike of the Gothic manner, one may see very well that in that age they were not, at least, in this country, arrived at the knowledge of the true way. The portal, for example, consists of a composite order unknown to the antients; the ornaments indeed are taken from them, but so put together, that you see the volutes of the Ionic, the foliage of the Corinthian, and uovali of the Doric, mixed without any regularity on the same capital. So the vault of the church, though broad enough, is incumbered with too many little tricks in sculpture. It is indeed supported with single columns, instead of those vast clusters of little pillars that one meets with in Gothic cathedrals; but at the same time these columns are of no regular order, and at least twice too long for their diameter. There are other churches in the town, and two or three palaces which are of a more modern make, and built with a good fancy. I was shewn the little Nôtredame that is handsomely designed, and topped with a cupola. It was made as an offering of gratitude to the blessed Virgin, for having defended the country of the Tirol against the victorious arms of Gustavus Adolphus, who could not enter this part of the empire after having over-

run

run most of the rest. This temple was therefore built by the contributions of the whole country. At about half a league's distance from Inspruck, stands the castle of Amras, furnished with a prodigious quantity of medals, and many other sorts of rarities both in nature and art, for which I must refer the reader to Monsieur Patin's account in his letter to the Duke of Wirtemberg, having myself had neither time nor opportunity to enter into a particular examination of them.

From Inspruck we came to Hall, that lies at a league distance on the same river. This place is particularly famous for its salt-works. There are in the neighbourhood vast mountains of a transparent kind of rock, not unlike allum, extremely solid, and as piquant to the tongue as salt itself. Four or five hundred men are always at work in these mountains, where, as soon as they have hewn down any quantities of the rock, they let in their springs and reservoirs among their works. The water eats away and dissolves the particles of salt which are mixed in the stone, and is conveyed by long troughs and canals from the mines to the town of Hall, where it is received in vast cisterns, and boiled off from time to time.

They make after the rate of eight hundred loaves a week, each loaf four hundred pounds weight. This would raise a great revenue to the Emperor, were there here such a tax on salt as there is in France. At present he clears but two hundred thousand crowns a year, after having defrayed all the charges of working it. There are in Switzerland, and other parts of the Alps, several of these quarries of salt, that turn to very little account, by reason of the great quantities of wood they consume.

The

The salt-works at Hall have a great convenience for fuel, which swims down to them on the river Inn. This river during its course through the Tirol, is generally shut up between a double range of mountains that are most of them covered with woods of fir-trees. Abundance of peasants are employed in the hewing down of the largest of these trees, that after they are barked and cut into shape, are tumbled down from the mountains into the stream of the river, which carries them off to the salt-works. At Inspruck they take up vast quantities for the convents and public officers, who have a certain portion of it allotted them by the Emperor; the rest of it passes on to Hall. There are generally several hundred loads afloat; for they begin to cut above twenty leagues up the river above Hall; and there are other rivers that flow into the Inn, which bring in their contributions. These salt-works, and a mint that is established at the same place, have rendered this town, notwithstanding the neighbourhood of the capital city, almost as populous as Inspruck itself. The design of this mint is to work off part of the metals which are found in the neighbouring mountains; where, as we are told, there are seven thousand men in constant employ. At Hall we took a boat to carry us to Vienna. The first night we lay at Rottenburg, where is a strong castle above the town. Count Serini is still a close prisoner in this castle, who, as they told us in the town, had lost his senses by his long imprisonment and afflictions. The next day we dined at Kuff-stain, where there is a fortress on a high rock, above the town, almost inaccessible on all sides: This being a frontier place on the dutchy of Bavaria, where we entered after about an hour's rowing from Kuff-stain. It was the plea-

O santest

santeſt voyage in the world, to follow the windings of this river Inn through such a variety of pleasing scenes as the course of it naturally led us. We had sometimes on each side of us a vast extent of naked rocks and mountains, broken into a thousand irregular steeps and precipices; in other places we saw a long forest of fir-trees, so thick set together, that it was impossible to discover any of the soil they grew upon, and rising up so regularly one above another, as to give us a view of a whole wood at once. The time of the year, that had given the leaves of the trees so many different colours, compleated the beauty of the prospect. But as the materials of a fine landskip are not always the most profitable to the owner of them, we met with but very little corn or pasturage for the proportion of earth that we passed through, the lands of the Tirol not being able to feed the inhabitants. This long valley of the Tirol lies inclosed on all sides by the Alps, though its dominions shoot out into several branches that lie among the breaks and hollows of the mountains. It is governed by three councils residing at Inspruck; one sits upon life and death, the other is for taxes and impositions, and a third for the common distributions of justice. As these courts regulate themselves by the orders they receive from the imperial courts, so in many cases there are appeals from them to Vienna. The inhabitants of the Tirol have many particular privileges above those of the other hereditary countries of the Emperor. For as they are naturally well fortified among their mountains, and at the same time border upon many different governments, as the Grisons, Venetians, Swiss, Bavarians, &c. a severe treatment might tempt them to set up for a republic, or at least throw themselves under the milder government

vernment of some of their neighbours: Besides that their country is poor, and that the Emperor draws considerable incomes out of its mines of salt and metal. They are these mines that fill the country with greater numbers of people than it would be able to bear without the importation of corn from foreign parts. The Emperor has forts and citadels at the entrance of all the passes that lead into the Tirol, which are so advantageously placed upon rocks and mountains, that they command all the valleys and avenues that lie about them. Besides that the country itself is cut into so many hills and inequalities, as would render it defensible by a very little army against a numerous enemy. It was therefore generally thought the Duke of Bavaria would not attempt the cutting off any succours that were sent to Prince Eugene, or the forcing his way through the Tirol into Italy. The river Inn, that had hitherto been shut up among mountains, passes generally through a wide open country during all its course through Bavaria, which is a voyage of two days, after the rate of twenty leagues a day.

INDEX.

INDEX.

A

ADDA, and the Addige, both described by Claudian, page 43, 44.
Albano for what famous, 219.
Alps; described by Silius Italicus, 256.
St. Ambrose, his resolute behaviour towards Theodosius the great, before the gates of the great church at Milan, 30.
Ambrosian library in Milan how furnished, 32.
Ancona, its situation, 90.
St. Anthony of Padua, his magnificent church, 47. a natural perfume issuing from his bones, ibid. a conjecture upon it, ibid. his famous sermon to an Assembly of fish, 47. the titles given him by a poor peasant, 53.
Antiquaries, wherein faulty, 189.
Antiquities, two sets in Rome, 176. the great difference between them, 177.
Antium, its extensive ruins, 170. for what famous formerly, 171.
Anxur, its pleasant situation, 117. described by Martial, &c. ibid.
Appenine mountains described by the Latin Poets, 246.
Ariosto, his monument in the Benedictine church in Ferrara, 75.

B

Baiæ, the winter retreat of the old Romans, 139.
St. Bartholomew, his famous statue in the great church in Milan, 28.
Bern, its public walks, 273. and arsenal, 274.
Bolonia, for wat famous, 248. its rarities, ibid.

Brescia,

INDEX.

Brescia, why more favoured by the Venetians than any other part of their dominions, 42. famous for its iron works, ibid.

C.

Calvin, his advice to the Genevois before his death, 287.
Caprea, described, 150, &c. its fruitful soil, ibid. some account of the medals found in it, 156.
Cassis, a French port, its pleasant neighbourhood, 13.
Cennis, a mountain between Turin and Geneva. 254.
St. Charles Boromeo his subterraneous chapel in Milan, 28. an account of that Saint, ibid. compared with the ordinary saints in the Roman church, 29.
Cimmerians, where placed by Homer, 167.
Civita Vecchia, its unwholsome air, 229.
Clitumnus, the quality of its waters, 95.
Colonna Infame, a pillar at Milan, 34. the occasion of it, ibid.
Confessionals, inscriptions over them, 31.

E.

English courted by the present Pope to settle at Civita Vecchia, 229.
Escargatoire, the use of it, 272.

F.

Fano, from whence so called, 90.
Felix the fifth, his story, 261, 262.
Ferrara, thinly inhabited, 75. the town described, ibid.
Florence, 235. an account of its public buildings, ibid. its famous gallery, 236. and rarities contained in it, ibid. &c. and in some chambers adjoining to it, 240. &c. famous for modern statues, 245. the great Duke's care to prevent Civita Vecchia from being made a free port, 228. incensed against the Lucquese, 231. for what reason, 232.
Fortune. Two Fortunes worshipped by the heathens at Antium, 170.

INDEX.

Fountains in Switzerland, a reason given for their periodical fluxes, 262.

Fribourg described, 271. with an hermitage near it, 272.

G.

St. Gaul, Abbot of, the extent of his territories, 279. manner of his election, ibid. the riches of the inhabitants, 280. their quarrel with the Abbot, 281, the abbey, 282, their arms, 283.

St. Gaul, the great apostle of Germany, some account of him, 283.

Geneva, its situation, 258. under the emperor's displeasure, and from what reason, 270. esteemed the court of the Alps, 287.

Genoese, their manners described, 17. their character from the modern Italians, and Latin Poets, 17, 18. an instance of their indiscretion, 21. why obliged to be at present in the French interest, ibid. their fleet, and its service, 22. their Doge claims a crown and scepter from their conquest of Corsica, ibid. and advantage arising to them from it, and a different maxim observed by the ancient Romans, 22.

Genoa, its description, 18, &c. its banks no burden to the Genoese, 21. why incapable of being made a free port, 229.

St. George, his church at Verona, 46.

Granaries, the administration of them in Switzerland, 287.

Grotto del Cani, some experiments made in it, 140, 141. reasons offered for the effects of its vapours, 141, 142.

Grotto Obscuro, 154.

Gulf of Genoa, its nature, 15.

H.

Hall, its salt works, 300. the method of preparing them ibid. its mint, 301.

Henry the eighth of England, his letter to Anne of Bullein, 211.

Her-

INDEX.

Hercules Monæcus, 16.
Homer, his Apotheosis, 199.

I.

Jesuits, their particular compliment to the Queen of the Romans in a comedy designed for her entertainment, 297.
Inspruck, its public buildings, 296.
Ischia, by the ancients called Inarime, 163. some account of it, ibid.
Italians, the usual furniture of their libraries, 32. compared to the French, 37. the difference of manners in the two nations, 38. the great aversion to the French observed in the common people, ibid. some reasons for it, 39. their extravagant tomb-stones, 46. the difference betwixt their poetical and prose language, 66. a great help to their modern poetry, 67. their comedies low and obscene, ibid. a reason for it, 68. the chief parts in all their comedies, ibid. a great custom among them of crowning the holy Virgin, 79.
Italy divided into many principalities, as more natural to its situation, 36. its present desolation, 112. compared to its ancient inhabitants, ibid.
Juno Sispita, or Sospita how represented, 240. Tully's description of this goddess, ibid.
St. Justina, her church one of the finest in Italy, 55.

L.

Lago di Como, formerly Larius, 42. described by Claudian, 44.
Lago di Garda, or Benacus, described by Virgil, 43.
Lapis Vituperii, what, and to what use applied, 55.
Lausanne, 267. a peculiar privilege belonging to one street in this town, ibid.
Lawyers, their great numbers, and continual employment among the Neapolitans, 127.
Leghorn, 226. a free port, ibid. the great resort of

INDEX.

other nations to it, 227. the advantage the great
  Duke receives from it, ibid. &c.
Lemanus, the lake described, 259, &c. with the towns
  upon it, 260.
Lindaw, 294.
Liris, or the Gariglano described, 116.
Loretto, its prodigious riches, 93. why never attacked
  by the Turks, *ibid.* or the christian Princes, *ibid.* a
  description of the holy house, 94.
Lucan, his prophecy of the Latian towns, 221.
Lucca, the industry of its inhabitants, 231. under the
  King of Spain's protection, 232. in danger of ruin,
  ibid. the great contempt the inhabitants have of the
  Florentines, 233. why never attempted as yet by the
  great Duke, ibid. the form of its government,
  234.
Ludlow, Edmund, his epitaph, 264.

M.

St. Marino, its situation, 84. the extent of its dominions, 85. the founder, and original of this little
  republic, ibid. the antiquity of it, 86. the form of
  the government, 87, &c.
Mary Magdalene, the deserts rendered famous by her
  penance, 13. described by Claudian, 14.
Maximilian, the first founder of the Austrian greatness,
  298.
Meldingen, a little republic in Switzerland, 277. the
  model of its government, ibid. and business of the
  councils of state, 278.
Milan, its great church, 27, &c. the relics and great
  riches contained in it, 30. the citadel, 36. the situation of its state, ibid. an affectation of the French
  dress and carriage in the court, 37. Milan described
  by Ausonius, 40.
Mincio, described by Virgil, 43. and Claudian, 44.
Miseno, its cape described, 162. its set of galleries,
  163.

Modena,

INDEX.

Modena, the extent of its dominions, and condition of the inhabitants, 250.
Monaco, its harbour described by Lucan, 16. dominions, ibid.
Monte Circeio, why supposed by Homer to have been an island, 168. Æneas his passage near it described by Virgil, ibid.
Monte Novo, how formed, 143.
Morge, its artificial port, 267.
Morpheus, why represented under the figure of a boy, 238, 239. in what manner addressed to by Statius, 239.

N.

Naples, 121. its many superstitions, 122. its delightful Bay, 124. described by Silius Italicus, 147. its pleasant situation, 126. the litigious temper of the inhabitants, 127. different from what it was in Statius his time, ibid. the great alteration of the adjacent parts from what they were formerly, 134, the natural curiosities about it, 140.
Narni, why so called, 102.
Neapolitans addicted to ease and pleasure, 129. the reason, ibid.
Nemi, why so called, 218.
Nettuno, for what remarkable, 170.

O.

Ocriculum, its ruins, 103.
Ostia, described by Juvenal, 173.

P.

Padua, its university, 55. the original of Padua from Virgil, 55, 56.
Parker an English ecclesiastic, his epitaph on his tomb in Pavia, 25.
Parma, its famous theatre, 249. the extent of its dominions, 250, and condition of the inhabitants, ibid.

INDEX.

Pavia, its description, 23, &c. why called Ticinum by the ancients, 26.

Pausilypo's Grotto, 132. the beautiful prospect of its mount, 161.

St. Peter's church at Rome described, 109. the reason of its double dome, 110. its beautiful architecture, 111.

Pietists, a new sect in Switzerland, 292.

Pisatello, see Rubicon.

Pisauro, Doge of Venice, his Elogium, 61.

Po, described by Lucan, 72. Scaliger's critic upon it, 73. described by Claudian, 252.

Pope, his territories very desolate, 112, and the inhabitants poor, 114. reasons for it, ibid.

Puteoli, its remains near Naples, 134. its mole mistaken for Caligula's bridge, 135. the error confuted, ibid.

R.

Ravenna, 75. its antient situation according to Martial, 76. and Silius Italicus, ibid. the city and adjacent parts described, ibid. &c. its great scarcity of fresh water, 107.

St. Remo, a Genoese town, described, 15.

Rhone, some account of it, 269.

Rimini, its antiquities, 80.

Rome, the modern stands higher than the ancient, 176. the grandeur of the commonwealth, and magnificence of the Emperors differently considered, 177. its rarities, ibid. &c. and considerations upon them, ibid. why more frequented by the nobility in summer than in winter, 220.

Romulus his cottage described by Virgil, 95.

Rubicon, called at present Pisatello, described by Lucan, 79, 80.

S.

Sannazarius, his verses upon Venice, 70.

Sienna, 224. its cathedral, ibid.

Snow

INDEX.

Snow monopolized at Naples, 146.
Soleurre, the residence of the French Ambassadors, 276.
Soracte, called by the modern Italians St. Oreste, 103.
Spaniards, their policy observed in the government of Naples, 126, 128, 129.
Spoletto, its antiquities, 95.
Suffolk, Duke of, buried in Pavia, 24. the inscription on his tomb; ibid. his history, 25.
Switzerland; its wonderful tranquility, 283. the reason for it, 284. the thrift of its inhabitants, 285. the reason for it, ibid. their dress, 286. their custom in bequeathing their estates, 289. their notion of witchcraft, 290.

T.

Terni, why called formerly Interamna, 97.
Theatines, their convent in Ravenna, 78.
Tiber, an account of it from Virgil, 173. its great riches, 196.
Ticinus, or Tesin, a river near Pavia, 26. described by Silius Italicus; ibid. and Claudian, 44.
Timavus, described by Claudian, 44.
Tirol, the particular privileges of its inhabitants, 302.
Turin, a convenience particular to it, 254. the aversion of the common people to the French, ibid.

V.

Valina Rosea Rura, why called so by Virgil, 99. the cascade formed by the fall of that river, 100.
Venetians, their thirst after too many conquests on the Terra Firma prejudicial to the commonwealth, 62. wherein, ibid. the public in a declining condition, ibid. on what terms with the Emperor, ibid. the Pope and Duke of Savoy, 63. their Senate the wisest council in the world, ibid. the refined parts of their wisdom, ibid. their great secrecy in matters of state, ibid. an instance of it, 64. the number of
their

INDEX.

their nobility, ibid. their operas; 65. a custom peculiar to the Venetians, 69. a show particular to them exhibited on Holy Thursday, ibid. described by Claudian, 70.

Venice, its advantageous situation, 57. convenient for commerce; 58. its trade declining, 59. the reason of it; ibid. its description, 59, 60. remarkable for its pictures from the best hands; 60. the moisture of its air, ibid. its arsenal; 61. its carnival; 65. the necessity and consequences of it, ibid. &c.

Venus, her chambers, 138.

Verona; its amphitheatre, 44. its antiquitties; 45.

Vesuvio described; 143; &c. much different from Martial's account of it; 152.

Virgil's tomb, 132.

Ulysses; his voyage undetermined by the learned, 14.

Volturno described, 116.

Z.

Zurich. an account of it, 278.

FINIS.

www.ingramcontent.com/pod-product-compliance
Lightning Source LLC
Chambersburg PA
CBHW022057230426
43672CB00008B/1196